READING THE 21ST CENTURY

Reading the 21st Century

Books of the Decade, 2000–2009

STAN PERSKY

McGill-Queen's University Press

Montreal & Kingston • London • Ithaca

© McGill-Queen's University Press 2011
ISBN 978-0-7735-3909-9 (cloth)
ISBN 978-0-7735-4047-7 (paper)

Legal deposit fourth quarter 2011
Bibliothèque nationale du Québec

Reprinted 2012
First paperback edition 2012

Printed in Canada on acid-free paper that is 100% ancient forest
free (100% post-consumer recycled), processed chlorine free

McGill-Queen's University Press acknowledges the support of the
Canada Council for the Arts for our publishing program. We also
acknowledge the financial support of the Government of Canada
through the Canada Book Fund for our publishing activities.

Library and Archives Canada Cataloguing in Publication

Persky, Stan, 1941–
Reading the 21st century: books of the decade, 2000–2009 / Stan Persky.

Includes bibliographical references and index.
ISBN 978-0-7735-3909-9 (bnd)
ISBN 978-0-7735-4047-7 (pbk)

1. Best books. 2. Books – Reviews. 3. Literature – 21st century – History
and criticism. I. Title

Z1035.AIP47 2011   028.1'090511   C2011-902169-2

This book was typeset by Interscript in 10.5/13.5 Sabon.

for Brian Fawcett

in memory of Robin Blaser

Contents

Introduction: In the Twilight of Literary Criticism   ix

1 The Storyteller: Larry McMurtry   3

2 Indelible: Philip Roth's *Human Stain*   9

3 Heroes: Javier Cercas's *Soldiers of Salamis*   22

4 Ignorance in the Desert   39

5 The Snowflake from the Snow: Orhan Pamuk   67

6 In the Land of Amos Oz: *A Tale of Love and Darkness*   83

7 Homeland Alone: 9/11, Afghanistan, Iraq   105

8 Lost and Found: Daniel Mendelsohn   137

9 Walking, Seeing, Shelving   144

10 The Gods That Failed: Richard Dawkins   160

11 Exit Strategies: Said, Coetzee, Saramago, Roth   180

12 Other Voices, Other Realms   201

13 Haunted by a Spectre: Krugman, Klein, Stiglitz   224

Conclusion: Code Red   253

Appendix: Some Prize Lists   261

Index   267

In the Twilight of Literary Criticism

Reading the 21st Century: Books of the Decade, 2000–2009 is my assessment of the important intellectual currents and the books that gave expression to them in the first decade of the 21st century. That period was volatile politically, economically, and culturally, particularly at the centre of empire in the United States. The decade really began with the terrorist assault on the World Trade Centre towers in New York on September 11, 2001, and reached its high point with the election on November 4, 2008 of Barack Obama, the first African-American president of the United States. The election campaign that put him in office coincided with a global economic crisis, the most severe recession since the Great Depression of the 1930s, and one that is likely to continue well into this decade. Those circumstances, and much more, are reflected and examined in the significant books of the first ten years of the new century.

There were also major disruptions within the literary world in the years since 2000, in terms of publishing, marketing, and the very forms of book "packaging," as well as a profound "withering away" of the pendant activity of literary criticism. But the problem I'm interested in is far more than "market disturbances" within the realm of writing.

The background thesis of this celebratory account of contemporary books is that we are simultaneously facing a cultural catastrophe whose major symptom is the decline of serious book reading, especially among young people, and a consequent array of "knowledge deficits" that makes it increasingly difficult to sustain democratic society, and intellectual life. The unresolved paradox of our present cultural condition is that while writing is flourishing, reading is in big trouble. We have greater technological access to information and knowledge than ever before, but our ability to understand our world is increasingly "dumbed down" by the content that is, according to the evidence, most frequently accessed on the very devices that are heralded as the informational wonders of our time. So, my praise of recent writing is heartfelt, but it is also a *cri-de-coeur* against what I perceive to be an encroaching cultural barbarism.

Reading the 21st Century doesn't purport to provide a full description of our present cultural crisis, much less a set of remedies, but I make a point of discussing several of the books of the past decade that address the crisis in reading, knowledge, and intellectual life generally. My apprehensive recognition of that cultural condition is the background assumption that informs many of my readings throughout this book. I should underscore that my concern about our intellectual situation is not simply aesthetic, but equally political, moral, and economic. My preference for the informed mind over the "invisible hand" applies to all those areas.

My qualifications for an overview of the books of the decade go back to my first brush with literary criticism as a ten-year-old fifth grader, when I wrote a critical essay about Herman Melville's *Moby Dick* under the sensationalist title of "Bloated Whale Beached" (I found the sea-going masterpiece a bit long). Since that precocious debut, it's been mostly downhill: I worked as the chief literary critic for the Toronto *Globe and Mail* and the *Vancouver Sun* for all of the decade of the 1990s, and since 2000 have steadily reviewed books at two Canadian journalistic websites, www.dooneyscafe.com in Toronto and www.thetyee.com in Vancouver, as well as for conventional print publications, several of which are now defunct, such as the *Globe's* stand-alone book section, *Books in Canada*, and *Saturday Night*. I've also published three book-length works during this period: *The Short Version: An ABC Book* (2005), *Topic Sentence: A Writer's Education* (2007), and a volume about pornography legislation in Canada, *On Kiddie Porn: Sexual Representation, Free Speech and the Robin Sharpe Case* (co-authored with John Dixon, 2001). Given the condition of contemporary literary criticism, I have also prudently retained my "day job" as a philosophy professor at Capilano University in North Vancouver, British Columbia, where I teach courses about philosophy and literature, aesthetics, and philosophy and culture.

As a way of giving a prefatory idea of the contents of this book, I want to make a few comments about the state of writing between 2000 and 2010 and provide some indication of how I intend to approach this subject. Most works of cultural and literary criticism that I've read not only treat the novel as the primary form of "literature" (a term that itself needs more explanation than it usually gets) but tend to ignore all other genres of writing. My first move in this assessment is to elevate the category of "writing" to a central position and to regard all genres of book-length writing within a given period as eligible for discussion. This has the advantage of reflecting my own (and many other readers') patterns of reading, as well as permitting a cross-pollination in the discussion of intellectual themes in fiction and non-fictional genres. My asssumption that "writing" is the relevant organizing category invites justificatory argument, but that theoretical debate can be reserved for another occasion. For now, I'll simply operate with the notion of "writing," on the grounds that it yields a better portrait of our current intellectual challenges than an approach that restricts itself to novels or "literature."

With respect to fiction, contrary to the expectations of many people, the often announced demise of the novel has not occurred. It's true that the serious novel, or "literary fiction" as it is sometimes called, now has a reduced status in cultural conversation, a more ambiguous role in intellectual life, and a diminished readership. Yet, I've been surprised by how many novels and other shorter fiction I've read and liked in the last decade. My enthusiasms range from Saul Bellow's *Ravelstein* (2000) and Philip Roth's *The Human Stain* (2000) to Javier Cercas's *Soldiers of Salamis* (2001; tr. 2003) and Orhan Pamuk's *Snow* (2002; tr. 2004); they include such works as J.M. Coetzee's *Elizabeth Costello* (2003) and *Diary of a Bad Year* (2007), Jose Saramago's *Death with Interruptions* (2005; tr. 2008), and Daniyal Mueenuddin's *In Other Rooms, Other Wonders* (2009). Much of this book will be an account of why I think those works are not only aesthetically engaging, but relevant to understanding our world and our times. I note that I prefer stories that are innovative with respect to storytelling to those that are more conventionally "realistic." I'm interested in fiction that is "necessary," that says things that can't be said in any other form. I've read and been engrossed by some of the more straightforward novels that have garnered wide attention and their share of literary prizes, but I've been

less inclined to write about them, an inclination that reflects a judgment about comparative worth.

For the most part, I call attention to fiction that I'm appreciative
of, and refrain from hatchet jobs. Although the work of the daily
and weekly literary critic understandably involves more pointing out
of what's wrong with a given season's crop of books than to cele-
brating the greatness of particular works, here, in a summing up of
what I regard as the most interesting books of the decade, I find myself engaged in the more pleasant, and perhaps more difficult task, of
meting out praise. My range of interest is international, and leans
toward what the American novelist and essayist Gore Vidal sometimes sneeringly calls Quality Lit.

My criteria for response to fiction invoke no grand theoretical principles, although I'm not naïve about literary theory and its powers.
My views are informed by an eclectic spectrum of theorists and critics
that ranges from Harold Bloom, author of *The Western Canon*
(1994), to the Marxist critic, Terry Eagleton, in such works as *Literary
Theory: An Introduction* (1983; 2008) and *The Task of the Critic*
(2009). I realize that a lot of people read novels primarily for entertainment, or as one friend replied when I asked my perennial and
despairing question, What are novels *for*?, "Novels are for people
who like reading novels." Well, yes. But what I look for in all writing,
including novels, are books that tell me something about "life," in the
sense that Virginia Woolf or the mid-20th century British critic F.R.
Leavis used that term, preferably something about life that I didn't
know, and in ways that I also didn't know. As the philosopher Richard
Rorty remarks in *Philosophy as Cultural Politics* (2007), "The point
of reading a great many books is to become aware of a great number
of alternative purposes, and the point of *that* is to become an autonomous self." One might equally emphasise that the social purpose of
reading books is to become a more effective participant in creating a
better world. Cultural critic Edward Said says in *On Late Style* (2006)
that the novel is "the Western aesthetic form that offers the largest
and most complex image of ourselves that we have." That may be true
historically, but today I just as often find that "most complex image"
of ourselves and our world in non-fiction, poetry, and drama (despite
saying very little about the latter two genres here, mostly for reasons
of economy, but also due to lack of knowledge). Again, that's the reason why I take "writing" as my organizing concept in this account.

This is as good a place as any to issue a few caveats. My selections are bound to be idiosyncratic, and the absence of various books and gaps in the discussion are likely more a function of my ignorance rather than an expression of distaste. I intend that remark about idiosyncrasy as more than a rhetorical politeness. I not only imagine other readers producing alternative readings of the first decade of the 21st century, but I'm aware that my account is shadowed by a considerable number of first-rate books which I don't discuss, but that easily could have become the basis for further investigation. By way of example: Alex Ross's resonant history of 20th century modern music, *The Rest Is Noise* (2007), is one of the liveliest surveys of the "lively arts"; Suketu Mehta's account of Bombay, *Maximum City* (2005), Roberto Saviano's *Gomorrah* (2006), an investigation of criminal networks in and around Naples, and Vancouver physician Gabor Mate's *In the Realm of Hungry Ghosts* (2008) all provide harrowing urban portraits; Tim Flannery's *The Weather Makers* (2006) is one of many good books about a crucial issue of the period, climate change; and even Gary Taubes's *Good Calories, Bad Calories* (2007), one of the few serious books about the science of nutrition, is fascinating and informative, especially in an era of burgeoning waistlines. Further, I regretfully ignore such literary genres as detective novels and "speculative" or science-fiction, which often produce work as or more interesting than general fiction. Finally, in this litany of omission, I leave aside a broad array of scholarly and academic books, many of which deserve extended reflection.

Beyond particular books I've omitted, it would have been possible to trace the work of other authors than the ones I choose: other readers would have looked at the recent books of such writers as Marilynne Robinson, Joyce Carol Oates, Don DeLillo, Cormac McCarthy, Thomas Pynchon, Toni Morrison, Alice Munro, and Margaret Atwood, just to name a few North American writers not included here. In the end, while I despair of my failures of inclusion, I'm heartened by the abundance of good work.

I write about Naomi Klein, Azar Nafisi, Chimamanda Adichie, Barbara Ehrenreich, and other women writers, but I notice that my text lists in the direction of male authors. I'm not sure how big a problem this is, but if it is one, it's complicated by a variety of factors. In a certain obvious sense, writers are writers and not divisible by gender, but at the same time it has been important, in recent times, to read

women writers, at least partially, *qua* women, both because of their
enlargement of the understanding of human experience and as a way
of resisting the sexism that stains the history of writing. I don't know
if the paucity of attention to women writers here reflects a lack of
sensitivity on my part or if it's simply that such writing has been less
urgent for me as a reader than in earlier periods, when I was preoccupied by the works of Nadine Gordimer, Doris Lessing, Marguerite
Duras, and Christa Wolf as well as various theorists and popularisers
of feminism, beginning with Simone de Beauvoir. Perhaps the success
of feminism in recent decades in alerting us to the question of gender
in writing has mitigated its urgency. That the issue of gender still matters can be gauged from the angry response to a *Publishers Weekly* list
of the purported top ten books of 2009 in which all of the selections
were authored by males; and more affirmatively, by the positive regard in which the Orange Prize, a literary award for women, is held.
In any case, I'm aware that there may be serious gaps here.

    The biographical circumstance that I've "divided" my time over the
last decade between Vancouver, Canada, and Berlin, Germany, results
in my paying more attention to international writing than would otherwise be the case. Nor have I been rigidly precise in terms of time boundaries, given that the notion of a decade as a defining measure for
literature or politics is an arbitrary one. This is especially relevant in the
case of translations, which, in English, are often quite belated. So, I discuss a few books from the very end of the 1990s, and I didn't close
down shop at midnight on New Year's eve of the last day of 2009. In
terms of critical temperament, I'd say I'm more of a cheerful reader
than a grumpy one, on the premise that if you don't basically like books,
it's probably not a good idea to pursue a vocation of reviewing them.

As I noted above, I treat both fiction and non-fiction simply as "writing." I organize my survey according to broad themes that I think
characterize the decade and its intellectual interests. I intersperse
those discussions with essays about, and reviews of, particular books
that I found interesting and significant. It would be a distortion of
those books to pigeonhole them in artificial categories and, in any
case, I want to convey some of the flavour of my encounter with
them. However, *Reading the 21st Century* is intended as a coherent
portrait of writing in a designated period and is not a critic's collection of occasional reviews or an overbroad survey that attempts to

put in a good word for everything worthy of note. Some of the themes I focus on are a direct reflection of political, economic and cultural processes that have unfolded during the past ten years, others have emerged more indirectly.

A discussion of books about 9/11, and the wars in Iraq and Afghanistan is grouped together in a chapter titled "Homeland Alone" and looks specifically at some of the many well-written and informative books about the period's global politics. In a chapter called "The Gods That Failed," I consider the development of what is known as "the new atheism" and the books that have pressed that argument, most notably Richard Dawkins's *The God Delusion* (2006). Thinking about the old age and recent passing of many significant writers, I look at their later works in a chapter on "Exit Strategies." The losses caused by death are irreparable, but there are also gains to consider. I take account of some of those gains in "Other Voices, Other Realms," a look at newly available international writing. In "Haunted by a Spectre" I examine some of the works that address the global economic crisis that has dominated public attention since 2008 and counting. As I said at the outset, the condition of 21st century intellectual life during this period weighs heavily on my mind. That theme is considered early on in a series of reviews of books, under the heading "Ignorance in the Desert," that worry about the decline of storytelling, historical memory, education, and book reading itself.

Reading the 21st Century is a book about the stories of our time, fictional and non-fictional, and since our time is also a self-reflexive one, my most persistent corollary theme is about the nature of storytelling itself. In fact, the book begins with reflections on Texas writer Larry McMurtry's *Walter Benjamin at the Dairy Queen* (1999), his ruminations on the state of storytelling at the end of the last century, and the subject recurrently appears in the text in chapters on Philip Roth, Javier Cercas, Daniel Mendelsohn, Azar Nafisi, and Amos Oz. As a way of demonstrating that my reading of the books under consideration is not an abstract exercise, I make use of my personal experiences in academia, journalism and as a citizen to show the relevance of books to our lives.

The project of engaging in a work of literary criticism at this time is marked by a certain irony, if not outright folly, given the technological and marketing changes now occurring in the publishing and distribution of books, and their effects on the subsidiary activity of criticism. Book publishing firms have been increasingly turned into dubious (read, insufficiently profitable) arms of larger "media convergence" corporations; book selling has shifted to the Internet (principally Amazon.com) and "big box" bookstores, with a consequent decline in "independent" outlets; and the transformation of the printed book into a digital version to be read and stored on an electronic device is in the offing, for better or worse.

I should note, for the sake of clarity, that I'm not engaging in the discussion of technological "delivery systems" here. I think the debate about printed books versus electronic ones that are read on digital devices has more to do with the "business plans" and "marketing strategies" of various "stakeholders" than it does with reading and writing or the content of intellectual life. I'm formally (and personally) indifferent to the form of books, though like other readers I'm interested in their availability and their role in public life. My concern is primarily with the content of books and their use by readers. I'm particularly interested in texts that can provide a sufficiently sustained reading experience that makes possible informed engagement with the political, cultural, and moral issues of our time. While such reading is possible through devices that utilize hyperlinked, interactive, electronic networks, there is little evidence to date that those devices are used with the "willed attention" required by sustained reading. In fact, the data so far suggests the contrary, but that is an interpretive argument that can be left to the larger analysis of our intellectual condition.

The effect of these developments on literary criticism has been a simultaneous diminution of print reviewing and a dispersion of online criticism, with debatable results concerning the quality of the reviewing. Stand-alone book sections of weekend newspapers, from the *Globe and Mail* in Canada to the *Washington Post* in the U.S., have disappeared, a trend that follows on a developing general tendency to reduce the number and length of book reviews in recent years. Publications like *Books in Canada* and *Saturday Night* have gone under, though *The New York Times Book Review*, and journals such as the *Literary Review of Canada*, *The New York Review of Books*, *Times Literary Supplement* (TLS), and the *London Review of Books* continue to exist, with limited readerships. Compared to, say, reviews of contemporary films, the number of reviews accorded to most books is now minuscule and seldom reaches the critical mass that adds up to a lively intellectual discussion. All of these developments are reflective of the diminishing importance of book reading in a world where "entertainment" products gradually replace art.

Reading Lewis Dabney's *Edmund Wilson: A Life in Literature* (2005) and Richard Cook's *Alfred Kazin: A Biography* (2007), the lives of two of America's best-known literary critics of the last century, brought home to me that we are possibly living in the twilight of literary criticism. Wilson (1895–1972), a critic, literary scholar, autobiographer, and historian, and Kazin (1915–1998), often seen as the successor to Wilson, both flourished in an early- and mid-20th century milieu where it was taken for granted that the worth and meaning of writing was a natural feature of cultural life. There was no debate about the value of books. It was a given. That's no longer the case. So, an endeavour at "reading the 21st century" is, perforce, a defense of a particular cultural practice, literary criticism. Since literary criticism is but a branch of a larger endangered activity, "reading the 21st century" is also a defense of *criticism* itself, in the broadest sense of that term.

ACKNOWLEDGEMENTS

My thanks to Brian Fawcett, John Dixon, and two anonymous readers for McGill-Queen's University Press for reading the manuscript and making helpful suggestions that I've incorporated into the text. In Vancouver, I'm grateful to Tom Sandborn, George Stanley, Don Larventz, Norbert Ruebsaat, and Dan Gawthrop, who are long-standing friends and members of the book reading group to which I belong; to my colleagues at Capilano University, especially Dan Munteanu and Jenny Penberthy, with whom I've enjoyed numerous discussions about the books of our era; and to David Beers, editor of *The Tyee*, where early versions of some of this material appeared. In Berlin, I'm appreciative of years of conversation about literature and life with Ilonka Opitz, Thomas Marquard, Nadja al-Wakeel, Frank Berberich, Arno Schmitt, and Damian Rytwinski; as well, I want to acknowledge the staff at Marga Schoeller bookstore, particularly Shirley Wray and Thomas Schaal, for their knowledgeable help and reading recommendations. Finally, my thanks to Don Akenson and his colleagues at MQUP for their encouragement and many courtesies.

May 2011
Vancouver-Berlin

READING THE 21ST CENTURY

The Storyteller: Larry McMurtry

I first learned of the Texas-based writer Larry McMurtry from my
friend Bobbie Louise Hawkins, herself a Texan and a writer. This was
many years ago, in the kitchen of Hawkins's house in the seacoast
town of Bolinas, California, where Bobbie, who is also an accomplished cook, was whipping us up a "Tex-Mex" lunch. Maybe that's
what started her thinking about McMurtry, already a well-known
popular novelist, some of whose books, such as *The Last Picture
Show* (1966), had been turned into successful Hollywood movies.

Hawkins's point was that McMurtry, someone who wrote primarily
about Texas for mass audiences, was neither merely a regional author
nor a potboiler pop writer. There was more to him than that. The implication was that it was through his appreciation of the specifics of the
local, in this instance Texas, that he arrived at a cosmopolitan intelligence, one that revealed something about the world. In due course, on
Bobbie's good advice, I read a couple of McMurtry's books. Whatever
else he was as an author, McMurtry was certainly, as anyone who's
read any of his twenty or so novels knows, a good storyteller, one of
those people who makes the telling of a tale seem almost effortless.

The broader range of McMurtry's interests is displayed in his in-
triguingly titled *Walter Benjamin at the Dairy Queen: Reflections at
Sixty and Beyond* (1999), published appropriately enough on the
cusp of a new century. It provides a pretty good account of what's on
his mind, as well as an introduction to questions of narrative, communication, and experience that will be germane to writing in the
first decade of the 21st century.

McMurtry starts off drolly, one summer day in 1980 in the Archer
City, Texas, Dairy Queen outlet. Archer County is where McMurtry

was born and raised. He's "nursing a lime Dr. Pepper (a delicacy strictly local, unheard of even in the next Dairy Queen down the road – Olney's, 18 miles south – but easily obtainable by anyone willing to buy a lime and a Dr. Pepper)." In addition to sipping his soda pop, McMurtry is reading Walter Benjamin's essay, "The Storyteller."

I, too, have read the famous "Storyteller" essay by Benjamin, the German-Jewish literary and cultural critic who died in 1940, by his own hand, while fleeing the Nazis. It's one of the three (maybe four, if you add McMurtry's reflections) indispensable works on the subject of storytelling that I know. The other two are John Berger's essay "The Storyteller" in his book *The Sense of Sight* (1986) and Mario Vargas Lllosa's extraordinary novel of that name, *The Storyteller* (1990).

Benjamin's essay is, as McMurtry says, "an examination, and a profound one, of the growing obsolescence of what might be called practical memory and the consequent diminution of the power of oral narrative in our twentieth-century lives." If the culture of oral storytelling is in decline, I'd add, that will have consequences for written narrative as well, with respect to the list of what's becoming obsolete and of diminishing power in our time.

In attempting to identify some of the correspondences between Benjamin's observations and his own situation, McMurtry's memoir is inevitably a story of what it's like to grow up in the bleak cowboy country of small west Texas towns, where the "aridity ... was not all a matter of unforgiving skies, baking heat, and rainlessness; the drought ... was social, as well as climatic."

In places like Vancouver, Toronto, Chicago, and other large cities, the Dairy Queens are now little more than unfashionably down-at-the-heels early exemplars of the fast-food chain-franchises of global capitalism. But in arid Archer City, circa 1980, the Dairy Queen served as one of the rare settings with the "potential for storytelling of the sort Walter Benjamin favoured."

As McMurtry says, "It was startling to sit in that Dairy Queen, reading the words of a cosmopolitan European, a man of Berlin, Moscow, Paris, and realize that what he was describing with a clear sad eye was more or less exactly what happened in my own small dusty county in my lifetime." I can add that it's still pretty startling to read Benjamin in the city of his birth, Berlin, as I've found myself doing more than once in recent years. McMurtry notes, "I was born, in the year of the essay [1936], into a world of rural storytellers," then asks, " – and what had become of them?"

Answering that question will require a hundred pages or so of telling the story of his pioneering ancestors and their futile scrabbling for a living (a tale of cowboys, cattle, and grass), but one possibility that McMurtry immediately canvasses is found in Benjamin's own speculations. "In every case," says Benjamin, "the storyteller is a [person] who has counsel for his readers. But if today 'having counsel' is beginning to have an old-fashioned ring to it, it is because the communicability of experience is decreasing." McMurtry notes that one reason Benjamin "offers in explaining why we no longer exchange experience (by telling or listening to stories) is that experience has fallen in value – 'and it looks as if it will continue to fall into bottomlessness.'" If experience and imagination, the sources of stories and books, have declined in value, that doesn't bode well for either practical or intellectual life. Or as a friend of mine dourly quipped, books have less intellectual credibility today because intellectual credibility has less credibility.

Whatever the explanation, we are well into the subject of experience and its communicability, and in the company of a writer who is neither merely regional or pop. When young McMurtry came along, about a half-century after the first McMurtrys settled Archer County, "there were still only a few people to be seen, but life had nonetheless accumulated, in all its puzzling but pregnant detail." In the evening, once the chores were done, the covey of McMurtrys gathered on the front porch or around the fireplace, depending on the season, and told stories.

"None of those stories was ever told to or directed at me," he says, "but I was allowed to listen to whatever stories the adults were telling one another." Except for the occasional square dance, "no one had any entertainment *except* the exchanging of experience that occurs in storytelling. So it was, no doubt, in rural places throughout the centuries; then, there was no media – now, it seems, there's no life."

McMurtry has considerably more to say about "the extent to which what's given us by the media is our memory now," and he wonders, "Does mere human memory, the soil that nourishes storytelling, still have any use at all?" McMurtry, writing at the end of the 20th century, is already living in a culture in which oral and written storytelling has been largely subsumed by the visual culture of movies and television and its consequent effects on "mere memory." A decade later, we have the Internet, ubiquitous iPod music players, incessant chattering on cellphones in public, and the truncated contact that various "social networking" websites enable – and sometimes all of these digital devices employed at once in a blur of distraction euphemistically known as "multi-tasking." McMurtry didn't have to be particularly prescient to see it coming.

Here, and in other parts of *Walter Benjamin at the Dairy Queen*, McMurtry provides an engrossing, often humourous tale of his own successful escape from the fate of being a cowboy, as well as his subsequent adventures as a reader, writer, and obsessive book collector. He also offers a grim, credible account of the wrong-headedness of what cowboys were fated to do.

"In a sense the whole range cattle industry, source of a central national myth, was a mistake, based on a superficial understanding of plains environment," he says. The fifty million buffalo that had once grazed the plains were wiped out in a scant twenty years, replaced by forty-five million cattle, "to the ultimate detriment of everyone's home on the range." One of the points that McMurtry makes, an insight that revises our understanding of a foundational American legend, is that the plump Hereford cattle were simply the wrong animals for the environment: McMurtry's grandparents and their descendents would have done better with skinny Mexican longhorns. "Now the plains are so overgrazed – the public lands particularly – that should a major drought occur, the potential for a new dust bowl is great." McMurtry's estimate of the accomplishments of his ancestors, as well as his own achievements in "word-herding" rather than cattle-herding, is a consistently thoughtful pleasure to read.

"It is usually when one is in one's sixties that one begins to wonder whether the customary yardsticks by which success is measured have any relevance at all," McMurtry says. (I've begun to wonder about that myself, ever since arriving at a similar age.) "My father, as he neared the end, counted himself lucky that he had owned a few good horses in his life ... Though he enjoyed great respect, and the love of his family, in his last years he often expressed to me his conviction that reality was more than a little cracked. Somehow, life hadn't really added up; his works and days hadn't been a harmony ..."

McMurtry has similar intimations in these stories told from the Archer City Dairy Queen. "When I consider my twenty and more books I sometimes feel the same uneasy breeze that my father felt at he contemplated the too meager acres where his life began and ended. My achievement may not be much different from his ... I think two or three of my books are good, just as he thought two or three of the many horses that he owned were good." As for the rest, so be it.

For all his self-deprecation, it's interesting to note that McMurtry is one of the storytellers of our time who most successfully made the transition from the printed page to the screens of movies and television. In addition to *The Last Picture Show*, his first novel, *Horseman, Pass By* (1961) became the hit film *Hud*. He turned his Pulitzer Prize-winning novel *Lonesome Dove* (1985) into a TV miniseries and co-wrote the Oscar-winning screenplay of *Brokeback Mountain* (2005) from an E. Annie Proulx short story.

In any case, there's plenty of McMurtry storytelling available for judgment, but what remains is the issue of what use or value memory and experience have, a question to which McMurtry, sensibly enough, doesn't attempt to provide a definitive answer, since there isn't one. Other than recognizing it as the question that any of us who aspires to storytelling must confront, I'm of two minds about it. There's not much practical difference for me between oral storytelling and writing, and the latter is as much peril in as the former. The social-political context, on many days, strikes me as being as bleak as those small west Texas towns McMurtry knows. It just can't get any dumber, or more vicious, I more-than-occasionally think, contemplating the latest vulgarity or atrocity.

But those dark thoughts don't encompass the whole of the territory. Not a year has gone by that hasn't brought a book, or several, at least an interesting as McMurtry's. That will turn out to be the case for the decade I'm contemplating, although the readers of those interesting books may find themselves increasingly isolated.

At this later stage of his life, McMurtry is more painfully aware of his limitations than before, but as a writer and critic he continues to fashion stories, essays, and meditations like *Walter Benjamin at the Dairy Queen*. In a practical sense, the conditions under which stories are told don't much matter. Writers like McMurtry will go on doing what he does in writing and storytelling, simply because doing so is pretty much inextricable from the rest of him. Such people also tend to be willing, as McMurtry has, to lend a hand to the social politics of it all, in which we struggle for the kinds of lives and communities we hope to have. My own sense of the matter is that my life and those of my friends continue to be replete with stories, from large narratives to everyday anecdotes, though, like McMurtry, I now keep a nervous eye on the darkening horizon. If "word-herders" are raising the wrong animal for the environment, the Internet will no doubt soon enough inform us.

As for Walter Benjamin, who died at forty-eight, "almost from the beginning he labored under the curse of the exaggerated expectation which his own early brilliance had created. He is the archtype of the self-disappointed writer," McMurtry claims. "What Benjamin ended up with was a few finished and admirable essays ... and a slag heap of notes, flashes of light that are just that, flashes." McMurtry adds, "But the sparks do have a white brilliance that in itself is enough."

It's impossible to read McMurtry's meditations on Benjamin without turning to the author of "The Storyteller" himself. Conveniently enough, in the same *fin-de-siecle* year as McMurtry's book was published, Harvard University Press was publishing part of a four volume series of Benjamin's *Selected Writings* in English, and in it we can read some of those "admirable" essays, including "Unpacking My Library," "Moscow," and "A Berlin Chronicle." McMurtry cites Benjamin's experimental, fragmentary book of extended aphorisms, *One Way Street* (one of the few books he published in his lifetime), and suggests that it was probably "the mode he might always have chosen had he not been seduced by the notion of size, of large ambition, or the masterpiece." It's a shrewd and fair assessment, I think, and perhaps even a recipe for some contemporary writers.

2

Indelible: Philip Roth's *Human Stain*

I

Philip Roth is quick to remind us, right near the beginning of *The Human Stain* (2000), that Western literature begins with a bitter argument, one that takes place in the midst of a bogged-down war. If "all of European literature springs from a fight," so does Roth's pugnacious novel, set in the midst of America's "culture wars" at the very end of the 20th century.

Coleman Silk, the book's protagonist, is a former professor of classics who spent his entire career, both teaching and in administration, at Athena College, located in the Berkshire hills of rural Massachusetts. When he was still teaching, before his angry resignation (more about that in a minute), Professor Silk, having taken the roll at the first class meeting of his ancient Greek literature course, would rhetorically ask his students, "You know how European literature begins?" and immediately supply the answer: "With a quarrel. All of European literature springs from a fight."

To demonstrate his point, Silk would pick up a copy of Homer's *Iliad* and read to the class its indelible opening lines, "Divine Muse, sing of the ruinous wrath of Achilles ... Begin where they first quarreled, Agamemnon the King of men, and great Achilles." Looking up from Homer, Silk would ask, "And what are they quarreling about, these two violent mighty souls? It's as basic as a barroom brawl. They are quarreling over a woman. A girl, really. A girl stolen from her father. A girl abducted in a war ..."

And we're off, as countless other Greek Lit in Translation survey courses have been, parsing the details of who said what to whom on the plains of Troy and what Apollo, Athena, Zeus, and other divinities thought and did. Not only does the *Iliad* begin with the Greek military leaders quarreling among themselves about sacrificed daughters, wives on the homefront, and girls who are the spoils of war but, it will be recalled, the whole quagmire of the Trojan War is predicated on an even more sensational outrage, the abduction or elopement of Helen, wife of a Greek king, seduced by the intemperate Paris, prince of Troy.

The Human Stain, in my view the first great American novel of the new millennium, opens a couple of years after the professor's last classroom peroration with the revelation of a semi-scandalous secret about a relationship. As the book's narrator puts it, "It was in the summer of 1998 that my neighbour Coleman Silk … confided to me that, at the age of seventy-one, he was having an affair with a thirty-four-year-old cleaning woman who worked down at the college," one Faunia Farley.

The voice of the narrator, Nathan Zuckerman, will be familiar to readers of Philip Roth. *The Human Stain* is the concluding volume of an "American" trilogy that Roth produced in his mid-60s, at a time in life when many writers are winding down. (I discuss Roth's late writings further in chapter 11, "Exit Strategies.") It is also the eighth of a nine-novel cycle in which Zuckerman, Roth's "alter brain," appears. Zuckerman is, in this incarnation, in his mid-60s, a reclusive, well-known Jewish novelist, now incontinent and impotent (the result of the removal of his cancerous prostate), who has retreated into the New England backwoods, Nathaniel Hawthorne country, to practice his solitary, exacting vocation, one that, as he says much later in the book, is "in professional competition with death."

But before Roth provides the details of Coleman's affair with Faunia and the quarrels it engenders, quarrels on the order of those between Agamemnon and Achilles, Zuckerman launches into a medium-decibel tirade about the broader cultural war in which this particular skirmish will play out.

"The summer that Coleman took me into his confidence about Faunia Farley and their secret," says Zuckerman, "was the summer, fittingly enough, that Bill Clinton's secret emerged in every last mortifying detail – every last *lifelike* detail, the livingness, like the mortification, exuded by the pungency of the specific data." Perhaps a decade or so on from President Bill Clinton's fling with a government intern,

Monica Lewinsky, the lifelike details of the forensics, including a semen-stained blue dress, and possibly even the ensuing congressional impeachment trial of the libidinous president will have faded from public memory. But not for Zuckerman.

> Ninety-eight in New England was a summer of exquisite warmth and sunshine ... and in America the summer of an enormous piety binge, a purity binge, when terrorism – which had replaced communism as the prevailing threat to the nation's security – was succeeded by cocksucking, and a virile, youthful middle-aged president and a brash, smitten twenty-one year-old employee carrying on in the Oval Office like two teenaged kids in a parking lot revived America's oldest communal passion, historically perhaps its most treacherous and subversive pleasure: the ecstasy of sanctimony. In the Congress, in the press, and on the networks, the righteous grandstanding creeps, crazy to blame, deplore, and punish, were everywhere out moralizing to beat the band; all of them in a calculated frenzy with what Hawthorne (who, in the 1860s, lived not many miles from my door) identified in the incipient country of long ago as 'the persecuting spirit'... No, if you haven't lived through 1998, you don't know what sanctimony is.

Whatever else is going to happen at ground level to Coleman and Faunia (and plenty will), Zuckerman wants us to be apprised of the larger context, the Olympian level, the quarrels of the gods. Not perhaps the magnitude of a war over Troy, but an American culture war over Trojan condoms, identity politics, Viagra, racial righteousness, family values, and sexual propriety. As Zuckerman says, if you weren't there, you don't know what sanctimony is.

Prior to his semi-forced resignation, Coleman Silk had been a paragon of academia, "one of a handful of Jews on the Athena faculty when he was hired and perhaps among the first of the Jews permitted to teach in a classics department anywhere in America." Moreover, for all those years, he'd been an ostensibly orthodox family man, married four decades to his wife, Iris, and father of four children. While reconstructing Silk's c.v., Zuckerman notes in an aside that a few years earlier Jews had been a rarity in those parts; indeed, the only Jew around Athena had been E.I. Lonoff, the all-but-forgotten short story writer, to whom, back when Zuckerman was a newly published apprentice, he had paid a "memorable visit." Faithful readers of Roth will get the little in-joke here, a reference to *The Ghost Writer* (1979), the first of the Zuckerman cycle, in which that memorable visit to Lonoff is recounted.

Not only was Silk a prominent professor, he was also the first and only Jew ever to become dean of faculty at Athena, and as dean, "Coleman had taken an antiquated, backwater, Sleepy Hollowish college and not without steamrolling, put an end to the place as a gentleman's farm ..." Then, in the mid-1990s, after stepping down as dean, in order to round out his career back in the classroom before full retirement, he resumed teaching in the newly combined languages and literature department, which had in postmodernist fashion absorbed "classics," and was run by the stylish French-born Professor Delphine Roux.

It was back in the classroom as a full-time professor "that Coleman spoke the self-incriminating word that would cause him voluntarily to sever all ties to the college – the single self-incriminating word of the many millions spoken aloud in his years of teaching and administering at Athens, and the word that, as Coleman understood things, directly led to his wife's death." Like profs everywhere, Silk had taken attendance at the beginning of the semester, partly to learn the names of his students. But there were two names that failed to get a response five weeks into the semester. At the next class, Coleman opened the session by asking, "Does anyone know these people? Do they exist or are they spooks?" *Spooks.*

Later that day, Professor Silk was "astonished to be called in by his successor, the new dean of faculty, to address the charge of racism brought against him by the two missing students, who turned out to be black, and who, though absent, had quickly learned of the locution in which he'd publicly raised the question of their absence."

Impatiently, Silk tells the dean, "I was referring to their possibly ectoplasmic character. Isn't that obvious? These two students had not attended a single class. That's all I knew about them. I was using the word in its customary and primary meaning: 'spook' as a specter or a ghost. I had no idea what color these two students might be. I had known perhaps fifty years ago but had wholly forgotten that 'spooks' is an invidious term sometimes applied to blacks. Otherwise, since I am a totally meticulous ..." Though he goes on (and on, as all of Roth's characters do), given the moment in American cultural life, whatever he says is going to be too much and not enough.

In due course, Silk angrily resigns from Athena, his wife Iris unexpectedly dies of a stroke in the middle of the dispute (which is why Coleman thinks of her death as a direct casualty of the bizarre incident of political correctness), and Coleman goes a little crazy – which is what brings him into contact with Zuckerman, with whom heretofore he'd had only a nodding acquaintance.

By then, it's two years later, the time of Clinton's fling and the attempted impeachment that followed it. The retired Silk has managed to right himself and is in the midst of his age-defying affair with Faunia, when trouble comes again. This time, it's double-barrelled: first, there's an anonymous letter that says, "Everyone knows you're sexually exploiting an abused, illiterate woman half your age," penned, it turns out, by no one other than the Fury-driven Professor Delphine Roux, who also had a hand in the "spooks" incident. Second, there's Les Farley, the ex-husband of Faunia, a damaged Vietnam vet still suffering from Post-Traumatic Stress Disorder a quarter-century after the war that gave rise to it, who's prone to stalking his ex-wife and her elderly Jewish lover. As Roth sets it up, there's no shortage of quarrels, no lack of elements of tragedy in an era "when some kind of demon had been unleashed in the nation and, on both sides, people wondered 'Why are we so crazy?'"

2

The high-tide waters of academic "identity politics," though they left vestigial flotsam in the form of campus "harassment officers" and "speech codes," have considerably receded since Roth's book appeared. And perhaps with the election of Barack Obama in 2008, so should the broader cultural war in America. Readers coming belatedly to *The Human Stain* may wonder if there really was a time when a misconstrued word on a college campus could lead to a witch hunt, or a cross-generational romance could excite the Furies, feminist or warrior, to a wrath equivalent to that depicted in Hawthorne's *Scarlet Letter*.

The year before Roth's novel was published, Richard Rorty (1931–2007), the most interesting American philosopher of the latter part of the 20th century, discussed the country's ongoing ideological

confrontation in "Trotsky and the Wild Orchids," an essay in his
Philosophy and Social Hope (1999), one of the defining books of the
era. "At the moment there are two cultural wars being waged in the
United States," Rorty observed. The first war, he said, is the important
one. It's the one between "decent, humanitarian liberals" versus fundamentalists of various stripes, promoting everything from born-
again religious revivalism to faith-based opposition to abortion,
homosexuality, gun control, and even government itself. The outcome
of that cultural war, Rorty predicted, "will decide whether our country continues along the trajectory" of everything from the Bill of
Rights to the New Deal to the civil rights, feminist, and gay movements of our own era. "Continuing along that trajectory would mean
that America might continue to set an example of increasing tolerance
and increasing equality." Rorty saw the fundamentalists, "the people
who think hounding gays out of the military promotes traditional
family values, as the same honest, decent, blinkered, disastrous people
who voted for Hitler in 1933." Rorty viewed the humanitarian liberals "as defining the only America I care about."

The second cultural war, he argued, is being waged primarily in
the universities and its attendant intellectual journals. "It is between
those who see modern liberal society as fatally flawed (the people
handily lumped together as 'postmodernists') and typical left-wing
Democrat professors like myself, people who see ours as a society in
which technology and democratic institutions can, with luck, col-
laborate to increase equality and decrease suffering. This war is not
very important," Rorty declared. It is, he said, "just a tiny little dispute" within the ranks of "upmarket progressives."

People on the harsher postmodernist left, Rorty claimed, operate
from the perspective that the U.S. "is not so much in danger of slip-
ping into fascism as it is a country which has always been quasi-
fascist. These people typically think that nothing will change unless
we get rid of 'humanism,' 'liberal individualism' and 'technologism.'
People like me," the social democratic Rorty admitted, "see nothing
wrong with any of these –isms, nor with the political and moral heritage of the Enlightenment."

The identity politics of the 1990s that raged in the corridors of
academia were far removed, in tone and temperament, from the earlier "counterculture" campus politics of the 1960s, a now legendary
time of turbulence frequently and falsely cited by conservatives as

the source of all of America's subsequent ills. Though the New Left student politics of the 1960s were not short of foolishness and self-inflation, they were interestingly utopian, sometimes imaginative, and even playful, before they dissipated into a home-grown version of terrorism. By contrast, the left-wing campus politics of the 1990s were rather a grim-lipped affair, humourless for the most part and possessed of a self-righteousness reflective of an academic left that was powerless outside the precincts of its own committee rooms, lacking influence in a world where the real inequalities reigned. Since absence of power is proportionally inverse to the savagery displayed in its own bailiwick, the excesses of political correctness were predictable, if not of primary importance.

Though Rorty regarded most of what got to be called "political correctness" and "identity politics" in the 1990s as "politically silly," and quickly picked up on the early-warning signs of academic tribalism, he nonetheless also saw that many of those attacking postmodernism were prone to a sort of "Blimpishness." They tended to ignore the criticisms of injustice that had motivated the postmodernists in the first place. Overall, Rorty displayed a level-headedness when it comes to the less important academic disputes, a cool demeanour not shared at Athena College. As for the important cultural war with the fundamentalists, whom Rorty believed to be "philosophically wrong as well as politically dangerous," that's the one to pay attention to, he insisted.

At the time of Rorty's essay, written in the mid-1990s, the first signs of calm on the turbulent waters of identity politics were about to appear, but the flood waters of the important cultural war continued to rage. It's the genius of Roth's *Human Stain* to inextricably intertwine both aspects of those culture wars that Rorty delineated.

The point is that Roth isn't making it up, even though he's writing satire. By happenstance, as a faculty member myself, at a post-secondary institution not all that different from Silk's Athena College, I was one of the people who "lived through it," as Zuckerman says, and thus got an intimation of "what sanctimony is."

The discussion of "sexual harassment" on campus, and corollary issues involving discrimination against people of different ethnic and racial identities, as well as those of differing abilities and sexual orientation, began plausibly enough. When the problem of sexual harassment was called to our attention, I and others were prepared to raise our hands at the appropriate time to vote for the resolution to stop that sort of thing.

The appropriate moment and the resolution soon arrived. But from the beginning, there was something curious about the issue for which we were devising preventive mechanisms. First, there already existed an extensive process of monitoring and evaluating the performance and behaviour of teachers and students, which included the acts now called "sexual harassment" and provided penalties up to and including expulsion. Second, our school (and similar ones) was already in the intellectual forefront of criticising sexism, racism, and homophobia in our society. But, on the other hand, maybe a proverbial "ounce of prevention" was worth the effort, we thought, to capture some acts lying between Criminal Code offenses and institutional regulatory codes.

In the end, the policy we (and many others) adopted, included, among much else, the notion that sexual harassment isn't just unwanted touching and threatening come-ons but also "comment of a sexual nature when the comment has the effect of creating an offensive [classroom or campus] environment, and it may include the expression of sexist attitudes." It didn't take much foresight to envision that the policy's virtues might be outstripped by its potential excesses.

I probably would have thought Coleman Silk's "spooks" incident rather farfetched if I hadn't seen a "decent, humanitarian liberal" professor at a neighbouring university get caught up in something similar. Protesting a graduate student's thesis defence at which male faculty and students had been barred, the professor penned a memo in which he described the dissertation examination as an "orgy of self-congratulation." He was promptly charged by the student and her faculty advisor with sexual harrassment – the use of "orgy" was construed to mean an outbreak of lesbian sexuality on campus – and for the next two or three years his career was entangled in the coils of various human rights' tribunals and commissions. There were other such incidents, not as many as conservative professors and commentators liked to claim, but enough of them.

Ultimately, a sort of sanity, or maybe only exhaustion from unreason, prevailed, and most of the circumstances that Roth sends up in *The Human Stain* have simply become an historical memory, along with "the persecuting spirit" Hawthorne detected in *The Scarlet Letter*.

3

About a quarter of the way into Roth's novel about identity politics, another far deeper secret about identity, with barely a hint of fore-warning, is suddenly revealed. Silk is consulting his ambitious young lawyer in Athena, Nelson Primus, about getting a restraining order against the possibly psychopathic Les Farley. Instead, Primus sub-jects Silk to an overbearing lecture about the foolishness of such a course of action and primly advises the elderly academic to simply drop his scandalous affair with Faunia. Silk is enraged. He tells Primus, "I never again want to hear that self-admiring voice of yours or see your smug fucking lily-white face."

A little aside here. The cameo characters, like Primus, who appear throughout *The Human Stain*, are never cut-outs, never mere carica-tures. Rather than simply dispatching the smug lawyer, as he might have done, Roth gives us the subsequent scene in which Primus goes home that evening and explains to his wife how he totally blew it with old Silk, perhaps as a result of some combination of intimida-tion ("the man is a force ... Somebody's *there* when he's sitting there") and a "wrong-headed attempt to be taken seriously by him, to im-press him." That is, Roth is sufficiently attentive to the nuances of human personality to show us that Primus is not just a self-righteous jerk. But Primus is left with a lingering question. "No, I don't fault him for unloading on me like that. But, honey, the question remains ... 'Lily-white'? Why 'lily-white'?"

With no more than that bare hint, Zuckerman begins a lengthy, richly detailed account of the youth of "Silky" Silk, growing up in a small New Jersey town, not unlike the one in which Zuckerman himself was raised, as the favourite son of a middle-class "model Negro family" of the late 1930s. They're middle-class enough to be shocked to discover that the adolescent, athletic Coleman has suc-cessfully taken up the pugilistic arts at the local boxing club. (How Zuckerman acquires all this deep background is only revealed near the novel's end, but as is typical of Roth's storytelling skills, the in-tricate plot is woven with adamant confidence.)

The revelation that Silk is a light-skinned black man who could and did pass as white (and Jewish), for most of a lifetime – and what about his kids? what if they display a recessive gene? (they don't) – only adds ultimate irony to his downfall, based as it is on a false accusation of uttering a racially derogatory remark. The improbable story of a man who reinvents himself at the cost of severing almost all ties to his past and breaking his mother's heart, is Roth's daring reversal of every celebration of "roots." If cultural politics is what the American left and right want to battle over, Philip Roth is prepared to lace up the gloves and take on America's deepest cultural shame, the "human stain" of skin colour itself.

The Human Stain was, for the most part, not only favourably received but listed as one of the *New York Times'* "10 best books of 2000," and it picked up a couple of lesser literary prizes, the Pen/Faulkner Award for Fiction and Britain's W.H. Smith Award. It didn't receive any of the bigger American prizes (the Pulitzer, National Book Award, or the National Book Critics Circle Award), and one critic, who otherwise praised the book, complained that the novel's weakest parts were the "hatefully rendered interior monologues" of Delphine Roux and Les Farley.

Well, it's true that Roth is less than fair to the French-born postmodern Fury, Delphine Roux, but it's also true that identity politics spewed up its share of unfairness as well. More important, Roth's unjust rendering is very funny. However, the charge about the portrait of Les Farley is unwarranted. Fairly early on in the story, Roth enters the Vietnam vet's tortured mind, and what ensues is a by now classic Roth full-rage riff that runs on for six, seven riveting pages. Here, and in subsequent chilling set pieces, Roth recreates the burntout psychopathology of a permanently damaged man, presented with no more squeamishness than Homer's portrait of battlefield carnage at Troy. By the time we get to the final scene, which finds Les ice-fishing at a remote pond and brandishing a large auger before Zuckerman's eyes, we are persuaded that such spectral casualties of war are afoot in the land.

Indeed, Roth's consummate mastery as a writer is repeatedly displayed in what I think of as the *filigree* work of the novel. As with the secondary character Nelson Primus, the lawyer, all of the lesser figures of the book – Coleman's children, or the first black professor that Silk hired at Athena, or the testosterone-fuelled ex-football star who now runs the college's maintenance department, even a cameo encounter with a cautious young policeman – are all drawn with full-bodied nuance, as Roth reveals their hypocrisies, strategic moves, and admirable strengths, in short, human complexities no less than those of the warriors in the old epics. Even the novel's presiding muse, Faunia, improbable and wounded as her life may be, is believable.

Roth can deliver a pitch-perfect filthy conversation (overheard by Silk) between three college employees on lunch-break lasciviously discussing the shenanigans between the American president and the smitten Monica Lewinsky and manage to slip in the underlying thematic. "She was talking to everybody," says one of them. "She's part of that dopey culture. Yap, yap, yap. Part of this generation that is proud of its shallowness. The sincere performance is everything. Sincere and empty, totally empty ... The sincerity that is worse than falseness, and the innocence that is worse than corruption."

Roth's characters talk and talk. No other American novelist so lets his characters ramble on, whether in interior monologues or aria-like orations. For all their loquaciousness, our attention seldom flags, so supple is Roth's grasp of the American conversation.

In almost every really first-rate novel, there's a moment or a scene where you know you're *inside* the story and are therefore prepared, as a reader, to let it carry you. That scene occurs early on in Roth's *Human Stain*. Silk first met Zuckerman by barging into the writer's cabin the day after his wife's death, demanding that Zuckerman write up the outrageous mistreatment that led to Silk's downfall and his wife's "murder." "All the restraint had collapsed within him, and so watching him, listening to him – a man I did not know, but clearly someone accomplished and of consequence now completely unhinged – was like being present at a bad highway accident ..." Ever since Zuckerman declined the proposal, Silk had been "at work on a book of his own about why he had resigned from Athena, a nonfiction book he was calling *Spooks*."

It's some time later. A friendship of sorts has grown, and Silk has gotten into the habit of inviting Zuckerman over to his place on a Saturday night for a drink or a game of cards while they listen to the radio playing old tunes from their youth. They're sitting in the screened-in side porch Silk uses as a summertime study, his notebooks stacked on his desk, and there's an epiphany.

"Well, there it is," said Coleman, now this calm, unoppressed, entirely new being. "That's it. That's *Spooks*. Finished a first draft yesterday, spent all day today reading it through, and every page made me sick ... That I should spend a single quarter of an hour at this, let alone two years ... But I read it and it's shit and I'm over it. I can't do what the pros do. Writing about myself. I can't maneuver the creative remove. Page after page, it is still the raw thing. It's a parody of the self-justifying memoir ..."

And then later that same evening, as the first bars of Frank Sinatra singing "Bewitched, Bothered and Bewildered" ooze from the radio, Silk says to Zuckerman, "I've got to dance. Want to dance?"

I laughed. No, this was not the savage, embittered, embattled avenger of *Spooks*, estranged from life and maddened by it – this was not even another man. This was another soul ...
     "Come, let's dance."
     "But you mustn't sing into my ear."
     "Come on, get up."
     What the hell, I thought, we'll both be dead soon enough, and so I got up, and there on the porch Coleman Silk and I began to dance the fox trot together. He led, and, as best I could, I followed ... One would have thought that never again would this man have a taste for the foolishness of life, that all that was playful in him and light-hearted had been destroyed and lost, right along with the career, the reputation and the formidable wife. Maybe why ... [I] let him, if he wanted to ... place his arm around my back and push me dreamily around that old bluestone floor was because I had been there that day when her corpse was still warm and seen what he'd looked like.
     "I hope nobody from the volunteer fire department drives by," I said.
     "Yeah," he said, "We don't want anybody tapping me on the shoulder and asking, 'May I cut in?'"
     On we danced. There was nothing overtly carnal in it, but because Coleman was wearing only his denim shorts and my hand rested easily on his warm back ... it wasn't entirely a mocking act. There was a semi-serious sincerity in his guiding me about on the stone floor, not to mention a thoughtless delight in just being alive, accidentally and clownishly and for no reason alive ...

Once you've seen those two old men dancing across the porch of a rural cabin on a summer Saturday night, you're willing to hear whatever Roth has to tell you about – to echo the final word of his novel – "America."

Heroes: Javier Cercas's *Soldiers of Salamis*

I

Javier Cercas opens his novel *Soldiers of Salamis* (2001; translated into English by Anne McLean, 2003), by telling us that he initially heard the Spanish Civil War story "about Rafael Sanchez Mazas facing the firing squad" in the summer of 1994, a half dozen years before the writing of the book we're reading and more than a half century after the events depicted in that story.

So, this is going to be a story about a story, an investigation into an historical "true tale," "constantly alert to its own constructs," as one reviewer, Colm Toibin, put it. But as Cercas is told much later in the novel, "Listen, those stories don't interest anyone any more, not even those of us who lived through them; there was a time when they did, but not any more. Someone decided they had to be forgotten and, you know what I say? They were probably right ... it would be best ... if you forgot about this nonsense and devoted your time to something else." Thus, the problem is how to interest people in stories, like the one about Sanchez Mazas facing the firing squad, that "don't interest anyone any more."

Cercas, the real-life narrator of *Soldiers of Salamis*, presents himself as a fortyish, sad-sack, failing writer, husband, and son. He's forced to abandon his unrealized literary ambitions and slink back to his old journalist's job (where they now make him "do everything but get the boss's coffee from the bar on the corner") at a newspaper in the northern Catalan city of Gerona. It's a provincial city in Spain's Catalonia region, located between the French Pyrenees and the regional capital of Barcelona, a part of the country to which George

Orwell famously paid tribute in his memoir of the Spanish Civil War, *Homage to Catalonia* (1938).

I probably should say "seemingly real-life narrator" in describing Cercas, because although it's true, as Cercas claims, that he published a couple of apparently less than memorable books a decade or so before this one, he also tells us at the outset that his father recently died and his wife left him. But in a later interview about his novel, which he insists is a "true tale," Cercas says that in fact his father is not dead and that "Javier Cercas" is a fictionalized version of Javier Cercas, the novelist and lecturer in Spanish literature at the University of Gerona. (Richard Lea, "Really intense tales," *The Guardian*, June 15, 2007.)

I don't have any information about the alleged wife who abandoned him as he sat in a blocked-writer's funk before a blank television screen, but Conchi, the ebullient, irrepressibly vulgar, improbable TV fortune-teller girlfriend who turns up shortly afterwards certainly seems like a work of the imagination (she's the one who will tell Cercas, "Well, honey, I don't think imagination is really your strong suit"). Whatever else is going on in the "true tale" of the now-seemingly ancient Spanish Civil War that Cercas is investigating, the scaffolding around it is designed to be playfully enticing and may be one of the ways of getting us "interested" in stories "that don't interest anyone any more."

Once his journalist colleagues get done razzing him about his apostasy as a reporter and his failed pursuit of the literary chimera, Cercas is soon back to his old chores at the paper, "editing the odd piece, writing articles, doing interviews." That's how, in the summer of 1994, he ends up interviewing the well-known Spanish writer Rafael Sanchez Ferlosio, who happens to be in Gerona, giving some lectures at the university. "I managed to get him to agree to talk to me for a while," Cercas says, then adds, "Calling that an interview would be going a bit far; if it was an interview, it was the weirdest one I've ever done."

Part of the weirdness is that when he meets Sanchez Ferlosio at a local bar, the Bistrot, the eminent writer is surrounded by an adoring entourage and moreover, refuses "to answer a single one of the questions I put to him." So, if Cercas asks him a literary question about the characters in his books, "he would contrive to answer me with a discourse on, say, the causes of the rout of the Persian fleet in the battle of Salamis"; if Cercas seeks Sanchez Ferlosio's opinion on the recent five hundredth anniversary of the conquest of the Americas, "he would answer me by describing with a wealth of gesticulation and detail, say, the correct use of a jack plane."

It's "an exhausting tug-of-war" which the journalist later attempts to salvage by rendering coherent an inchoate set of answers, occasionally reduced to the desperate device of more or less "making it up." Then, almost as an afterthought, Cercas remarks that "it wasn't until the last beer of the evening that Ferlosio told the story of his father facing the firing squad, the story that's kept me in suspense" ever since.

Sanchez Ferlosio's father was Rafael Sanchez Mazas, one of the founders of the Spanish Falange, the right-wing group that provided the ideological fodder for the Nationalist forces, led by General Francisco Franco, that overthrew the Spanish Republic and those loyal to it in 1939, after a three-year civil war. At the very end of the war, in January 1939, Sanchez Mazas, then a prisoner of the Republican forces, is taken, along with other prominent Nationalists, to the Collell Sanctuary, a former monastery and boarding school near Banyoles in northern Catalonia, to be executed, even as the defeated remnants of the Republican army and a river of civilian refugees are streaming north to cross the French border.

In the mass execution, which took place in the woods near the sanctuary, Sanchez Mazas unexpectedly survived. "The bullets only grazed him," Ferlosio recounts, "and he took advantage of the confusion to run and hide in the woods."

> From there, sheltering in a ditch, he heard the dogs barking and the shots and the soldiers' voices as they searched for him knowing they couldn't waste much time searching because Franco's troops were on their heels. At some point my father heard branches moving behind him; he turned and saw a militiaman looking at him. Then he heard a shout: "Is he there?" My father told how the soldier stared at him for a few seconds and then, without taking his eyes off him shouted, "There's nobody over here!", turned and walked away.

After that, Sanchez Mazas spent several days hiding in the woods, until he encountered some young men, former Republican soldiers, from a nearby village, who fed and protected him until the Nationalists arrived. They did so partly as an act of decency, but also because they shrewdly saw in Sanchez Mazas a sort of "insurance policy" against the fortunes of war once the regime change was accomplished. "I don't think he ever saw them again," Ferlosio concludes, "but he talked to me about them more than once. I remember he always called them by the name they'd given themselves: 'the forest friends'."

In salvaging his "interview" with Sanchez Ferlosio, both the battle of Salamis and the instructions on the use of a jack-plane are dropped in favour of the prominent writer's views, inchoate or made up, on characters in novels and the recent anniversary celebrations of the discovery of America, and the story about Sanchez Mazas facing the firing squad isn't mentioned. "At the time I'd not read a single line of Sanchez Mazas," confesses Cercas, "and to me he was no more than a mist-shrouded name, just one more of the many Falangist politicians and writers that the last years of Spanish history had hastily buried, as if the gravediggers feared they weren't entirely dead."

Perhaps they weren't. The story sufficiently intrigues Cercas that he becomes curious about Sanchez Mazas and "about the Civil War, of which till then I'd known not much more than I did about the battle of Salamis ... and about the horrific stories that war produced, which till then I'd considered excuses for old men's nostalgia and fuel for the imagination of unimaginative novelists." For a while, Cercas takes an interest in Sanchez Mazas, one of the Falangist writers who "had won the war but lost literature," as the scholar Andres Trapiello put it in a book about writing and the Spanish Civil War. It doesn't take long for Cercas "to conclude that Sanchez Mazas was a good writer, but not a great writer." In any case, "Time passed. I began to forget the story."

It's not until five years later, in February 1999, the year of the sixtieth anniversary of the end of the Civil War, that Cercas is assigned to write a commemorative article about the tragic last days of the famous left-wing Spanish poet Antonio Machado, who "in January 1939 (together with his mother, his brother Jose and some hundreds of thousands of their utterly terrified compatriots), driven by the advance of Franco's troops, fled from Barcelona to Collioure, on the other side of the French border, where he died a short time later." It was a well-known episode that "not a single Catalan (or non-Catalan) journalist would manage to avoid recalling." Cercas resigns himself to doing "the standard time-honoured" hack job. That's when he remembers Sanchez Mazas and his botched execution, which had occurred at more or less the same time as Machado's death.

The beleaguered journalist has a tiny inspiration. "I then imagined that the symmetry and contrast between these two terrible events – a kind of chiasmus of history – was perhaps not coincidental and that, if I could manage to get across the substance of each within the same article, the strange parallel might perhaps endow them with new meaning."

What follows is the text of the article, which is presented as a document called "The Essential Secret" (I haven't checked to see if it was indeed published in a Gerona newspaper in 1999, but Cercas presents it as such). And, as promised, the journalist weaves together the two stories, the poet's death and the Falangist writer's escape, adding, "We'll never know who that militiaman was who spared Sanchez Mazas's life, nor what passed through his mind when he looked him in the eye," just as we'll never know what was said by Machado's surviving family members as they stood before the grave of the poet. "I don't know why, but sometimes I think, if we managed to unveil one of these parallel secrets, we might perhaps also touch on a much more essential secret," the article concludes, suggesting that perhaps the secret is contained in the well known lines of another poet, Jaime Gil, who wrote, "Of all the stories in History / the saddest is no doubt Spain's / because it ends badly."

I reprise all of this because the self-reflexive sub-theme of Cercas's novel is about how we become not only interested, but obsessed, with a story, a small story that opens the door to the historical memory of an entire country. After publishing his article, to Cercas's mild surprise, he receives some letters about his piece in the paper.

One of them is from a young local historian in nearby Banjoles, Miquel Aguirre, who writes to Cercas to tell him that someone else besides Sanchez Mazas had escaped from the execution at Collell and had written a now forgotten book about it, a copy of which Aguirre offers to provide. The two men meet at Cercas's favourite watering hole, the Bistrot bar, for dinner and drinks, where Aguirre delivers the obscure book about the firing squad and fills Cercas in on the background of the story. But there's something more. At the end of their conversation, Aguirre, polishing off his chocolate cake dessert, drops the crumb that changes everything.

"Did Ferlosio tell you about the 'forest friends'?" Aguirre asks.

"Do you know about them?" Cercas asks, surprised, since he had cited Ferlosio as the source of the story about the firing squad but hadn't mentioned the "forest friends" in his piece.

"I know the son of one of them," Aguirre tells him.

"You're kidding," says Cercas.

"I'm not kidding."

Suddenly, like Cercas, we perk up. What had been a casual, meandering war story is now a recoverable mystery, given a little persistence and luck. One thing will lead to another. There will be dead-ends, misunderstood clues, unexpected revelations. The trail through the forest is a time machine. We stop worrying about whether we're interested in the distant Spanish Civil War, or how Spaniards in the 21st century see it retrospectively, or whether we can keep track of the welter of names, characters, and documents that the investigation will turn up. Cercas stops worrying, too. We simply follow the story to see where it takes us.

First, it takes us on holiday to a Cancun, Mexico, resort with Conchi and Javier. That's where Cercas realizes "that the character and his story had over time turned into one of those obsessions that constitute the indispensable fuel for writing … I decided that, after almost ten years without writing a book, the moment to try again had arrived, and I also decided that the book I'd write would not be a novel, but simply a true tale, a tale cut from the cloth of reality."

Once back in Spain, the story takes us everywhere the story has to go: to dusty provincial archives, to obscure phone conversations with civil war literary scholars in Madrid, to minute comparisons of versions of the story, which in its many re-tellings has practically become a folktale, to Sanchez Mazas's own notebook (a page of which is reproduced in the text), to former sanctuaries and killing grounds, and most of all, to people, like the son of one of the "forest friends." He's the one who says to Cercas, "Anyway, if you do plan to write about Sanchez Mazas and my father, you should really talk to my uncle. He definitely knows all the details."

"What uncle?" Cercas asks.

"My uncle Joaquim … My father's brother. Another one of the forest friends."

Cercas is stunned. It's as if the son of the forest friend had "just announced the resurrection of one of the soldiers of Salamis." "He's alive?" Cercas asks, having assumed that all of the forest friends were long since dead. Not only Uncle Joaquim, it turns out, but others, too, old Catalans in their 80s, who are perfectly happy to chat with the young writer up from Gerona. (In the film version of Cercas's book, made by director David Trueba in 2003, the Catalan-speaking "forest friends" are there in person, their words sub-titled in Spanish.)

When Cercas formally announces to Conchi at a restaurant where they're having dinner that he's writing a book, she's happy that it's not a novel, since, as noted previously, she's of the opinion that "imagination" isn't really Cercas's "strong suit." But she's distressed to learn what the proposed book is about. "How can you want to write about a fascist with the number of really good lefty writers there must be around!" Conchi wonders. "Garcia Lorca, for example. He was a red, wasn't he?"

Later, one of the elderly forest friends says to Cercas that Sanchez Mazas told them he was going to write a book about his brush with death. "He was going to call it *Soldiers of Salamis*; strange title, don't you think? He also said he'd send it to us, but he didn't ... Do you know if he wrote the book?"

Part two of Cercas's novel, also titled "Soldiers of Salamis," is an account of the life of the right-wing "good but not great" writer, Falangist politician, and melancholic aristocrat Rafael Sanchez Mazas.

2

There's a translation problem with *Soldiers of Salamis*. I'm not referring to Anne McLean's translation of it into English, which is eminently readable, but to a problem of cultural translation. The most extreme example of this that I encountered happened when I tried to teach Cercas's novel to first-year university students in a Philosophy and Literature class a couple of years ago. I figured we'd have some philosophic fun with "true tales" and "fiction," with "unreliable narrators," the ironies of history, characters invented out of necessity, and that sort of thing. It would be a lesson about the ambiguities of "reality."

But as soon as I started talking about Cercas's book, I felt one of those holes in the classroom that teachers are trained to notice. I looked up and half-realized what it was. "Have you heard of the Spanish Civil War?" I asked in my most non-accusatory possible voice.

They hadn't. And since I could hardly expect them to sit down and read the two standard, thick texts on the subject, Hugh Thomas's *The Spanish Civil War* (1961; revised, 2001) or Antony Beevor's *The Battle for Spain* (1982; revised 2006), neither of which mentions Rafael Sanchez Mazas, I brightly chirped, "Oh, I'll tell you about the Spanish Civil War then and try to explain why it was so important." They looked up, like flightless fledglings in the nest, and opened their beaks in preparation to receive a tasty historical worm.

I quoted Albert Camus's eloquent remark about what the experience of the Spanish Civil War meant: "It was in Spain that men learned that one can be right and yet be beaten, that force can vanquish spirit, that there are times when courage is not its own recompense. It is this, doubtless, which explains why so many men, the world over, regard the Spanish drama as a personal tragedy." I paused to ask them if they knew who Albert Camus was. They didn't. When I mentioned in passing George Orwell's famous memoir about the Spanish Civil War, *Homage to Catalonia*, there was a similar problem. They hadn't heard of it. Nor did most of them know who George Orwell was, or, well, maybe one or two of them did, because Orwell's *Nineteen Eighty-Four* had been on the high school reading list.

Later, we stumbled over the cultural problem again. I noted that one of the characters in Cercas's book is a Chilean novelist who had been in Chile in 1973 at the time of the overthrow of Salvador Allende by General Augusto Pinochet and the American CIA. Again, I felt the chilling abyss-like vacuum in the room. They hadn't heard of Salvador Allende or Chile in the 1970s, much less the Chilean novelist character in Cercas's book. "Um, I'll tell you about it," I said, my bird-chirpy feathers slightly drooping.

I didn't ask them whether they'd ever heard of the Soviet Union, which had expired in 1991, or thereabouts, a year or two after their births. I wasn't sure I wanted to know the answer. And I just straight-out told them that the battle of Salamis, between the Greeks and the Persians, happened in 480 BCE and that the story, if they were interested, is told in Herodotus's *Histories*. No doubt I'm exaggerating the extent of their ignorance but, I mean, how do you discuss a novel about the nature of historical memory with people who have no historical memory?

The problem isn't exclusive to ill-educated North American uni-versity students. The problem of how to address the historical mem-ory of the Spanish Civil War was one that Cercas faced in Spain, and his elegant solution to the problem is one of the reasons that *Soldiers of Salamis* became a prize-winning bestseller in his native land.

As the Irish-born novelist Colm Toibin, who lived in Barcelona for a time and wrote a book about it, *Homage to Barcelona* (1990), ex-plains in his review of Cercas, "The transition from dictatorship to democracy in Spain after the death of Franco in 1975 was a model of decorum, choreographed with skill. There were to be no recrimina-tions against the old regime, which was to be consigned to the dust-bin of history through silence rather than show trials ... The silence worked wonders; it allowed for a new constitution, great autonomy for the regions, and a strong sense of democracy ... But strangely, in those years of easy and friendly freedoms, the silence exerted its sin-ister power and influence in the private realm more than in the pub-lic, and there, in families and villages, it did a great deal of harm." Toibin adds, "History resided then in locked memories, half-told sto-ries, unread archives. In some families the silence was complete; the children, as they grew up in the bright new democracy, simply did not know what their parents had done in the war" (Colm Toibin, "Return to Catalonia," *The New York Review of Books*, Oct. 7, 2004).

For a new generation, that of Cercas (he was born in 1962), the time had come to unlock some of those memories, to re-tell those half-told tales, to read the unread archives. "The civil war as a battle between good and evil," Toibin notes, "no longer works in Spain. Just as on the right, no one wants to be reminded of the cruelties in the name of fascism, on the left, no one is proud of what happened either." Instead, as Toibin says, "Forgetting and reconciliation have made their way into the core of Spanish political life." Today, a story merely telling of the bravery of the Republican left and the evil of the fascist right "would seem to some too simple, too old-fashioned; and to others too obvious to be of any interest." What Cercas has managed to do is enact in the pages of *Soldiers of Salamis* "the same process of reconciliation which Spain has been striving for, while reminding readers, with considerable tact and some wryness, that the shadow of the civil war is a shadow they live with, and that what creates this shadow continues, whether they like it or not, to obscure the light."

It is that achievement, of allowing the past "beauty and the possibility of redemption," of telling a tale that "is not a story of tragedy, although there is tragedy all around it, but of the irony of history," that accounts for Cercas's book not only winning most of his country's major literary prizes but achieving a national popular success, selling more than half a million copies in Spain alone.

Those factors, astutely delineated by Toibin, don't fully account for its enthusiastic reception by critics outside Spanish-speaking lands or its winning the British newspaper *Independent's* Foreign Fiction Prize for 2004. For readers not directly engaged by the delicate issues that engross Spanish readers, the reason that *Soldiers of Salamis* is one of the notable books of the decade must have something to do with the unique place that the Spanish Civil War holds in the memory of many of us as, as Camus noted, an instance where totalitarianism utterly defeated democracy. Equally compelling is its more generally applicable investigation of the questions of historical memory and of storytelling itself.

I'm partial, I notice, to writing that moves back and forth across the always- permeable boundary between true tales and made-up stories. The interesting thing about this kind of genre-bending is that the writer can approach the borders of truth and fiction from either side of the divide.

In contemporary non-fiction, the use of novelistic techniques to tell a true story became widespread in North America with the appearance of what was called "the new journalism" in the 1960s and 70s. Books like Truman Capote's *In Cold Blood* (1966), about two murderers in the American Midwest, were labelled "non-fiction novels"; Michael Herr's hallucinogenic *Dispatches* (1977), about the Vietnam War, and the "gonzo" writings of Hunter S. Thompson and Tom Wolfe are also exemplars of the method. The masterpiece of the genre is Norman Mailer's *Armies of the Night* (1968), an account of an anti-Vietnam War demonstration in Washington, D.C., in which the novelist "Mailer" appears as a picaresque third-person character that the author (Mailer) treats with no more solemnity or piety than he bestows on the rest of the cast he assembles on the steps of the American Pentagon.

The tangled boundaries of truth and fiction can equally be reached from the fictional side. The *roman a clef*, in which a true story is only lightly fictionalized, such as Saul Bellow's *Ravelstein* (2000), a portrait of his friend, the social critic and scholar Allan Bloom, is one way of doing it. Philip Roth's novel *Operation Shylock* (1993), in which Roth appears as "Philip Roth" and other actual public figures make substantial appearances, is another and more elaborate way of blending fiction and truth. Tomas Eloy Martinez's elegant *Santa Evita* (1995), the story of the eerily peripatetic corpse of Eva Peron, is one more strategy for getting at certain strange realities.

I should mention, just to dispel any possible misunderstandings, that I'm not talking about purportedly true stories that are exposed as false. The scandal of the decade in this category was James Frey's *A Million Little Pieces* (2003), a so-called "misery memoir" about the author's recovery from various addictions that was revealed, two years and a million copies later, to contain significant elements that were false. A somewhat similar but more complicated case from the previous decade was Benjamin Wilkomirski's *Fragments: Memories of a Wartime Childhood* (1996), a purported Holocaust memoir that turned out to be a fabrication. Those are not the mixtures of truth and fiction under consideration here.

While I'm at it, it's also appropriate to note that self-reflexiveness in fiction, in which the author talks about himself and about the book we're reading, as Cercas does, is not, as is often suggested, a recent "postmodern" invention of the late 20th century. Novelists have been doing this sort of thing ever since Cervantes, Sterne, Defoe, and Denis Diderot put quill to paper in the 17th and 18th centuries.

Of all the contemporary novels prior to Cercas's *Soldiers of Salamis* that play with real and fictional persons, while challenging the conventions of the novel, the masterpiece of the form is the Peruvian novelist and 2010 Nobel Prize winner Mario Vargas Llosa's *The Storyteller* (1990). It's the account of a young anthropology student who literally goes native, joining a tribe in the Amazonian jungle whose central and binding figure, because of the tribe's ecologically scattered state, is a "storyteller." In fact, Vargas Llosa's novel is the story of two storytellers. It's not only about the man who becomes a tribal storyteller but also about the unnamed narrator, who is obviously Vargas Llosa himself. Apart from the uncertain identity of the storyteller whom Vargas Llosa claims was a friend and university classmate of his, all other aspects of the book, from references to various Peruvian professors to an account of

Vargas Llosa's own adventures as a storyteller on Peruvian TV, appear to be purely factual.

Vargas Llosa's challenge in writing *The Storyteller* was the problem of creating the tribal storyteller's perspective, as he confesses in the pages of his novel. "Why, in the course of all those years, had I been unable to write my story about storytellers?" Vargas Llosa asks. "The answer I used to offer myself, each time I threw the half-finished manuscript of that elusive story into the wastebasket, was the difficulty of inventing, in Spanish and within a logically consistent intellectual framework, a literary form that would suggest, with any reasonable degree of credibility, how a primitive man with a magico-religious mentality would go about telling a story."

In the end, Vargas Llosa "makes it up," writing a series of credible chapters in the voice of the tribal storyteller. In a sense, Vargas Llosa, in writing a "true tale," is forced to "make it up" in order for the story to become real. That is, there are some "true" stories in which fiction is imperative. It's the necessity of fiction that turns Javier Cercas's *Soldiers* from simply an ingenious book into one of the memorable novels of the decade.

3

Cercas's monograph on the life of Sanchez Mazas is, as Cercas might say, "good but not great." It provides an account of an upper middle-class gentleman, born at the end of the 19th century, whose literary ambitions lead him both to poetry and a journalistic stint in Italy in the 1920s, where he becomes an admirer of the Italian fascist Mussolini. On his return to Spain, he helps to found the Falange, Spain's version of fascist ideology, and, though mild-mannered himself, his violent rhetoric in numerous articles and speeches ultimately contributes to the deaths of thousands of his countrymen in a civil war, even though he personally makes good on his promise to protect his "forest friends" from recrimination and jailing after the war. Making use of the testimonies of the "forest friends" and other surviving documentation, Cercas reconstructs in some detail the central episode in Sanchez Mazas's life, his near execution and the inexplicable act of mercy by a Republican soldier who doesn't shoot him. After Franco's triumph, Sanchez Mazas serves briefly as a minister in the Nationalist government, but soon retires, on inherited wealth, to a fading and rather melancholy literary life as an obscure minor writer that ends with his peaceful death in 1966.

At first, Cercas reads the manuscript that he's written in a white heat with considerable euphoria. "At the second rereading my euphoria gave way to disappointment: the book wasn't bad, but insufficient … it was missing a part. The worst of it was I didn't know what part it was." He confesses his failure to Conchi. "Shit!" Conchi replies, "Didn't I tell you not to write about a fascist? … What you have to do is forget all about that book and start another one. How about one on Garcia Lorca?" Cercas slumps into writerly despair, plopping himself down in "an armchair in front of the television without turning it on."

The depressed author cuts his book-writing leave short and returns to the newspaper, where his editor takes pity on him and suggests that he get out of the office and conduct a series of interviews with various transplanted intellectuals, businessmen, and athletes who have settled in Catalonia. One of the first persons Cercas interviews is the Chilean-born novelist Roberto Bolaño, a man in his late 40s with "the unmistakable air of a hippy peddler that afflicted so many Latin Americans of his generation exiled in Europe." Although Cercas mentions that Bolaño, after years of penury, had recently won a major literary prize, most English speaking readers wouldn't have recognized Bolaño's name at the time that Cercas was writing. (Though Cercas doesn't say so, the prize was for Bolaño's novel *The Savage Detectives*, published in Spanish in 1998 but only posthumously translated into English in 2007.)

Cercas gives us a thumbnail sketch of Bolaño's life, which includes, in addition to his Chilean birth and an adolescence in Mexico, a short stint as a would-be revolutionary in Salvador Allende's Chile in the early 1970s, brief imprisonment in General Augusto Pinochet's subsequently authoritarian Chile, followed by exile in Mexico. Then there's a wandering resettlement in Europe, some complicated medical problems concerning his liver (which will ultimately shorten Bolaño's life; he died in 2003), and finally a rather ascetic literary life with his wife and children in a small Catalonian coastal town. We're filled in on this background as Cercas and Bolaño are having a drink at a bar down by the harbour and talking about Pinochet. "Naturally, I asked him what it'd been like to live through Pinochet's coup and the fall of Allende. Naturally, he regarded me with an expression of utter boredom," Cercas reports.

Then Bolaño replies, "Like a Marx Brothers' movie, but with corpses. Unimaginable pandemonium   Look, I'll tell you the truth. For years I spat on Allende's name every chance I got. I thought it was all his fault, for not giving us weapons. Now I kick myself for having said that about Allende   [He] thought about us as if we were his kids, you know? He didn't want them to kill us. And if he'd let us have those guns we would have died like flies. So ... I think Allende was a hero."

"And what's a hero?" Cercas asks.

Bolaño pauses, then says, "I don't know. Someone who considers himself a hero and gets it right. Or someone who has courage and an instinct for virtue, and therefore never makes a mistake, or at least doesn't make a mistake the one time when it matters, and therefore can't *not* be a hero. Or someone, like Allende, who understands that a hero isn't the one who kills, but the one who doesn't kill or who lets himself get killed. I don't know. What's a hero to you?"

The answer to that question, it will turn out, is the epic subject matter of Cercas's book. A week later, when the interview is published, Bolaño phones to tell Cercas he'd liked the piece. "Are you sure I said all that about heroes?" Bolaño asks.

'Word for word,' I answered, suddenly suspicious, thinking the initial praise was just a preamble to the reproaches, and that Bolaño was one of those loquacious interviewees who attribute all their verbal indiscretions to journalists' spite, negligence or frivolity. 'I've got it on tape.'

"No shit! Well, it sounded pretty good!" Bolaño reassures him, and suggests they meet for lunch the next day since Bolaño has to be in Gerona to update his residence permit. So, they spend a rambling day together, talking about the vicissitudes of writing, life, and all the rest. At the end of the day, in a hotel bar near the train station, between cups of tea for the liver-damaged Bolaño and gin and tonics for the depressed Cercas, Bolaño tells him, almost as accidentally as Ferlosio told Cercas about his father, the heroic story of Miralles.

Miralles was an old battle-scarred warrior who'd fought in Spain to the very end, then crossed into France, joined the Foreign Legion, got shipped to North Africa where he fought the Italian fascists, then back to Europe to fight the Nazis in World War II. A quarter-century after the wars, in the late 1970s, Bolaño had gotten to know the ancient veteran, then a French resident living in Dijon, at a Catalan summer caravan camp where Bolaño was working as a watchman.

It's a good story, as Cercas reprises Bolaño's version of it, of a warrior for whom the war never ends, and for whom the dead, although dead, never go away. As they're walking to the train, Cercas asks Bolaño if in all the subsequent years he'd ever heard anything more about Miralles.

> 'Nothing,' he answered. 'I lost track of him, like so many people. Who knows where he is now. Maybe he still goes to the campsite; but I don't think so. He'd be over eighty ... Maybe he still lives in Dijon. Or maybe he's dead, really. I guess that's the most likely, no? Why do you ask?'
> 'No reason,' I said.
> But it wasn't true.

Sometime in the middle of the night, something clicks. "And at that moment, with the deceptive but overwhelming clarity of insomnia, like someone who finds, by unbelievable chance, having already given up the search (because a person never finds what he's searching for, only what reality delivers), the missing part ... I heard myself murmur, in the pitch-black silence of the bedroom: 'It's him.'"

After checking with Bolaño to make sure that the Chilean isn't already writing the story of Miralles, he tells Bolaño what's on his mind. "You've got a hell of a novel there," Bolaño enthusiastically replies. "I knew you were writing something.'

"I'm not writing," Cercas insists. "And it's not a novel. It's a story with real events and characters."

"Same difference," Bolaño replies. "All good tales are true tales, at least for those who read them, which is all that counts."

Cercas does find Miralles at the end of a circuitous search, after the almost-giving-up, the dead-ends, the clues that fade away. In fact, during one of the impasses, Bolaño says to Cercas, "You'll have to make it up."

"Make what up?" Cercas asks.

"The interview with Miralles. It's the only way you can finish the novel," Bolaño tells him.

Either way, made-up or not, there's an old man at the end of the road, or sitting in the TV room of an old people's home in Dijon, and he hasn't forgotten anything. Yes, he was at the sanctuary of Collell in the last days of the Spanish Civil War; yes, he knew Sanchez Mazas ("How could I not know? He was the biggest of the big shots"); and yes or no, was he the gun-toting soldier in the woods who looked Sanchez Mazas in the eye before saying, "There's no one here," and turning away?

Cercas's readers of a tale that mixes real people with fictionalized characters will wonder about the status of Miralles. Does Miralles exist? Did Bolaño really know such a person? Did Cercas actually find and interview him?

Cercas's book, you see, is a demonstration of what a really good writer does when he or she runs out of facts. As in life, we simply don't know what the factual truth is. But here we don't care because the tension between it and invention, if the writer is good enough, more than compensates. If Miralles is fictional, the fiction is informative to the truth.

For Cercas, he gets closer, perhaps only in imagination, to one of the "essential secrets": the meaning of the look in the hero's eyes. If there's no yes or no answer to any of this, there is this:

> Beneath the sodden hair and wide forehead and eyebrows covered in raindrops, the soldier's look doesn't express compassion or hatred, or even disdain, but a kind of secret or unfathomable joy, something verging on cruelty, something that resists reason, but nor is it instinct, something that remains there with the same blind stubbornness with which blood persists in its course and the earth in its immovable orbit and all beings in their obstinate condition of being ...

But that's not what's on the mind of Miralles. It's not his act of heroism that he returns to, but the dead.

"Sometimes," Miralles tells Cercas, "I dream of them and then I feel guilty. I see them all: intact and greeting me with jokes, just as young as they were then, because time doesn't pass for them ... and they ask me why I'm not with them, as if I'd betrayed them, because my place was there ..."

"At some point Miralles had started to cry," Cercas says, "his face and his voice hadn't changed, but inconsolable tears streamed down the smooth channel of his scar, rolling more slowly down his unshaven cheeks."

Nobody remembers them, you know? Nobody. Nobody even remembers why they died, why they didn't have a wife and children and a sunny room; nobody remembers, least of all, those they fought for. There's no lousy street in any lousy town in any fucking country named after them, nor will there ever be. Understand? You understand, don't you? Oh, but I remember, I do remember, I remember them all, Lela and Joan and Gabi and Odena and Pipo and Brugada and Gudayol, I don't know why I do but I do, not a single day goes by that I don't think of them.

Old heroes don't think about their heroic deeds, but about the innocence of those who were once alive.

4

Ignorance in the Desert

One of the central intellectual themes of the decade, whose justifiably rising murmur can be heard by anyone willing to listen, has to do with the public state of mind and our methods for understanding the world. It is also one of the central themes of this book. As I wrote in my introduction, I see the decline of book reading and the deterioration of knowledge as an impending cultural catastrophe.

Intellectuals have perennially observed that among the activities at the heart of human understanding are reading and conversation. While there is a degree of public awareness about various critical situations – the crisis of the earth, and that of the state or the economy – there is far less awareness of a significant aspect of what I think of as the human crisis. That crisis encompasses the practical conditions of human life, such as widespread poverty and other forms of suffering, but it also includes an intellectual crisis that affects even the most developed industrial nations. Several writers at the beginning of this century have argued cogently that our methods for comprehension are in the process of atrophying, that much of conversation has been reduced to mere chatting and twittering, and that the decline of serious reading threatens our ability to sustain thought. The dangers include the prospect of the diminution of memory, imagination, and our sense of history. These are warnings we ignore only at our peril.

I. CAN YOU READ THIS?

A couple of decades ago, back in the 1980s, a friend of mine in Vancouver displayed a jokey bi-lingual poster on his front door that said in big letters: "*Fin de lire.*" At the bottom of the poster, in small print, its punch line asked, "Can you read this? Don't you wish you couldn't?" I.e., wouldn't you like to be as dopey as everybody else?

Susan Jacoby's *The Age of American Unreason* (2008) suggests that today, in the United States (and elsewhere), that old poster's hiply expressed qualm about the decline of literacy is no joke. It's not that people are unable to read but rather that they're not very interested in serious reading or much else of substance, and they're too distracted to care whether or not it's a problem.

For Jacoby, a former *Washington Post* journalist and the author of *Freethinkers: A History of American Secularism* (2004), the decline of intellectual engagement is not simply a matter of reading; rather "the inescapable theme of our time is the erosion of memory and knowledge ... Anti-rationalism and anti-intellectualism flourish in a mix that includes addiction to infotainment, every form of superstition and credulity, and an educational system that does a poor job of teaching not only basic skills but the logic underlying those skills."

The Age of American Unreason obviously plays on the title of Tom Paine's 18th century polemic, *The Age of Reason*. But it draws more directly on Richard Hofstadter's groundbreaking *Anti-Intellectualism in American Life* (1963) and the work of such other mid- and late-20th century social critics as Paul Goodman and Neil Postman. It says what a lot of people (including me) believe about the public state of mind, even though those of us holding this view are admittedly a minuscule, beleaguered minority whose voices are pretty much lost in the din of advertising for the new distractions.

Jacoby writes in a straightforward, non-academic style – her book is intentionally rather "middlebrow" in its appeal to a general readership – but my fear is that, insofar as she receives much notice at all, she will either be shrugged off as merely alarmist (the "oh, come on, things aren't that bad" line) or rebutted by techno enthusiasts who tout the wonders of the Internet's cornucopia of infinite information (the "it's all there, you just need to know where to look and have the will to find out" defence). Both of those ploys against Jacoby's thesis strike me as woefully wrong-headed.

American Unreason begins with Jacoby's sketch of the current situation, as a prelude to tracing the historical sources of a gathering intellectual darkness in recent decades. "It is difficult to suppress the fear," she says, "that the scales of American history have shifted heavily against the vibrant and varied intellectual life so essential to functional democracy. During the past four decades, America's endemic anti-intellectual tendencies have been grievously exacerbated by a new species of semiconscious anti-rationalism, feeding on and fed by an ignorant popular culture of video images and unremitting noise that leaves no room for contemplation or logic."

Jacoby examines various strands that make up the present cultural context, several of which have a particularly American tinge. They include a three-decade resurgence in fundamentalist Christian religion, coupled with a propensity to hold nutty paranormal beliefs. As well, there's a media system that dumbs down public events to soundbites and sensationalism and for the rest of prime time ensures that we're "amusing ourselves to death" (to recall the title of Neil Postman's 1985 book). Add to that a national Attention Deficit Disorder fuelled by a cascade of gadgets that makes sure there are no idle hands, eyes, or ears, because we're kept busy pushing cellphone buttons, clicking computer mouses, poking touch screens, and pouring iTunes into our heads, often all at once. Finally, there's the decline of reading and writing, and the erosion of what was once a functioning mid-level culture.

All of this is institutionally underpinned in the U.S. by a system of local school boards without effective national (or state) standards. It's a school system that reproduces educational poverty and backwardness in the worst school districts and allows flaky school boards to drop such topics as evolution or sex education from the curriculum if the school trustees' religious or ideological beliefs are offended.

Of the various "endemic anti-intellectual tendencies" afoot, Jacoby cites anti-evolutionary dogma as emblematic of the situation. "Americans are alone in the developed world in their view of evolution by means of natural selection as 'controversial' rather than as settled mainstream science," she observes. "The continuing strength of religious fundamentalism in America (again, unique in the world) is generally cited as the sole reason for the bizarre persistence of anti-evolutionism …" and there's no doubt that Biblical literalism plays its part in recent squabbles over such matters as "intelligent design." But Jacoby suspects that the problem may be deeper. "The real and more complex explanation may lie not in America's brand of faith," she suggests, "but in the public's ignorance about science in general and evolution in particular."

Jacoby cites a range of recent surveys showing that only about a third of the American population has any idea that evolution is a well-founded scientific theory, and that even the minority that thinks it is science believes that it is a process guided by the hand of God. Half the population is content with the Genesis version that human beings were created by divine intervention more or less in their present form and it all happened relatively recently, rather than the scientific view that humans have gradually developed through changing forms over a period of several million years.

Beyond the evolution conundrum, Jacoby reels off a string of statistics indicating that masses of Americans also have problems with everything from whether the sun revolves around the earth to the function of DNA. There's a temptation here to reprise all the gory details and stats of her case, but an "executive summary" of her argument is precisely the opposite of what her book invites, namely, a contemplative reading.

Her thumbnail historical survey stretches from the American Revolution, led by such Enlightenment-era founding fathers and intellectuals as Jefferson, Franklin, and Madison, to the present digital moment, which tends to be led by software moguls, talk show hosts, and self-help gurus. Jacoby has some particularly interesting things to say about her own mid-20th century experiences growing up in the 1950s in small-town Michigan, when there was still a fairly vibrant and cohesive "middlebrow" culture available.

She's also thoughtful about the subsequent turbulent era of the 1960s, which has been retrospectively transformed by conservatives into the source of all present-day evils. Jacoby was for part of that decade on an extended journalistic assignment in Moscow that buffered her from the available enthusiasms of a radical counterculture. That distance perhaps contributes to her balanced perspective on the period, one that is neither nostalgic nor inclined toward "blaming it on the Sixties," as she titles one chapter. It also allows us to see that there was what she calls "the Other Sixties," which featured born-again religious fundamentalism, the Campus Crusade for Christ, the birth of neo-conservative think tanks, and the election (and re-election) of the Nixon administration. Jacoby astutely points out that the 1960s wasn't all campus radicalism, anti-Vietnam War protests, and the rise of modern feminism, but insofar as it was, she ably defends a good deal of it.

One crucial focus of Jacoby's critique is the issue of reading and writing. She offers at least two cheers for the "middlebrow" American culture of the 1950s which has long since collapsed. Although we now think of the 1950s as a conservative and conformist era, Jacoby recalls that it was also a decade of burgeoning American symphony orchestras, community art museums, a substantial market for recordings of classical music, "art" movie houses, encyclopedias, Book-of-the-Month clubs, and "the years of the paperback book revolution, a development of fundamental importance to middlebrows because middlebrowism was, above all, a *reading* culture."

In examining the present "culture of distraction," Jacoby makes the point that "the willed attention demanded by print is the antithesis of the reflexive distraction encouraged by infotainment media, whether one is talking about the tunes on an iPod, a picture flashing briefly on a home page, a text message, a video game, or the latest offering of 'reality' TV." The ability of all these sources to simultaneously engender "distraction and absorption accounts for much of their snakelike charm."

But what about the "reasonable-sounding proposition that all we have to do to control the influence of the media in our lives is to turn off the television set, the iPod, the computer," and turn to more substantial materials? Jacoby notes that it's not so easy to turn off media "that make up, as a once ubiquitous television commercial for cotton clothing proclaimed, 'the fabric of our lives.'" Here, Jacoby is pointing to the crucial notion of a "cultural context." You don't just click the power button if you have nothing in your cultural context to give you a reason to do so and everything encouraging you to cheer on the contestants of "American Idol," the last "Survivor," or some fading pop star's latest bout with detox and rehab. This is one of the arguments that the philosopher Herbert Marcuse made in the 1960s in his critique of *One Dimensional Man* when he emphasized the all-enveloping nature of a cultural box that didn't allow one to think outside it. Or, as Jacoby puts it, "The more time people spend before the computer screen or any screen, the less time and desire they have for two human activities critical to a fruitful and demanding intellectual life: reading and conversation."

Jacoby could have said more about what the difference is between reading as an act of thought and the mere consumption of visual infotainment, but with respect to current arguments about whether there is a decline in reading, she leaves little doubt. "There is really no need to make a case for the proposition that video watching displaces reading," she says. "When four out of ten adults read no books at all (fiction or non-fiction), the facts speak for themselves," and in case they don't, she cites the details of the National Endowment for the Arts survey documenting the case.

"These recent statistics are particularly important because they document the decreasing popularity of books in a largely literate society," Jacoby adds. "Even if such figures had existed two centuries ago, it would be pointless to compare the proportion of readers [today] to the proportion in 1800, when only a small minority of the population could read at all." That is, the issue isn't whether there was or wasn't a Golden Age of Reading in the past, but that the proportion of readers has diminished since the middle of the last century despite the vastly increased technological and institutional opportunities for reading today. What's taking place looks more like an intellectual paradigm shift than mere disaffection with Gutenburg's printing press.

Not only is there less reading, but there are corollary side effects: published writing tends to be shorter and more superficial, book reviewing is in decline across the U.S., and even conversation and letter-writing have given way to talk shows and text messages. And if you're wondering about writing skills in the school population at large, a *New York Times* story reports that only "about one-third of America's eighth-grade students, and about one in four high school seniors, are proficient writers," according to the results of the latest nationwide test (Sam Dillon, "Students Lack Writing Skills in Test," *New York Times*, Apr. 3, 2008). Since the proficiency level of the test was a grade of about 55 per cent, not exactly a high hurdle, that means 75 per cent of America's high school teens are failing. They're also failing when it comes to matters of history, geography, and the structure of government – not a good sign for sustaining a democratic polity.

The response to Jacoby's mild-mannered jeremiad was mixed at best. It was faintly praised by Michiko Kakutani as "smart, well researched and frequently cogent," but faulted for "failing to pull these observations together into a coherent, new argument." (Michiko Kakutani, "Why Knowledge and Logic Are Political Dirty Words," *New York Times*, March 11, 2008.) More typical was reviewer Carlin

Romano, who wonders, in a sort of "what, me worry?" *Mad Magazine* style, if there's even a problem out there. (Carlin Romano, "The Age of American Unreason," *Philadelphia Inquirer*, March 20, 2008.) In his best Junior Chamber of Commerce manner, Romano cites as counter-evidence international elites who send their kids to elite American universities, the preponderance of U.S. Nobel Prize winners in various fields, and foreign book publishers who furiously compete for rights to American books.

Romano suggests that Jacoby "needs to get out of her apartment" and secure a professorship. "Ensconced at a first-class university or college, she's likely to find that her 'Age of American Unreason' never happened." Leave aside Romano's smug tone. I don't know if the place where I teach is first-class, but as someone "ensconced" in a university classroom, I can assure Romano that Jacoby's description of our intellectual ills is pretty much spot on. More important, the issue is not whether there's an intellectual pulse in elite educational institutions but the state of mind of the 60 or 70 per cent of college age youth who are not in post-secondary education at all, first-rate or otherwise. They're the generation that will be faced with the maintenance of a venerable republic. Jacoby's doubts that they're up to it are not, um, unreasonable.

2. HOW DUMB CAN YOU GET?

I'm a feet-on-the-ground kind of guy, so I seldom have visions. But a year or so prior to the publication of Mark Bauerlein's *The Dumbest Generation* (2008), while I was in the library of the university where I teach, something odd happened. At first, I didn't notice anything out of the ordinary. Downstairs, the students were busily at the computer terminals, looking up stuff on Wikipedia, or checking their Facebook "wall," or doing whatever it is students do on the library computers.

I went upstairs to the stacks, where the library's collection of books is housed, and where, off to the side, are the carrels, filled with students in various states of study and/or slumber. Clutching the slip of paper on which I'd scribbled the call number of a book that I was looking for – a book written in the 1930s by literary scholar Edmund Wilson – I slipped into the forest-like rows of bookshelves. Maybe it was the odd silence that engulfed me as I browsed in the stacks, or maybe it was something else, but a moment or two later when I arrived at the shelf where Edmund Wilson's books are kept and reached up for the one I wanted, I was hit by a multiple realization.

First, I was the only person browsing in the stacks. There were lots of people around, but none of them was browsing in the book stacks. I was all alone in the forest of books. Second, it became clear to me why, whenever I looked for a book in the school library, it was almost always there: because the students seldom took out books to read. The collection was pretty much intact. Finally, as I began glancing at the spines of the books on the nearby shelves, which often included the year of their publication, I realized that very few of the books there had been published or purchased in the last ten years. That's because the library, I immediately understood, had bought very few books in recent years (I later checked with the librarians and confirmed my intuition). The "acquisitions budget," as it's called, had been diverted to buy the computers and computer "data bases."

That's when I had my little vision. The spines of the books, instead of reminding me of trees in a forest, as they often do, suddenly began to look like tombstones. Each date on a book spine recorded the death of a book. I was standing in the middle of The Dead Library. Book reading was over.

The vision lasted about five or ten seconds. Then I snapped back to my ordinary pedestrian existence, skipped down the stairs, passed the students crowded around the computer terminals, checked out my book at the checkout counter, and went off to read a few pages of Edmund Wilson.

The library is still a fairly busy place, filled with students and librarians and computers and places to study, but the students cheerfully ignore the collection. The Dead Library is up there, silent, like an unexplored forest or an unvisited old graveyard.

Like most visions, my vision of The Dead Library isn't exactly true. There are still book readers, and books are still being borrowed from school libraries. But I notice that Mark Bauerlein, in *The Dumbest Generation*, has also experienced this moment of bibliodesolation. "At every university library I've entered in recent years," says Bauerlein, who's a professor of English at Emory University in Atlanta, Georgia, "a cheery or intent sophomore sits at each computer station rapping out emails in a machine-gun rhythm. Upstairs, the stacks stand deserted and silent," he adds, reassuring me that I'm not just imagining things.

In a front cover book-jacket blurb, the prominent literary scholar Harold Bloom – who is sort of the Edmund Wilson of the present generation – rightly calls Bauerlein's *The Dumbest Generation* "an urgent ... book on the very dark topic of the virtual end of reading among the young." That's true. But there's more.

Bauerlein suggests that young people are suffering not only a decline in reading but also significant "knowledge deficits" about history, geography, science, and art and an ignorance of civic life that poses a threat to democratic society. However, if Bauerlein accurately alerts us to an important problem, it's equally the case that his *Dumbest Generation* is a polemic that suffers from serious defects (which I'll get to in a moment).

When he isn't being an English prof, Bauerlein works in research and analysis for the U.S. National Endowment for the Arts (NEA). He's a report writer and reader, quite a good one, and in *The Dumbest Generation* he provides a painstaking and persuasive summation of a raft of recent reports. The reports reveal that young people in the U.S. have more schooling, more disposable income, more leisure time, and more access to news and information than at any time in the recent past. What do they do with all that time and money? They download, upload, post, chat, and network (nine of their top ten sites are for social networking), and they watch television and play video games two to four hours per day.

What don't they do? They don't read, even online, and two-thirds of them are not proficient in reading. They don't follow or engage in politics, notwithstanding the hopeful Obama-boom/blip among the young during the 2008 presidential election; they don't vote regularly (nearly half of them can't comprehend a ballot); and they can't find Iraq on a map. They know who the current "American Idol" is, but they've no idea that Nancy Pelosi was the first woman speaker of the U.S. House of Representatives.

Bauerlein's book intentionally doesn't attempt to assess behaviours and values of under-thirty-year-olds. "It sticks to one thing," Bauerlein says, "the intellectual condition of young Americans, and describes it with empirical evidence, recording something ... insidious happening inside their heads." It charts, he says, "a consistent and perilous momentum downward."

Bauerlein is aware that his pessimistic findings may be dismissed "as yet another curmudgeonly riff. Older people have complained forever about the derelictions of youth, and the 'old fogy' tag puts them on the defensive."

But Bauerlein (age forty-nine at the time of his book's publication) insists that the facts are the facts. Despite the "Information Age," the "Digital Revolution," and all the other slogans about access to knowledge, "young Americans today are no more learned or skilful than their predecessors, no more knowledgeable, fluent, up-to-date or inquisitive, except in the material of youth culture." The last is a point Bauerlein reiterates throughout his book. What the young are knowledgeable about is confined to their own rather narrow, narcissistic milieu.

Further, "they don't know any more history or civics, economics or science, literature or current events. They read less on their own, both books and newspapers, and you would have to canvas a lot of college English instructors and employers before you found one who said they compose better paragraphs." The wellsprings of knowledge are everywhere, "but the rising generation is camped in the desert, passing stories, pictures, tunes and texts back and forth, living off the thrill of peer attention."

Bauerlein documents this ignorance in the desert by examining a dozen or more recent, major, reputable, mass surveys of the intellectual condition of young people, including one he directed for the NEA. The whole story is almost too depressing, so just a sampler:

"On the 2001 National Assessment of Educational Progress history exam, the majority of high school seniors, 57 per cent, scored 'below basic.'" That's a polite way of saying they failed. "Only 1 per cent reached 'advanced' ... Two-thirds of high school seniors couldn't explain a photo of a theatre whose portal reads 'Colored Entrance.'"

In a 2003 National Conference of State Legislatures citizenship study, "While 64 per cent knew the name of the latest 'American Idol,' only 10 per cent could identify the speaker of the U.S. House of Representatives." Less than half knew which party controlled the American Congress; a 2004 National Election Study found that barely over a quarter could correctly identify the Chief Justice of the U.S. Supreme Court; a 2006 Pew Research report learned that only a quarter of eighteen to twenty-nine-year-olds knew that Condoleezza Rice was then U.S. secretary of state while a mere 15 per cent knew that Vladimir Putin was then the president of Russia.

And so it goes, in every field surveyed, from math and science, to fine arts participation to geography, where the 2006 Geographic Literacy Survey found that 63 per cent of test takers "could not identify Iraq on a map." Maybe that's why GPS devices are a hot shopping item. But marketing aside, not only is there a knowledge deficit. When you ask the young to interpret some bit of the world in terms of what it means, things only get worse.

Beyond Bauerlein's discussion of "Knowledge Deficits," his chapters on "The New Bibliophobes," "Screen Time," and "Online Learning and Non-Learning," make what amounts to a pretty irrefutable case about what is and isn't on the minds of the present generation. If you aren't convinced by the tidbits presented here, you're invited to check out the text itself.

The standard rebuttal of Bauerlein's case, which usually appears under a rock-song heading that declares "The Kids Are Alright," claims that while book reading may have changed, the young are reading more than ever, via the Internet. One review of *The Dumbest Generation* published by Canada's most influential newspaper, *The Globe and Mail* ("Are the kids all right? Depends upon whom you ask," July 19, 2008), is a case in point.

The reviewer, Don Tapscott, chairman of nGenera Insight (a business consulting firm) and the author of *Grown Up Digital* (2008), claims that the young are "reading plenty of non-fiction on the Internet," which, he assures us, "can be just as intellectually challenging as reading a book." Well, if they were reading any of a dozen first rate magazines and newspapers available online or researching their philosophy papers with an article from the online Stanford Encyclopedia of Philosophy rather than just Wikipedia, that might be true. But as Bauerlein documents, that's not what they're reading. They're reading each other's post-it notes on Facebook, and viewing pop star gossip on YouTube (or YouPorn or PornTube). Predictably, the deniers and would-be refuters of Bauerlein's thesis have little to offer beyond bromides about the wonders of technology.

The problem is not with Bauerlein's "empirical" account of the decline of reading and much else. That rings true, at least to quite a few of us in the teaching profession. What doesn't ring true is the book's "packaging," its skewed explanation of the source of the deficit in reading, knowledge, and civics and, ultimately, its sense of the big picture.

The first problem, which may be caused by Bauerlein's publisher rather than by Bauerlein himself, is the over-hyped packaging of the book. Calling the book *The Dumbest Generation,* a phrase meant to play on Tom Brokaw's paean to World War II veterans, *The Greatest Generation* (1998), simply invites pointless challenges. Since Bauerlein isn't offering an in-depth historical account of knowledge levels over several generations, or even any comparisons with other cultures, the use of "dumbest" is needlessly provocative. And while Bauerlein makes clear in his text that he's using "dumb" to mean "ignorant" rather than "stupid," it's bound to cause confusion of the "who-are-you-calling-stupid?" variety.

To make matters worse, there's a glibly earnest sub-title, *How the Digital Age Stupefies Young Americans and Jeopardizes Our Future,* that also over-hypes the problem and sounds like a publicity department's efforts to make sure that all the right hot-buttons are pressed. And just in case potential readers still don't get it, there's even a sub-sub-title, *Or, Don't Trust Anyone Under 30*, an ironic reversal of a 1960s over-the-top admonition about not trusting people over 30. I guess it wouldn't have been sexy enough to more modestly call the book *An Ignorant Generation: The Decline of Reading, Knowledge, and Citizenship Among Young People Today*.

A far more serious defect mars the book when Bauerlein departs from his sound empirical findings and attempts to identify the source of the present decline. In the latter third of the book, under chapters headed "The Betrayal of the Mentors" (an echo of the title of Julian Benda's 1920s critique, *The Treason of the Intellectuals*), and "No More Cultural Warriors," Bauerlein decides that the decline of reading was initiated by the youth culture of the 1960s, and especially by the "indulgence" of their mentors, who should have known better.

"Spend some hours in school zones," Bauerlein advises, "and you see that the indulgent attitude toward youth, along with the downplaying of tradition, has reached the point of dogma." Adds Bauerlein, "Like so many dominant cultural attitudes today, the final ennobling of youth motives and attribution of youth authenticity derive from the revolutionary heat of the 1960s." Soon, we're into a full-blown case of "blaming it on the '60s." "The benighted mental condition of American youth today," Bauerlein tells us, "results from many causes, but one of them is precisely a particular culture-war outcome, the war over the status of youth fought four decades ago.

From roughly 1955 to 1975, youth movements waged culture warfare ... and the mentors who should have fought back surrendered."
Bauerlein's portrait of the 1960s is simplistic, shallow, and skewed
beyond caricature. In his version of the 1960s there's no civil rights
movement, no resistance to an American imperialist war in Vietnam,
no feminist or gay movements, no birth of modern environmentalism. There's barely a Bob Dylan song blowin' in the wind.

Not only is this a shabby intellectual account, it also thoroughly
vitiates a lot of the hard work Bauerlein has done in empirically
demonstrating the decline of reading and knowledge. It isn't at all
clear why Bauerlein doesn't blame the obvious culprits: the present-
day manufacturers and advertisers of devices and trivial content
who relentlessly push their wares upon young customers and con-
vince them that it's cool.

Isn't the aggressive marketing of the panoply of digital distractions
something like the recent Sports Utility Vehicle (suv) fiasco? There,
manufacturers and advertisers created a "need" for suvs where none
existed, and in North America brainwashed half the driving public
into purchasing gas-guzzling, unsafe, "off-road" vehicles that 90 per
cent of them weren't going to drive off-road, unless the Wal-Mart
parking lot can be seen as an off-road adventure.

No, it's not the makers of *Grand Theft Auto* or the latest Batman
superhero entertainment who are responsible for the dumbing down
of the young, it's a band of youthful radicals from a half-century
ago, according to Bauerlein.

Bauerlein conveys almost no sense of the market-driven, mindless
– okay, let's say it – *capitalist,* cultural context driving the present era.
There's good data, but no big picture. And there's little inclination to
go on to ask that famous political question, "What is to be done?"

Bauerlein doesn't attempt to discuss any solutions, apart from a few
handwaving gestures. In a sense, the answers are obvious: to reverse
the decline in reading, knowledge, and democracy, we would have to
transform the relationship between the marketplace culture and society. In an equally obvious sense, the problem is too big: nobody knows
how to transform, or even slightly change, globalized capitalism and
its cultural productions. In any case, there are historical reasons to be
cautious about answering big questions too quickly. So, I don't fault
Bauerlein for failing to produce workable remedies, but I would prefer a clearer perspective on the big picture.

And, of course, when the next teaching season starts up again, I'll try to persuade my students to enter The Dead Library and discover that it's a living, magic forest.

3. DECLINE AND DISTRACTION

Chris Hedges, *Empire of Illusion: The End of Literacy and the Triumph of Spectacle* (2009)

One end-of-the-semester morning, while taking attendance in the "philosophy and literature" course I teach at Capilano University, I checked off the name of a student who had missed the previous class. "Where were you last week?" I asked. Since attendance-taking is a desultory ritual, I try to liven it up with some low-level banter. But this time, instead of the equally desultory dog-ate-my-homework excuse, there was something new.

"Modern warfare was released at midnight," he said.

It took me a nano-second of mental double-take to realize that he wasn't announcing an apocalyptic event that had been forecast by Nostradamus or the biblical Book of Revelations. In that same micro-instant I saw that I needed to make an orthographic tweak to his sentence to understand what he was saying. I had to italicize the subject of the remark: it wasn't "modern warfare," but instead "*Modern Warfare*." Actually, *Modern Warfare 2*, *Call of Duty 6*, accompanied by the ubiquitous "TM" trademark logo.

But he didn't have to say all that because it was common knowledge. As I could tell from the collective chuckle, almost everyone in class got the picture immediately or, like me, an imperceptible nanosecond later. *Modern Warfare* is a popular series of videogames and a new version of it had been recently released. Like Harry Potter novels, vampire movies, or certain musical/video releases, part of the marketing strategy is to begin selling them at midnight, giving early customers a more vivid prestige-enhancing sense of being the first one on their block to own one.

So, my student had dutifully lined up outside the mall emporium, purchased a copy of the game ($59.95 a pop, according to Amazon.ca) in the middle of the night, gone home and blasted away until the wee hours, and was of course fast asleep by the time morning class rolled around. He wasn't the only one. In the initial marketing surge (or should that be, in these days of military metaphors, "surge"?), 4 million-plus copies were sold, according to the *Modern Warfare 2* website, and the company quickly raked in about a half billion dollars in sales. So, this is not merely an anecdote about the latest cute excuse for missing class.

Naturally, I took the opportunity of the occasion to deliver a medium-level rant about the vacuity, shallowness, and dopey nature of the pop culture foisted on young people today, although I soften the blow by pointing out that their consumption of such junk isn't entirely their fault. Since attendance-taking is generally agreed to be a desultory chore, the students are prepared to put up with these diverting rants as long as I don't go on too long and turn it into *nagging*.

I offer this little story of cultural catastrophe in support of Chris Hedges's critique of American culture, politics, and economics, *Empire of Illusion*. However, I have to admit that I view such scenes with a bit more wry amusement than Hedges, who tends to be rather grim-lipped about the whole thing. Hedges is a Pulitzer Prize-winning former foreign correspondent for *The New York Times* who subsequently turned into a political radical and became a senior fellow of the leftist Nation Institute, a columnist for *Truthdig.com*, and the author of *War Is a Force That Gives Us Meaning* (2002).

He begins his account of the "triumph of spectacle" with a protracted description of "entertainment" wrestling (as contrasted to the sport found in schools and Olympic contests). It's a ghoulishly fascinating fifteen-page portrait of the larger-than-life superheroes and lower-than-snakes villains of WWE, the World Wrestling Entertainment tour, one of the spectacles of U.S. cultural life. Instead of old-fashioned half-nelsons and body slams, WWE is apparently more about bizarre storylines involving provocative taunting, cuckolding, and derogatory genealogies. But Hedges' main point is that the popular culture in which the masses, as they used to be known, are immersed, willingly or otherwise, is trivial, salacious, distracting, intellectually mind-numbing, and, above all, a terrible illusion that signals the decline and fall of the Empire.

Subsequent vignettes in the opening chapter about celebrity culture include a visit to a "celebrity cemetery," beauty makeover shows, "reality" TV fare like *American Idol*, *Survivor*, and *Big Brother*, and "humiliation" programs of the Jerry Springer type, where sub-proletarians duke it out over paternity DNA and who slept with whom. All of it serves to drive home Hedges' message about the mindlessness of "mass-cult."

Eventually, Hedges moves from the ring to Plato's cave and spells it out. "We are chained," he says, "to the flickering shadows of celebrity culture, the spectacle of the arena and the airwaves, the lies of advertising, the endless personal dramas, many of them completely fictional, that have become the staple of news, celebrity gossip, New Age mysticism and pop psychology." This is not exactly news, as Hedges readily admits. Not news then, but apparently there are more distortions of reality than ever, and perhaps there's some usefulness in pointing them out. Though shudder-inducing in places, Hedges' book is nonetheless strangely unsatisfying, and it's not immediately clear why. Its tone, which my students would identify as "nagging"? But it's more than tone.

In an opening chapter called "The Illusion of Literacy" (and in a book partly sub-titled "The End of Literacy"), Hedges has surprisingly little to say about the subject, almost as if he's not particularly interested in the possibility of literacy as a remedy for cultural mindlessness. There are a scant couple of paragraphs citing an approximately 40 per cent functional illiteracy rate in North America, but nothing about the decline of book reading, especially among young people, nor anything about other "knowledge deficits" in history, geography, science, and civics, and really not much about how the Internet is actually used by its consumers. For that sort of information you have to go to Bauerlein's *The Dumbest Generation*, Jacoby's *The Age of American Unreason,* or Andrew Keen's *Cult of the Amateur*.

The paucity of literacy discussion in a book that advertises itself as being about that topic is only part of a larger problem. The "illusion of literacy" chapter is followed by others that explore the "illusions" of love, wisdom, happiness, and America itself. There's a lot about porn, the pretensions of higher education, pop psychology, and the dismaying condition of a pseudo-democracy. Most of what Hedges says is factually true, yet I found myself periodically surfacing from the account of cultural and political sludge to mumble, "Yes, yes, but this isn't what *all* of life is about or how I experience it." At least in some monastic corners of the world, the kid who's playing *Modern Warfare* is also reading the books on the philosophy and literature reading list. That Hedges thinks bleak catastrophe is indeed the whole of contemporary life appears to be Hedges' own illusion.

It's never quite clear who Hedges is writing for nor what he wants his readers to do. Certainly, his unrelieved polemical essay is not aimed at the benighted masses watching Ultimate Fighting Challenge and poker on TV, clicking onto YouTube or YouPorn, "friending" strangers on Facebook, or blowing up imaginary worlds on *Grand Theft Auto* and *Modern Warfare* videogames. It's not for them, since they're not reading at all.

So, it's a book *about* rather than *for* the unwashed but shampooed masses whose minds are inundated by junk culture. Hedges must be writing for the rest of us, the – let's be generous – 10 or 20 per cent of us who read books, participate in politics and civic culture, and keep a worried eye on the CO_2 counts in the atmosphere.

The chapter on the "illusion of love," which is entirely devoted to a journalistic visit to a pornmakers convention in Las Vegas, is characteristic of Hedges' perspective. He presents an Inferno-esque, "graphic" account of heterosexual commercial porn that emphasizes its increasing violence and degradation of women. Interviews with porn performers, peddlars, and recovering porn actors reiterate the sadistic nature of this particular illusion, and in case we're unfamiliar with its contents, Hedges provides extended snatches of porn video dialogue and detailed descriptions of how tab A is slotted into inserts B, C, etc., in such productions.

This *cinéma vérité* presentation builds to the climactic message that "porn reflects the endemic cruelty of our society. This is a society that does not blink when the industrial slaughter unleashed by the United States and its allies kills hundreds of civilians in Gaza or hundreds of thousands of innocents in Iraq and Afghanistan." Hedges goes on (and on). Porn is soon linked to the plight of the mentally ill and the unfairly imprisoned, as well as the dangers of gun ownership, obnoxious nationalism, and "rapacious corporate capitalism." Predictably enough, porn is eventually equated to the infamous Abu Ghraib prison in Iraq and we're assured that "torture and pornography inevitably converge."

I'm puzzled by the rhetorical overkill, both here and throughout Hedges' tract. While it's reasonable to sharply criticize both the content of hetero porn and the conditions under which it's made, it's not immediately clear what the purpose is of a hyperbole that insistently ties porn to all of the world's assorted ills. It's as if, in the name of some form of radicalism, Hedges's intent is to crush all possible discourse about the subject. In this leftist vision of liberation, one can sense the mirthless commissars just over the horizon.

In any case, Hedges' edicts about the meaning of porn seem designed to render any further discussion of sexual representation either trivial or irresponsible, or both. He shuts down debate. Yet, the discussion of attitudes toward, and practices of, sex have had a lot to do with both feminist and homosexual political struggles in the last half century. No recognition of that will be found in Hedges' *Empire*. Nor, when it comes to cruelty and wanton killing, will readers find anything about porn-deprived *jihadis*, who manage a good deal of slaughter and torture without the aid of salacious imagery. I'm not offering a brief intended to mitigate the sexist horrors of heterosexual porn, I'm just suggesting that the world is more various and complicated than Hedges, in the grip of an ideology, allows.

Subsequent chapters on higher education and positive psychology are similarly uneven. Hedges opens his chapter on the "illusion of wisdom" by saying, "The multiple failures that beset the country, from our mismanaged economy to our shredding of Constitutional rights to our lack of universal health care to our imperial debacles in the Middle East, can be laid at the door of institutions that produce and sustain our educated elite. Harvard, Yale, Princeton, Stanford, Oxford, Cambridge, the University of Toronto and the Paris Institute of Political Studies ... do only a mediocre job of teaching students to question and think." I suppose you could also lay at the door of those elite universities, employing the same loaded method of interpretation, such things as the end of slavery, free speech, civil rights, notions of ethnic and gender equality, sexual orientation, or even the attempt to reform health care in the U.S. But that's not what Hedges wants to do.

If Hedges offers sweeping, half-true, generalizations about elite education, he's also capable of astutely pointing out that in our "deteriorated educational landscape," it's the case that "there has been a concerted assault on all forms of learning that are not brutally utilitarian." He cites the continuing decline of teaching jobs in the liberal arts and notes that the humanities' share of college degrees is less than half of what it was during the mid-to-late '60s. "Bachelor's degrees in business, which promise to teach students how to accumulate wealth, have skyrocketed. Business majors since 1970-71 have risen from

13.6 per cent of the graduating population to 21.7 per cent. Business has now replaced education, which has fallen from 21 per cent to 8.2 per cent, as the most popular major." All too true.

Hedges is also good on the "illusion of happiness." That's where he skewers various self-help gurus peddling "positive thinking" and punctures the intellectual pretensions of various psychology departments to put "Positive Psychology" on a scientific footing. Barbara Ehrenreich's *Bright-Sided: How the Relentless Promotion of Positive Thinking Has Undermined America* (2009) does a more extensive and thorough job on the topic, but Hedges' acerbic view of the matter ought to be enough to get you to stash your "Smiley" buttons and shelve your copy of Rhona Byrne's *The Secret*. My complaint is not that Hedges isn't onto something important, but that his version of the big picture strikes me as just as skewed as Mark Bauerlein's more conservative view of the larger scheme of things in *The Dumbest Generation*.

The worst is saved for last. It's Hedges' chapter on the "illusion of America," and clearly the one he was most itching to write. As is his wont, the screed is unrelieved, but tinged with bitter affection for a land that once was. "The country I live in today uses the same civic, patriotic, and historical language to describe itself ... but only the shell remains," Hedges laments. "The America we celebrate is an illusion. America, the country of my birth, the country that formed and shaped me, the country of my father, my father's father and his father's father ... is so diminished as to be unrecognizable. I do not know if this America will return, even as I pray and work and strive for its return."

In place of the recognizable America, "our nation has been hijacked by oligarchs, corporations, and a narrow, selfish, political and economic elite, a small and privileged group that governs, and often steals, on behalf of the moneyed interests ... During this plundering we remained passive, mesmerized by the enticing shadows on the wall, assured our tickets to success, prosperity, and happiness were waiting just around the corner."

Hedges makes it clear that Barack Obama and the "bankrupt Democratic Party" is not the "hope" he "can believe in." About the only closing-line relief Hedges can offer is "love," whose power is greater than the power of death. "Love will endure," Hedges asserts, "even if it appears darkness has swallowed us all, to triumph over the wreckage that remains." For all love's power, it sounds pretty vague as an antidote to the wreckage and darkness.

Somewhere in the course of Hedges' final sermon (he was trained, he remarks in passing, as a seminarian), I think I figured out who he's writing for. The intended readership, I suspect, is left liberals and social democrats, and Hedges' polemic is designed to persuade moderate progressives that they/we don't fully understand the gravity of the situation. In failing to understand the situation, the moderate leftists become, in Hedges' view, the real enemy, more culpable than the right wing conservatives, because they prop up the shell of the system, even when they should know better. If that's what's going on here, it echoes the 1920s Communist Party's verbal and physical assault on social democrats as "social fascists," and at least some of us remember where that revolutionary strategy led.

Hedges's *Empire of Illusion* is a difficult book to deal with because much of it contains more than a grain of truth. Even if he could persuade left liberals and social democrats to repent and see the revolutionary light, I'm not sure what he wants them to do. It might be more helpful to see the situation as one of a divided polity, a divided culture in the midst of "culture wars," in which there are left-of-centre Democrats and social democrats, Obama included, and right-wing Republicans, angry anti-government libertarians, and self-proclaimed "independents."

That perspective at least makes possible an answer to the question, "What is to be done?" What we should do is continue to teach people to read books and to criticize the gadgets and content of capitalist pop culture. We should continue to try to reform health care, regulate and restrain capitalism, and attempt to save the planet. We should do the little things in our neighbourhoods, and we should join political parties and other organizations and try, as we used to say, to change the world.

This modest program is admittedly less spectacular than Hedges' despairing vision of spectacle and decline. But what's the alternative? I saw an ad on television recently advertising the latest apocalyptic movies and games, the screen filled edge-to-edge in high definition exploding objects. The voice-over punchline said, "The end of the world never looked so good."

4. THE YEARS THE LOCUSTS ATE

Historian Tony Judt's telling use of the biblical phrase, "the years the locusts ate," which he employs to describe the years since the fall of communism in 1989, can pretty well be applied, as he demonstrates, to our memory of almost everything after World War II. The British-born Judt (1948-2010) directed New York University's Erich Remarque Institute and is the author of the deservedly praised, Pulitzer Prize-nominated *Postwar* (2005), a history of Europe since 1945, as well as several more narrowly focused studies of French politics and intellectual life. His *Reappraisals: Reflections on the Forgotten Twentieth Century* (2008) collects some two dozen of his essays written over the past decade or so, all of which reflect on aspects of what he fears is an already forgotten era.

Wide-ranging, *Reappraisals* offers retrospective evaluations of such thinkers as Arthur Koestler, Primo Levi, Albert Camus, Hannah Arendt, Edward Said, and other intellectuals from the last century, as well as considerations of contemporary England, Belgium, Romania, and Israel, and a critical look at "The American (Half-) Century." Yet the book is strikingly more coherent and tightly argued than one might expect from a compilation of seemingly disparate essays. Some of the reasons for its quality of sustained thought are that Judt's essays are unfailingly interesting, knowledgeable without being pedantic, well-written, contentious but not cranky, and straight-from-the-headlines relevant. As well, anchor essays at the beginning and end of the book not only set out the themes and sum up the re-flective investigations in between but underscore the haunting phrase from the biblical Book of Joel about the years the locusts ate.

In the introductory "World We Have Lost," Judt lays out his con-cerns. At the broadest level, he is interested, first, in "the role of ideas and the responsibility of intellectuals" in societies like ours, hence his survey of various provocative thinkers. Second, Judt reflects on "the place of recent history in an age of forgetting: the difficulty we seem to experience in making sense of the turbulent century that has just ended and in learning from it." Judt fears that, if we look back at all, we shall "look back upon the half generation separating the fall of communism in 1989-91 from the catastrophic American occupation of Iraq as ... a decade and a half of wasted opportunities and political incompetence on both sides of the Atlantic." It was with "too much confidence and too little reflection" that we put the past century behind us and strode into the new one wrapped "in self-serving half-truths: the triumph of the West, the end of History, the unipolar American moment, the in-eluctable march of globalization and the free market."

Paradoxically, though we wear the last century "rather lightly," Judt observes, "we have memorialized it everywhere: museums, shrines, inscriptions, 'heritage sites,' even historical theme parks are all public reminders of 'the Past'." But there is something odd about this semi-commercial commemoration. "We encourage citizens and students to see the past – and its lessons – through the particular vector of their own suffering (or that of their ancestors). Today, the 'common' interpretation of the recent past is thus composed of the manifold fragments of separate pasts, each of them (Jewish, Polish, Serb, Armenian, German, Asian-American, Palestinian, Irish, homosexual …) marked by its own distinctive and assertive victimhood." In short, the past is reduced to a sort of wounded tribalism. "Whatever the shortcomings of the older national narratives once taught in school" – and the shortcomings, whether of the "Manifest Destiny," "Dictatorship of the Proletariat," or "Peace, Order and Good Government" variety, were many – "they had at least the advantage of providing a nation with past references for present experience."

In an era whose slogan is an injunction to put the traumas of the past "behind us, seek closure, and move on," Judt asks, "What, then, is it that we have misplaced in our haste to put the twentieth century behind us?" First, "curious as it may seem, we (or at least we Americans) have forgotten the meaning of war."

For much of the world, the 20th century "was a time of virtually unbroken war: continental war, colonial war, civil war." And war meant occupation, destruction and mass murder. But "the United States avoided all that … The U.S. was never occupied. It did not lose vast numbers of citizens or huge swaths of national territory, as a result of occupation or dismemberment. Although humiliated in neocolonial wars (in Vietnam and now in Iraq), it has never suffered the consequences of defeat."

The result, Judt suggests, is that for "many American commentators and policymakers the message of the last century is that war *works*. The implication of this reading of history has already been felt in the decision to attack Iraq in 2003. For Washington, war remains an option – in this case the first option. For the rest of the developed world it has become a last resort."

Judt is right both about American geopolitical rashness and about the former George W. Bush administration's doctrine of "pre-emptive war," but the one reservation I would offer concerns his declaration that war is a "last option" for the rest of the world (to be fair, Judt qualifies that as the "developed" world). Still, I didn't notice much restraint when it came to violence in the European civil wars of the 1990s in the former (more-or-less-developed) Yugoslavia, nor have various governments and militias in the (unevenly developed) Middle East hesitated about taking up arms, to say nothing of even less developed regions of Africa, Asia, and the former Soviet Union. But that's about my only caveat when it comes to Judt's large introductory generalizations, which are about war, followed by considerations of the state and the place of politics in our time.

Judt is on firm ground, I think, when he says, "After war, the second characteristic of the twentieth century was the rise and subsequent fall of the state." The former refers to the emergence of autonomous nation-states throughout the century, from the redrawing of national boundaries and the invention of new states in the wake of World War I, to the independence of India, Pakistan, Israel, and many former colonies in Africa at mid-century, to such contemporary events as the emergence of autonomous states in regions of the former Soviet Union or the contested declaration of independence in Kosovo.

Judt, however, is appropriately more focused on the diminution of state power "at the hands of multinational corporations, transnational institutions, and the accelerated movement of people, money and goods outside their control." While there's little dispute that the process of globalization is an unfolding juggernaut, Judt warns that "those who regard the outcome as both desirable and inevitable may be in for a surprise."

In exploring what is perhaps the central underlying theme of his reappraisals, Judt notes that "the twentieth century state acquired unprecedented capacities and resources. In their benevolent form these became what we now call the 'welfare state'... Malevolently, these same centralized resources formed the basis of authoritarian and totalitarian states in Germany, Russia, and beyond."

One of Judt's worries is about the diminishing allegiance to the notion of the state during the course of the last century. For the post-World War II period, "it was widely accepted that the modern state could – and therefore should – perform the providential role; ideally without intruding excessively upon the liberty of its subjects." But in the last third of the 20th century, "it became increasingly commonplace to treat the state not as the natural benefactor of first resort but as a source of economic inefficiency and social intrusion best excluded from citizens' affairs wherever possible." Here, Judt is referring to the now familiar triumph of both conservative ideology and unrestrained capitalist globalization.

The result is that "when now we speak of economic 'reform' or the need to render social services more 'efficient,' we mean that the state's part in the affair should be reduced ... The state, it is conventionally assumed on all sides, is an impediment to the smooth running of human affairs." Judt returns to this theme in a core section of his book called "Lost in Transition," a series of essays about England, Belgium, Romania, and Israel.

What Judt wants us to remember is that "it was not always self-evident that the state is bad for you; until very recently there were many people in Europe, Asia, and Latin America, and not a few in the U.S., who believed the contrary." If they hadn't, says Judt, neither the New Deal, nor the 1960s Great Society programs, nor the social democratic institutions of Western Europe would have come about.

In the end, Judt is arguing that "we need to learn once again to 'think the state,' free of the prejudices we have acquired against it in the triumphalist wake of the West's cold war victory." We're all aware, as of the end of the last century, "that you can have too much state. But ..." – and here's the punchline – "you can also have too little."

The antagonism toward the state, and the concomitant undermining of a concept of the citizen, leads directly to Judt's third broad theme of forgetfulness: "We have forgotten how to think politically."

Paradoxically, "the very success of the mixed-economy welfare state ... has led a younger political generation to take that same stability and ideological quiescence for granted and demand the elimination of the 'impediments' of the taxing, regulating, and generally interfering state." The striking result of this is "how far we have lost the capacity even to conceive of public policy beyond a narrowly constructed economism." This is what Judt means by the notion of forgetting how to think politically.

Instead, "we describe our collective purposes in exclusively economic terms." There's a clear and present danger: "Democracies in which there are no significant political choices to be made, where economic policy is all that really matters – and where economic policy is now largely determined by nonpolitical actors (central banks. international agencies or transnational corporations) – must either cease to be functioning democracies or accommodate once again the politics of frustration, of populist resentment." Some would say that that's exactly what happened in the U.S. during the George W. Bush period.

Canadian readers of Judt who find his arguments somewhat familiar are hearing an echo of John Ralston Saul's 1995 Massey Lectures, *The Unconscious Civilization,* where a similar plea for the public good, against corporate partial interests, and for the renewal of citizenship was eloquently rehearsed. It was Ralston Saul who said, "The most powerful force possessed by the individual citizen is her own government ... Government is the only organized mechanism that makes possible that level of shared disinterest known as the public good. Without this greater good, the individual is reduced to a lesser, narrower being limited to immediate needs."

If it's true that we've forgotten how to think politically, then it's only natural for Judt to worry about the ominous disappearance of intellectuals from the present public forum and to turn to recollections of specific thinkers of the recent past, which is precisely what he does in the succeeding sections of his book. Most of Judt's essays are occasioned by, and are a response to, recently published books he's reviewing. Often, the books are biographies, as in his essays about Arthur Koestler and Primo Levi, or occasioned by the reappearance of works by writers like Hannah Arendt, Manes Sperber, and Edward Said. Repeatedly, the reader comes away from Judt's reappraisals thinking, Yes, I've got to give Said, or historian Eric Hobsbawm, or philosopher Leszek Kolakowski another look (or maybe even a first look). The strength of Judt's essays is that they're persuasive invitations to the life of the mind.

When not writing about particular minds, the second kind of reappraisal that Judt engages in concerns the perilous state of The State and why we need to re-learn how to "think the state." Judt's most savage essay, about England's Tony Blair, circa 2001, just as the British New Labour prime minister was securing his first re-election, is perhaps representative.

Judt argues that Blair was not so much the creator of a "third way" of politics as the grateful inheritor of former PM Margaret Thatcher's extremely conservative politics, a politics which destroyed the old Labour Party as well as fracturing her own Tory ranks for the next decade – a politics which Blair was quite content to continue under the guise of something much more moderate. Above all, Thatcher "'normalized' the radical dismantling of the public sector in industry and services and its replacement with the 'privatized' Britain whose praises Blair enthusiastically" sang.

British-born and knowledgeably steeped in the Cambridge culture that educated him, Judt nails the phoniness of the former prime minister. "What seems to grate most is the ersatz quality of Tony Blair and his politics," Judt notes. "He doesn't exactly believe in privatization (but nor is he against it ...), he just likes rich people. He talks the talk of devolution, but as prime minister he is notoriously obsessed with control ... He conveys an air of deep belief, but no one knows in quite what. He is not so much sincere as Sincere." Judt thinks he can identify the British nerve that Blair touched. "The English capacity simultaneously to invoke and to deny the past – to feel genuine nostalgia – for fake heritage – is, I think, unique ... The remarkable alacrity with which industry, poverty, and class conflicts have been officially forgotten and paved over, such that ... even the most recent and contested past is available only in nostalgic plastic reproduction, is what makes Tony Blair credible. He is the gnome in England's Garden of Forgetting."

Beyond the shredding of a political personality, the deeper subject of Judt's essay is the catastrophic privatization of the British rail system under Thatcher, John Major, and Blair. "The outcome has been a chronicle of disasters foretold," Judt says, and then proceeds to detail the greed, dis-service, and literal dangers contained in that chronicle.

Judt's point is that "railways are a public service. That is why the French invest in them so heavily (as do the Germans, Italians and Spanish). They treat the huge subsidy given their train system as an investment in the national and local economies, the environment, health, tourism, and social mobility." And that's a good thing, says Judt. For most Europeans, "railways are not a business but a service that the state provides for its citizens at collective expense ... To treat trains like a firm, best run by entrepreneurs whose shareholders expect a cash return on their investment, is to misunderstand their very nature."

If Judt's essay about Blair's England is his most excoriating prose, his writings about Israel are the expression of his most controversial thoughts, and they deserve mention perhaps simply because they are controversial. As with most issues he tackles, Judt knows whereof he speaks: he was raised in a radical Jewish household and did a tour of service as a teenager on an Israeli kibbutz in the mid-1960s. His Marxism eventually was tempered toward left liberalism of the variety made respectable by one of Judt's intellectual heroes, the French writer Raymond Aron, and it's a liberalism that he continues to advocate and lament in his essay about "the strange death of Liberal America." Judt was also friends with the Palestinian-American Edward Said and wrote a fond essay (included in *Reappraisals*) that prefaces the posthumous collection of Said's late political writings.

What's controversial about Judt's views is that he aligns himself with Said's eventual advocacy of what's known as a "one-state solution" to the Israeli-Palestinian conflict – that is, a democratic, secular, egalitarian state rather than the standard "two-state" proposal, which retains the present theocratic, ideologized, antagonistic relations. This isn't the place to argue that argument – and at the moment, neither proposal looks even vaguely likely, or likely to bring peace – but one can see how unorthodox views like Judt's led to his revilement, especially by other, mostly North American, Jews.

At the end of his book, Judt comes full circle with an essay about what the French call "the excluded," those large numbers of people who are or who have become hopelessly and brutally marginalized in their societies, and this returns Judt to the question of the state. That's because, in his view, only the state can ameliorate the inhuman condition. As a pluralist, Judt doesn't believe that "any single set of political or economic rules or principles is universally applicable." What interests him is why, "in continental Europe the state will continue to play the major role in public life." Judt cites three general reasons.

"The first is cultural," he says. "People expect the state – the government, the administration, the executive offices – to take the initiative or at least pick up the pieces ... Thus, although the state has had a bad press ... there has been little loss of faith in the importance of the things it can do, properly led. Only a state can provide the services and conditions through which its citizens may aspire to lead a good or fulfilling life." Coincidentally echoing John Ralston Saul once more, Judt says, "Most important, only the state can represent a shared consensus about which goods are positional and can be obtained only in prosperity and which are basic and must be provided to everyone in all circumstances."

Judt warns against "the idealization of the market, with the attendant assumption that anything is possible in principle, with market forces determining which possibilities will emerge." He calls that idealization "the latest (if not the last) modernist illusion: that we live in a world of infinite potential where we are masters of our destiny (while somehow simultaneously dependent on the unpredictable outcome of forces over which we have no control)." Though we may cling to the illusion, it is, argues Judt, contradictory.

The second reason for preserving the state today is pragmatic, Judt suggests. "Because global markets *do* exist ... there is greater need than ever to hold on to the sorts of intermediate institutions that make possible normal civilized life." What we need to recognize is that the state is such an intermediate institution. Judt calls it "the only institution that can effectively interpose itself between those [global] forces and the unprotected individual in the national state." Indeed, such states are "all that can stand between their citizens and the unrestricted, unrepresentative, unlegitimated capacities of markets."

Finally, the need for representative democracy "is also the best argument for the traditional state ... Just as political democracy is all that stands between individuals and an overmighty government, so the regulatory, providential state is all that stands between its citizens and the unpredictable forces of economic change. Far from being an impediment to progress, the recalcitrant state, embodying the expectations and demands of its citizenry, is the only safeguard of progress to date."

Judt's reminders of what we have forgotten, and his moderate plea for the reconstruction of the social welfare or social democratic state, may or may not add up to "change that we can believe in," to once more cite Barack Obama's hopeful presidential campaign slogan. But Judt's essays are free of political "spin," suffused in intelligent thought, and just may save us from another plague of locusts.

5

The Snowflake from the Snow: Orhan Pamuk

I

A man is riding on a bus across Turkey, more than a thousand kilometres, from Istanbul in the west, to Kars, a provincial city in the far northeastern corner of the country near the Armenian-Georgian borders. It's wet and snowy. He's a Turkish poet, in his early 40s, known as Ka, the acronym of his given and family names, Kerim Alakusoglu. For the past dozen years he's lived in political exile in Frankfurt, Germany ("even though he had never been much of an activist"), but was permitted to return to Istanbul for his mother's funeral. And now, a few days later, he's on his way to Kars, ostensibly as a journalist sent to cover the municipal election (which the local Islamist party is poised to win) and to investigate a rash of mysterious teen suicides by what are known as "headscarf girls." His editor in Istanbul also mentioned in passing that a former university classmate of Ka's, the beautiful Ipek, divorced from her husband, Muhtar, was living in Kars at the old family hotel, the Snow Palace, with her father and sister.

Three-quarters of the way across the country, Ka has to change buses at Erzurum for the local one to Kars. It begins to snow. "It was heavier and thicker than the snow he'd seen between Istanbul and Erzurum. If he hadn't been so tired, if he'd paid more attention to the snowflakes swirling out of the sky like feathers, he might have realized that he was travelling straight into a blizzard; he might have seen from the start that he had set out on a journey that would change his life for ever." The word for "snow" in Turkish, *kar*, can be seen as snugly nesting between the names of Ka and Kars; and perhaps even K., the protagonist of Kafka's *The Castle,* is lurking somewhere in the shadows of these alphabetical affinities. Ka might have turned back, says the narrator of Orhan Pamuk's novel *Snow* (2002; translated into English by Maureen Freeley, 2004).

Instead, Ka is thinking only about the weather and poetry. "The silence of snow, thought the man sitting just behind the bus driver. If this were the beginning of a poem, he would have called what he felt inside him 'the silence of snow'." He sees the "snowflakes whirling ever more wildly in the wind" not as portents of a blizzard but as "a sign pointing back to the happiness and purity he had once known as a child," as a memory of innocence that allows him to momentarily "believe himself at home in the world." Ka, wrapped in an elegant charcoal-grey overcoat bought in Frankfurt, slips from reverie into long-sought sleep.

While he dozes, the narrator, who is named "Orhan," takes a moment to quickly fill us in on Ka's background. "But I don't wish to deceive you," says the narrator, "I'm an old friend of Ka's and I begin this story knowing everything that will happen to him during his time in Kars." With that, we're on our way into a fairy tale for adults in which the snow never stops falling, into A Thousand and One Turkish Nights where the magic of the magic realism is real, into a book about politics, God, love, and poetry. *Snow,* by the winner of the 2006 Nobel Prize for Literature, is also, I'm pretty certain, one of the great novels of the decade.

Once in snowbound Kars, after a night's sleep at the Snow Palace, Ka notices on an early morning walk that the snow, "veiling as it did the dirt, mud and the darkness," continues to speak to him of purity,

> but after his first day in Kars, it no longer promised innocence. The snow here was tiring, irritating, terrorising. It had snowed all night. It continued snowing all morning, while Ka walked the streets playing the intrepid reporter – visiting coffee-houses packed with unemployed Kurds, interviewing the voters, taking notes – and later, when he climbed the steep and frozen streets to interview the former mayor, the governor's assistant, and the families of the girls who committed suicide. But it no longer took him back to the snowy streets of his childhood... Instead, it spoke to him of hopelessness and misery.

In the poorest part of Kars, the Kaleati district,

The scenes he saw as he hurried under the ice-covered branches of
the plane trees and the oleasters – the old, decrepit Russian buildings with stovepipes sticking out of every window, the thousand-
year-old Armenian church towering over the wood depots and the
electric generators, the pack of dogs barking at every passer-by
from a five-hundred-year-old stone bridge as snow fell into the
half-frozen black waters of the river below, the thin ribbons of
smoke rising out of the tiny shanty houses of Kaleati sitting life-
less under their blanket of snow –made him feel so sad that tears
came to his eyes ... These sights spoke of a strange and powerful
loneliness. It was as if he were in a place that the whole world
had forgotten; as if it were snowing at the end of the world.

Within a few pages, Pamuk has immersed us in a world that is like
a children's snow globe, and yet simultaneously presents a grimly
realistic panorama of the various contradictions and circumstances
– secularism versus faith, ethnic minorities, poverty and backwardness, a society of surveillance, gossip, and violence – that engulf contemporary Turkey and beyond, the whole played out in a remote
crossroads of the world's troubles.

On that first morning in Kars, Ka checks in with his eastern
Anatolian journalistic colleague, Serdar, editor of the *Border City
News* (circulation: 320, most of which are government agency sub-
scriptions). The journalist takes the poet through the snowy city,
with its architectural vestiges of the Russian-Armenian-Ottoman
past, for requisite visits to the police, the deputy governor, and the
families of the dead girls. Kasim, the beer-bellied assistant chief of
police, offers Ka "protection" in the form of a plainclothes tail,
which will be provided whether or not it's wanted, and despite Ka's
protest, "If Kars is a peaceful place, then I don't need protection."
But, then, Kars is not a peaceful place; rather, it's a nexus of suspi-
cion where all strangers, and much of the citizenry, are under constant and mutual scrutiny. The deputy governor, "a squirrel-faced
man with a brush mustache," is primarily concerned with damage
control in the presence of a journalist from Istanbul who might
spread bad news about the suicide girls and make the local authorities look bad; or worse, news that might be picked up by the

European press, thus further humiliating tension-ridden Turkey. Then there are the homes and families of the girls who committed suicide, and tales of the "never-ending woes of Kars."

Among those woes is the intractable and puzzling epidemic of self-murder, as suicide is known in some languages. The girls are inspired by the Islamic revival to don headscarves, but in secular Turkey, the authorities, backed by the ever-present spectre of the coup-prone army, ban the wearing of head coverings in public institutions, such as the schools the girls attend. Unaccountably, some of the girls kill themselves. But why? As declarations of belief, or for more mundane reasons, like boyfriend trouble? The government's anti-suicide posters, which proclaim "Human beings are God's masterpieces and suicide is blasphemy," an idea reinforced even by the local Islamic establishment, appear to have little effect and may only inflame the situation. It is a mystery unlikely to be solved, but one that ominously pulsates within the snow-blanketed city.

Back at the Snow Palace for a brief mid-day pause of warmth and rest in his room, Ka receives a message from Serdar to return to the newspaper office. Just as he's about to exit the lobby,

> he was stopped dead in his tracks; for just at that moment, coming through the doors behind the reception desk, was Ipek, even more beautiful than in Ka's memory ... His heart began to pound. Yes, exactly – that's how beautiful she was. First they shook hands in the manner of the Westernized Istanbul bourgeoisie, but after a moment's hesitation they moved their heads forward, embracing without quite letting their bodies touch, and kissed on the cheeks. "I knew you were coming," Ipek said as she stepped back.

All of this – the first morning's walkabout in Kars, the initial forays into the themes of Pamuk's novel, the encounter with Ipek (they agree to meet at a nearby pastry shop in an hour) – is but a curtain-raiser to a plot of Byzantine complexity and velocity. It's an entangled narrative made more dense by the propensity of the characters to tell further tales, parables, and premonitions of their own, and by the appearance of transcripts, manuscripts, and descriptions of inspired poems. Finally, there's the sub-textual principle of the text, a continuous suggestion of the half-hidden symmetry or doubling of characters and events.

"Orhan," the narrator, turns out to be a kind of doppelganger or mirror of Ka the poet and is fated to retrace much of Ka's own odyssey. Ka's beloved Ipek has a refracting sister, Kadife; both of the sisters will turn out to be involved with an alleged Islamic terrorist who bears the curious moniker "Blue"; Blue has a counterpart in a revolution-minded actor named Sunay; a fundamentalist student from the local religious high school, Necip, whom Ka shortly meets, has a best friend, Fazil, who is his psychological twin; and the mirror-like pairings extend to the novel's horizons. Pamuk's characters are persuasive as people, but they are also a schematic of possibilities. Yet the resultant pattern, woven as elaborately as a Turkish carpet, is surprisingly easy to follow in the hands of its skilled storyteller. As the Canadian novelist Margaret Atwood, one of many enthusiastic reviewers of *Snow*, aptly puts it, Pamuk is "narrating his country into being," providing an "in-depth tour of the divided, hopeful, desolate, mystifying Turkish soul."

2

Back at Serdar's office, where his two sons are running off tomorrow's edition on an ancient German press, Ka reads an item headed, "Night of Triumph for the Sunay Zaim Players at the National Theatre." When Ka arrived in Kars the night before, he had briefly glimpsed, among the travellers waiting for their luggage, the vaguely familiar faces of Sunay Zaim and his touring theatre company, "leading lights of the revolutionary theatre world" back in the 1970s, now reduced to down-at-the-heels shows in the remote provinces.

But in Serdar's *Border City News*, that night's performance, which has yet to occur, is reviewed with lavish praise in a journalese of clichés and press release puffery. The show was received with "thunderous applause," the paper reports. "The people of Kars, who have long been yearning for an artistic feast of this calibre were able to watch not just from the packed auditorium but from the surrounding houses," thanks to Kars Border Television's first live broadcast. The story describes the station's "tireless" efforts to string cable from their transmission headquarters through the city's snow-clogged streets to the theatre, and salutes the civic spirit of citizens who allowed the cable to pass through their open front windows into their apartments and out through their back gardens "to avoid snow damage."

At the bottom of the item, the article records that "Ka, the celebrated poet, who is now visiting our city, recited his latest poem, entitled 'Snow,'" in a guest appearance at the evening's performance.

Ka looks up from the freshly-inked sheet. "I don't have a poem called 'Snow,' and I'm not going to the theatre this evening. Your newspaper will look like it's made a mistake," he says.

"Don't be so sure," Serdar tells him. "There are those who despise us for writing the news before it happens … You should see how amazed they are when things turn out exactly as we've written them. And quite a few things do happen only because we've written them up first. This is what modern journalism is all about."

The newspaper that reports on the future, and the clunky running of cables through people's living rooms for the first live TV broadcast in Kars, is Pamuk's neat bit of satiric (and oddly plausible) magic realism, both about the nature of the media and the quest for modernization. "I know you won't want to stand in the way of our being modern," Serdar adds, "you don't want to break our hearts, and that is why I am sure you will write a poem called 'Snow' and then come to the theatre to read it."

So, the story about to unfold will include a real theatre, and its real curtain is about to go up on the "former leading lights of the revolutionary theatre world," except that their concern will be less with "revolutionary theatre" and more with a revolution *in* a theatre. The famous gun that always hangs on the mantelpiece in the first act, will not only be fired in the last act but will contain real bullets and be aimed at the audience. By now we have enough of an idea of what's in store for us that a scene-by-scene reprise is unnecessary. The concluding symmetry that awaits us, one that we can anticipate and has been signalled in the narrator's opening remarks, will be the mirror-journey "Orhan Pamuk" makes to Kars some four years later to gather the details of the story he's telling.

Although there are frequent passing references to Turkish history, Pamuk doesn't need to dwell on them, because he can take it that his Turkish readers will be familiar with details they absorbed in their tattered schoolbooks. For those of us who lack such ingrained knowledge, about the only Wikipedia-level bit of potted history that's helpful is the story of Mustafa Kemal Ataturk (1881–1938), the founder and first president of the modern Turkish republic that emerged from World War I and the collapse of the Ottoman Empire.

During the approximately decade-and-a-half reign by Turkey's most prominent former military-leader-turned-politician there was a change in Turkey that didn't really occur in any of the neighbouring Middle Eastern and Central Asian countries. Ataturk, who was familiar with the European democracies, appeared in his native land garbed in a Panama hat and suit rather than the traditional fez, rode in touring motorcars, and offered a thorough-going program of 20th century political, religious, economic, and social modernization.

The program is wreathed in historical debate and details that need not detain us here, but its broad primary strokes deserve mention. First, there was a substantial change in the relationship between religion and the state: while Ataturk didn't seek the strict separation of mosque and state, there was a subordination of religious institutions and personnel to the state, with the secularism of the latter clearly predominant. Other reforms included the formal liberation of women; an attempt at multi-party, multi-ethnic democracy (albeit a democracy guaranteed by military force prepared to step in to prevent religious or tribal backsliding); and a sweeping array of social transformations. Ataturk even called in U.S. philosopher John Dewey in the early 1920s to help set up a modern educational system in Turkey. The Arabic script in which Turkish had been written was changed to Latin letters.

The variable successes and failures of those efforts can be left to interested readers willing to pursue the topic. The point here is a recognition that the republic straddling the Bosphorous Straits that link the Black Sea to the Sea of Marmara (and ultimately the Mediterranean) can legitimately claim to be a genuine gateway between East and West (as its romantic tourist advertising incessantly proclaims).

As Pamuk says in "In Kars and Frankfurt," his acceptance speech in October 2005 for the Peace Prize of the German Book Trade Association, "Of course there is an East-West question, and it is not simply a malicious formulation invented and imposed by the West," even though "most of the time it carries an assumption that the poor countries of the East should defer to everything" proposed by the West. Rather, Pamuk insists, "The East-West question is about wealth and poverty and about peace." Addressing his listeners, members of a European Union in which Turkey seeks membership, Pamuk reminded them that "those who believe in the European Union must see at once that the real choice we have to make is between peace and nationalism. Either we have peace, or we have nationalism."

By contrast, much of the rest of the region has retained or re-turned to many of its traditional institutions. Monarchic and/or au-thoritarian rule, religious sectarianism, patriarchal tribalism, theocracy and near civil war continued to be the source of much of the turbulence in places like Iran, Iraq, Pakistan, and Afghanistan throughout the first decade of the present century (as I discuss in chapter 7, "Homeland Alone"). This is not to claim that Turkey is without a repressed history (of the Armenian genocide of World War I), or a history of repression (against the minority Kurds). The country of the mid- and late-1990s portrayed by Pamuk in *Snow* is tensely poised between its ambitions for membership in the European Union and its own Islamic "revival," but its political and social strains are recognizably modern in ways that make nearby national entities appear entrapped in feudal backwardness, not withstanding their penchant for modern technology, up to and including nuclear weapons. If the claim that Pamuk is "narrating his country into be-ing" is a bit grandiose, his tour of the convoluted and divided na-tional "soul" succeeds in making Turkey interesting far beyond the tourist attractions of beautiful, melancholy Istanbul.

In Kars, Ka falls in love, meets the local Islamist politicos, imams, and on-the-lam terrorists, becomes inadvertently involved in a local revolution that occurs in the town theatre, and, most important of all, is unexpectedly visited by his long-absent poetic muse and is impelled to write an extraordinary serial poem, whose structure is based on the shape of, what else?, a snowflake.

Snow is a book of conversions and apostasies. The theme that I somehow missed in my first reading of Pamuk and found most poi-gnant when I re-read it a few years later is the longing for God that afflicts so many of the characters in this snowstorm of a novel, in-cluding Ka himself. Of the dozen or more scenes in which spiritual yearning is thrashed out, Ka's visit to Ipek's ex-husband, Muhtar, epitomizes the lure of the Islamic revival, a subject not only central to *Snow* but one that of necessity has become a preoccupation of the West in the present decade.

Ka, Ipek, and Muhtar were all university classmates in Istanbul a dozen years before, in the early 1980s. Typical of their generation, Ka and Muhtar were secularists, aspiring poets, young Marxists.

When Ka visits his former school acquaintance at the headquarters of the Prosperity Party in Kars, "now here was Muhtar running on the Islamic fundamentalist ticket" as its mayoral candidate, "something he would have found despicable ten years earlier ..."

Muhtar relates the story of his conversion, how he was transformed from an unhappy, raki-inebriated, failed poet with a failed marriage, into a believer through his fateful meetings with a local religious teacher, the Kurdish sheikh, Saadettin Efendi. "I was accepted into the group and taken into this bright and warm little house," Muhtar recalls.

> Inside, the people were nothing like the hopeless and downtrodden folk who populate Kars: they were happy ... Something was happening that I had secretly dreaded for a long time and that in my atheist years I would have denounced as weakness and backwardness: I was returning to Islam ... A feeling of peace spread through me. I had not felt that way for years and immediately understood that I could talk to [the sheikh] about anything, tell him all about my life. And he would bring me back to the path I had always believed in, deep down inside, even as an atheist: the road to God Almighty. Just the promise of salvation brought me joy.

Yet the conversions are attended by inevitable doubts. Already Ka hears "not serenity but disillusionment in Muhtar's voice." But the longing for meaning is mutual. Ka tells Muhtar, "I live a very solitary life in Germany. When I look over the rooftops of Frankfurt in the middle of the night, I sense that the world and my life are not without purpose. I hear all sorts of sounds inside me." What sorts of sounds, Muhtar wants to know. "It may just have to do with fear of getting old and dying," Ka says, then adds, "If I were an author and Ka were a character in a book, I'd say, 'Snow reminds Ka of God.' But I'm not sure that would be accurate. What brings me close to God is the silence of snow."

Pamuk takes seriously the possibility of God as one of the paths to happiness, and "happiness," that seemingly banal notion, is one of the recurrent, constant themes of *Snow*. For all its shopworn quality, the incessant desire for happiness is one of the dimensions that makes Pamuk's novel a "large" work. Certainly, it's a motivation for "love," but in the tempest-tossed relationship Ka has with Ipek, the certainties of mutual possession and boundless happiness spill over suddenly into agonies of waiting, doubt, and intimations of betrayal.

If the belief in God or love resembles a storm that alternately rages and subsides, one source of happiness that leaves at least an artifactual remainder on the page is the poem. At one point, fairly early on in the story, Ka is in the town's bleak railway station disputing theology with three boys from the religious high school. One of them, brasher than the others, sneers, "Mr. Poet, Mr. Ka, you've made no secret of the fact that you were once an atheist. Maybe you still are one. So tell us, who is it who makes the snow fall from the sky? What is the snow's secret?"

> For a moment they all looked across the empty concourse to watch the snow falling on the tracks.
> What am I doing in this world? Ka asked himself. How miserable these snowflakes look from this perspective; how miserable my life is. A man lives his life, and then he falls apart and soon there is nothing left ... Like a snowflake, he would fall as he was meant to fall; he would devote himself heart and soul to the melancholy course on which his life was set. His father had a certain smell after shaving, and this came back to him now. Then he thought of his mother making breakfast, her feet aching inside her slippers on the cold kitchen floor. He had a vision of a hairbrush; he remembered his mother giving him sugary pink syrup when he woke up coughing in the middle of the night; he felt the spoon in his mouth.

There is no ellipsis between the gloomy ruminations in the middle of a seemingly inconsequential debate with the schoolboys and a sudden avalanche of childhood memories.

> As he gave his mind over to all such little things that make up a life, as he thought how they all added up to a unified whole, he saw a snowflake.
> And so it was that Ka heard the call from deep inside him, the call he heard at moments of inspiration, the only sound that could make him happy: the sound of his muse. For the first time in four years, a poem was coming to him. Although he had yet to hear the words, he knew that it was already written ... He told

the three youths that he was in a hurry and left the deserted, filthy station. He hurried through the snow, thinking all the while of the poem he would write when he was back in the hotel.

Ka threw off his coat the moment he entered his room. He opened the green notebook he'd brought with him from Frankfurt and wrote down the poem as it came to him, word by word. It was as easy as following dictation whispered into his ear, but nevertheless he gave the words on the page his full attention …

The poem comprised many of the thoughts that had come to him in a rush a short while earlier: the falling snow, cemeteries, the black dog that had been frolicking happily around the station, an assortment of childhood memories, and the image that had lured him back to the hotel, Ipek – how happy it made him just to imagine her face. But also how terrified! He called the poem "Snow."

The prediction of Serdar, the publisher-editor of the *Border City News*, is fulfilled, and Ka will recite his poem at the theatre that evening. What's more, in addition to recording extensive notes in his journal about what he saw in Kars, Ka will write 18 more interlinked poems in his green notebook that together add up to a book-length work bearing the name of its first poem. It's the quest for that missing book that will provoke Orhan Pamuk's own journey to Kars and Frankfurt and eventuate in a novel about that search, titled *Snow*. Like Javier Cercas's *Soldiers of Salamis*, a story about a story, Pamuk's *Snow* is a novel about, amid much else, a book of poems called *Snow*.

In modern English-language poetry, the sort of interlinked poems that Ka writes in Kars was discovered or invented by the mid-20th century San Francisco poet Jack Spicer in his book *After Lorca* (1957). Spicer and his poet colleague Robin Blaser dubbed this form the "serial" poem, a form whose unit of composition is the "book" (using that word in a way slightly different from its conventional reference).

Distinguishable from the modern "epic" and other "long" verse forms, in the serial poem each poem stands on its own and yet is integrally connected to the other poems that make up the "book." As Spicer once described it, citing his friend Blaser, "It's as if you go into a room, a dark room, and the light is turned on for a minute, then it's turned off again, and then you go into a different room where a light is turned on and off." Sometimes that succession of briefly lighted rooms becomes a house, or a book. Furthermore, as is the case with Ka's *Snow*, Spicer links the serial poem with an Orphic theory that the poem is transmitted, from an unknown outside source, by a process of "dictation." The source of the poem, whether muse, Martians, or whatever, of necessity makes use of the poet's own biographical details, memories, and ideas (what Spicer called "the furniture in the room"), but the poem that eventuates is not an "expression" of the poet's life so much as it is a message transmitted from "outside," even if the outside is not outside ourselves but is something more like our collective linguistic consciousness.

The authenticity of Pamuk's account of what it's like to write poems reinforces the reader's trust in the other aspects of the novel, from its ambivalent politics to its recreation of the streets, buildings, and people of distant Kars. In *Snow*, the act of writing the poems is described, as are their contents, and even theorized (by Ka) as structured by the axes of a hexagonal snowflake. Of course, the poems never appear on the pages of *Snow* but dissolve like those self-same snowflakes, serving as one of the powerful enticements that draw us into Pamuk's snowy labyrinth of desire, spiritual yearning, politics, and art.

3

Pamuk recurrently describes himself as a man "who shuts himself up in a room." In his Nobel Prize speech of December 2006, "My Father's Suitcase," he says, "When I speak of writing, what first comes to my mind is not a novel, a poem, or literary tradition, it is a person who shuts himself up in a room, sits down at a table, and alone, turns inward; amid the shadows, he builds a new world with words." In "The Implied Author," a talk given at an American university in spring 2006, Pamuk reiterates this image: "For thirty years I've spent an average of ten hours a day alone in a room, sitting at my desk." He adds, "Literature does not allow such a writer to pretend to save the world; rather it gives him a chance to save the day. And all days are difficult. Days are especially difficult when you don't do any writing. When you cannot do any writing. The point is to find enough hope to get through the day ..." In any case, as Pamuk told his Nobel audience, "The starting point of true literature is the man who shuts himself up in a room with his books."

However, Pamuk admits that "once we shut ourselves away, we soon discover we are not as alone as we thought. We are in the company of the words of those who came before us, of other's people's stories, other's people's books ... the thing we call tradition." Pamuk affirms literature "as the most valuable hoard that humanity has gathered in its quest to understand itself." Societies flourish insofar as "they pay attention to the troubled words of their authors, and, as we all know, the burning of books and the denigration of writers are both signals that dark and improvident times are upon us." The writer who shuts himself up in a room has the possibility of discovering "literature's eternal rule: he must have the artistry to tell his own stories as if they were other people's stories, and to tell other people's stories as if they were his own."

For English-language readers, Pamuk emerged from the room in which he had shut himself up only in the first decade of this century. Though he had written a half dozen novels since the early 1980s, it was only with his sixth novel, *My Name Is Red* (1998; translated into English, 2001), which won the 2003 Impac Dublin prize, that he achieved broader literary recognition. That was the impetus for further translations, honours, and life as a sometimes reluctant public figure which followed in quick succession. *Snow*, published in Turkey in 2002 where it was a 100,000-copy bestseller, was translated into English in 2004 to wide acclaim; in 2005 Pamuk was awarded the prestigious Peace Prize of *the German Book Trade Association; Istanbul: Memories of a City* also appeared in 2005 in multiple translations, including English.

In the same year, 2005, Pamuk rather unwillingly became the focus of political debate when he was charged with uttering remarks about the Armenian genocide and the situation of Turkish Kurdish people that allegedly violated certain nationalist laws against insulting Turkey, charges that were eventually dropped on the eve of the trial, in the wake of international protest.

The following year, Pamuk was named the winner of the Nobel Prize for Literature. There was, as often occurs with the Swedish Academy's choices, some grumbling that Pamuk had been selected for political reasons. Sometimes, complaints about the Nobel Prize winner are justified. But in this instance, the body of Pamuk's work suggests that he is a worthy companion to such other 21st century Nobel recipients as Doris Lessing, Harold Pinter, J.M. Coetzee, and V.S. Naipaul.

In 2007, Pamuk published *Other Colors*, a volume of essays, talks, and interviews that had been significantly expanded from an earlier volume of the same title that had appeared in his native tongue in 1999. A new novel, *The Museum of Innocence*, already published in Turkish (and which Pamuk, in passing, "announces" in *Snow*), appeared in English translation in 2009. Apart from requisite but sporadic public appearances, Pamuk, as he told a *Paris Review* interviewer in 2005, remains shut up in a room in a "flat overlooking the Bosphorus with a view of the old city. It has, perhaps, one of the best views of Istanbul." It also has within it one of the best observers of Istanbul and points East and West.

The near-unanimous chorus of acclaim elicited by the publication of *Snow* requires some reprise of the book's reception among English-language reviewers. John Updike immediately picked up on the novel's abundance of "modernist tracer genes. Like Proust's *Remembrance of Things Past*, it bares its inner gears of reconstituted memory and ends by promising its own composition." Its setting echoes "the mountainous, debate-prone microcosm of Thomas Mann's sanitorium in *The Magic Mountain* ... Like Italo Calvino, Pamuk has a passion for pattern-making; he maps Kars as obsessively as Joyce did Dublin ..." Updike presciently suggested that "Pamuk, young as he is [born in 1951], qualifies as [Turkey's] most likely candidate for the Nobel Prize ... To produce a major work so frankly troubled and provocatively bemused ... entirely contemporary in its settings and subjects, took the courage that art sometimes visits upon even its most detached practitioners" (John Updike, "Anatolian Arabesques," *The New Yorker*, Aug. 30, 2004).

Margaret Atwood, as noted, credits Pamuk with "narrating his country into being," and also finds *Snow* "not only an engrossing feat of tale-spinning, but essential reading for our times." She says, "Kars is finely drawn, in all its touching squalor, but its inhabitants resist 'Orhan's' novelizing of them. One of them asks him to tell the reader not to believe anything he says about them, because 'no one could understand us from so far away.' This is a challenge to Pamuk and his considerable art, but it is also a challenge to us" (Margaret Atwood, "Headscarves to Die For," *The New York Times*, Aug. 15, 2004). Christian Caryl identifies Dostoyevsky as "the literary forebear whose spirit haunts this book most palpably ... *The Possessed*, driven by moral quandaries posed by terrorism and political extremism is a particularly strong influence ... Where Pamuk really excels in this novel is in the deftness with which he allows these forces to tug at one another." (Pamuk provided the introduction to the Turkish translation of *The Possessed*, which he declares it to be "the greatest political novel of all time.") Says Caryl, "Pamuk the novelist illuminates his country's quandaries of identity, and the crisis of confidence between Islam and the West, with an imaginative depth we had not known before" (Christian Caryl, "The Schizophrenic Sufi," *The New York Review of Books*, May 12, 2005).

One significant voice of dissent from the general praise bestowed on Pamuk is that of the self-professed "contrarian" critic Christopher Hitchens, who is suspicious of the search "for a novelist in the Muslim world who could act the part of dragoman, an interpretive guide to the East," a role into which he sees Pamuk as being too-conveniently cast. Hitchens finds the novel's characterizations "disappointing, precisely because its figures lack the crystalline integrity of individuals," the work as a whole "prolix and often clumsy," and he's not at all happy that "the author leaves no room for doubt that he finds the Islamists the most persuasive and courageous." This last is a curiously skewed reading of Pamuk's refusal to demonize the book's religious characters. But at the time he was reviewing *Snow*, Hitchens was embroiled in an acrimonious debate regarding both Islamists and his own support for the U.S. occupation of Iraq, which might have warped his perception of other writers' treatment of similar issues (Christopher Hitchens, "Mind the Gap," *The Atlantic*, October 2004).

The occasional dissent aside, *Snow* made readers ask what Pamuk calls "the question we writers are asked most often, the favorite question: Why do you write?" In his Nobel Prize acceptance speech, Pamuk replies,

> I write because I have an innate need to write! I write because I can't do normal work like other people. I write because I want to read books like the ones I write. I write because I am angry at all of you, angry at everyone. I write because I love sitting in a room all day writing. I write because I can only partake in real life by changing it. I write because I want others, all of us, to know what sort of life we lived, and continue to live, in Istanbul, in Turkey ... I write because I believe in literature, in the art of the novel, more than I believe in anything else ... I write to be happy.

Even the dissenting Hitchens grants that Pamuk's Ka moves between "visions of snow in its macrocosmic form – the chilly and hostile masses – and its microcosmic: the individual beauty and uniqueness of each flake. Along the scrutinized axes that every flake manifests he rediscovers his vocation and inspiration as a poet." It was Yeats, in "Among School Children," who famously asked, "How can we know the dancer from the dance?" Among the lengthy list of reasons to write, Pamuk might add that he writes to distinguish the snowflake from the snow.

6

In the Land of Amos Oz:
A Tale of Love and Darkness

I

The "tale" that Israeli writer Amos Oz tells in his memoir, *A Tale of Love and Darkness* (2003; translated into English by Nicholas de Lange, 2004), is at once a writer's coming-of-age story, a boy's heart-breaking experience of coming-to-grief, grief that permanently tempers the innocence of childhood, and, because of when and where the tale takes place, a man's account of coming-to-terms with being a citizen of a nation born in violence and against the wishes of its political neighbours.

Immediately upon its publication in Hebrew, *A Tale of Love and Darkness* became the best-selling literary work in Israeli history At home and in various foreign translations (especially in Germany, where Oz was honoured with the Goethe Prize in 2005), *A Tale of Love and Darkness* was recognized as the masterpiece of Oz's lengthy writing career. Oz, who was already among the first rank of his country's most widely regarded writers, along with Aharon Appelfeld, David Grossman, and A.B. Yehoshua, is the author of a dozen well-received novels, from the early *My Michael* (1968) to a post-modernist fable about writing and writers, *Rhyming Life and Death* (2007; tr. 2009), as well as the passionate author of several volumes of social and political reportage, the best known of which is probably *In the Land of Israel* (1983). But the reception of Oz's memoir went beyond anything his previous books had elicited.

Fellow novelist David Grossman was among the first to pronounce *A Tale of Love and Darkness* "his masterpiece." The Israeli scholar Amos Elon noted that Oz's "moving and frank autobiography" was rightly "praised as his finest book so far" upon publication in his native land (Amos Elon, "In Abraham's Vineyard," *The New York Review of Books*, Dec. 16, 2004). John Leonard called "this indelible memoir" a "glorious, masterly lamentation, these 'Speak, Memory!' Dead Sea Scrolls" (John Leonard, "'A Tale of Love and Darkness': Motherland," *The New York Times*, Dec. 12, 2004). For novelist Linda Grant, it was "one of the funniest, most tragic and touching books I have ever read" (Linda Grant, "The Burden of History," *The Guardian*, Sept. 11, 2004).

I add my "amen" to the chorus of praise accorded *A Tale of Love and Darkness*. Oz's book also provides an opportunity to pause to recognize a few of the other eminent autobiographies and memoirs, as well as literary biographies, that mark the first decade of the 21st century. Nobel Prize winner Gabriel Garcia Marquez's *Living to Tell the Tale* (2002; translated into English by Edith Grossman, 2003) is an equally shimmering evocation of a childhood home in a remote corner of the world; Daniel Mendelsohn's *The Lost* (2006) is the enactment of a remarkable autobiographical quest; Edmund White's *My Lives* (2005) is an innovative memoir by the pre-eminent writer to emerge from the late-20th century gay movement; and Patrick French's *The World Is What It Is: The Authorized Biography of V.S. Naipaul* (2008) is about as unvarnished a literary life story of a Nobel Prize winning author as can be imagined. But Oz's *Tale* tears at the heart in ways unsurpassed by any of its peers. When I began re-reading it, I thought I'd only read 50 or so pages, just to refresh my memory in order to write about it. Instead, I re-read the whole 500 pages and at the end felt the same shuddering sorrow that I experienced the first time I read it.

Love and Darkness begins, unprepossessingly enough, in a "tiny, low-ceilinged, ground-floor flat" in the city of Jerusalem, where Oz was born in 1939.

> My parents slept on a sofa bed that filled their room almost from wall to wall when it was opened up each evening. Early every morning they used to shut away this bed deep into itself, hide the bedclothes in the chest underneath, turn the mattress over, press it all tight shut, and conceal the whole under a light grey cover, then scatter a few embroidered oriental cushions on top, so that all evidence of their night's sleep disappeared. In this way their bedroom also served as study, library, dining room and living room.

That troubled marriage bed, which concealed the evidence of night, and whose daily folding up of its two large "jaws" provided a child's giant "barking dog" fantasy image, recurs in Oz's book and the presence or absence of its occupants, in states of sleep and insomnia, is carefully charted.

The cramped family quarters were located on Amos Street in the lower-middle-class neighbourhood of Kerem Avraham ("Abraham's Vineyard") at the edge of northern Jerusalem. That's where Amos Klausner – he didn't change his name to Oz, a Hebrew word signifying "strength," until he was in his mid-teens – grew up in the 1940s, the only child of Arieh Klausner and Fania Mussman (Klausner), two recent Jewish immigrants to the British-ruled protectorate of Palestine who had come from what were then parts of inter-war Poland.

Writing about all of this retrospectively from a desert outpost on the outskirts of the town of Arad, Israel, where he's lived for the last quarter-century, Oz meticulously re-imagines a childhood amid streets named for minor Biblical prophets, in a neighbourhood whose parched ground, with unintentional irony, was meant to recall the fertile vineyard of one of Judaism's mythical fathers, although, apart from "a dusty cypress tree," the only other bit of vegetation within view, "a pale geranium planted in a rusty olive can, was gradually dying for want of a single ray of sunshine."

Oz's parents, who had been driven to Palestine by the spectre of impending genocide, thrived no better than the dying geranium. Well-educated Jews from the edges of Europe, they despised the *stetl*, or village-life, of most of their compatriots. They longed not for the Zion to which they had reluctantly relocated but for the cultured capitals of Europe. As Amos Elon observes of the disappointed lives of such European Jews, they had "escaped in time to the Promised Land but never found there what they expected." Oz himself writes, "Both my parents had come to Jerusalem straight from the 19th century." His father had grown up "on a concentrated diet of operatic, nationalistic, battle-thirsty romanticism, whose marzipan peaks were sprinkled, like a splash of champagne, with the virile frenzy of Nietzsche." His mother drew on "the other romantic canon, the introspective, melancholy menu of loneliness in a minor key ..."

A rumour of born-anew, "blond-haired, muscular, sun-tanned Hebrew Europeans," a futuristic mythical race, circulated in Oz's childhood. Occasionally representatives of that glorious future would appear in Jerusalem's marketplace, having come by truck from the local collective farm, or kibbutz. The surprising appearance of young Amos, a blond-haired, light-eyed son in the Klausner family, was hailed, as Oz jokingly told *New Yorker* writer David Remnick, as a kind of "genetic-ideological miracle" (David Remnick, "The Spirit Level," *The New Yorker*, Nov. 8, 2004).

Amos's father, Arieh, was the nephew of a famous Jewish scholar and professor, Joseph Klausner, who taught at Jerusalem's Hebrew University on the slopes of Mount Scopus. But Arieh's own academic aspirations would be permanently disappointed. He had a degree in literature from the University of Vilna (now Vilnius in Lithuania) as well as a second degree from the university on Mount Scopus, "but he had no prospect of securing a teaching position in the Hebrew University at a time when the number of qualified experts in literature in Jerusalem far exceeded that of the students." In the end, he had to settle for a job as a librarian in the National Library; after work he stayed up late at night writing books about literature, privately pursuing a frustrated career as an independent scholar. Oz tells us that

> My father was a cultivated, well-mannered librarian, severe yet also rather shy, who wore a tie, round glasses, and a somewhat threadbare jacket, who bowed before his superiors, leaped to open doors for ladies, insisted firmly on his few rights, enthusiastically cited lines of poetry in ten languages ... and endlessly repeated the same repertoire of jokes (which he referred to as "anecdotes" or "pleasantries").

He was, for young Amos, an oddly detached figure, a man who dreaded silence and felt compelled to forestall every potential instant of it with his "pleasantries." As Amos Elon characterizes him, "The father was a dry pedant, a walking dictionary unable to have close relations with either his wife or child." He jokily addressed his son in the third person as "His Highness" or "His Honour," and delicately navigated among spouse, mistress, employers, relatives, and neighbours.

In Kerem Avraham, the neighbours "were petty clerks, small retailers, bank tellers or cinema ticket-sellers, schoolteachers or dispensers of private lessons, or dentists. They were not religious Jews ... yet they lit candles on Friday night, to maintain some vestige of Jewishness and perhaps also as a precaution, to be on the safe side, you never know." They were, however, people with tenacious opinions on everything from Zionism to morning calisthenics "that would keep gloom at bay and purify the soul."

Elsewhere, in a volume of reportage, *Under This Blazing Light* (1975), Oz describes the Jerusalem of his childhood as a "lunatic town, ridden with conflicting dreams, a vague federation of different ethnic, national and religious communities, ideologies and aspirations ... My Jerusalem childhood made me an expert in comparative fanaticism."

In Kerem Avraham, "these neighbours, who would congregate in our little yard on Saturday afternoons to sip Russian tea were almost all dislocated people." Though they all "knew how to analyse, with fierce rhetoric, the importance for the Jewish people to return to a life of agriculture and manual labour ... whenever anyone needed to mend a fuse or change a washer or drill a hole in the wall, they would send for Baruch, the only man in the neighbourhood who could work such magic."

> As a child I could only dimly sense the gulf between their enthusi-astic desire to reform the world and the way they fidgeted with the brim of their hat when they were offered a glass of tea, or the ter-rible embarrassment that reddened their cheeks when my mother bent over (just a little) to sugar their tea and her decorous neckline revealed a tiny bit more flesh than usual: the confusion of their fin-gers, that tried to curl into themselves and stop being fingers.

That's one of the first appearances in the book of the enigmatic woman at the centre of the emotional labyrinth whose Ariadne-like thread Oz seeks to follow. His mother, Fania Mussman, one of three sisters, was the daughter of a former mill owner in the lakeside city of Rovno, in eastern Poland (now Ukraine), a mixed town of Poles and Russians in which Jews made up the majority. She graduated from an elite Hebrew high school and later studied briefly in Prague. Her education included an extensive curriculum of Jewish philoso-phy, ancient and modern Hebrew writers, and readings, in Hebrew translation of everyone from Tolstoy and Dostoevsky to Shakespeare and Goethe.

Oz makes an interesting literary move in order to vividly recon-
struct his mother's childhood in Rovno in the 1920s. He visits his
surviving aunt Sonia (one of Fania's sisters) in present-day Tel Aviv.
She tells him stories of her youth. About a quarter of the way into
the book, Oz lets her take over and for about fifty pages there is only
the voice of his octogenarian aunt Sonia remembering her and her
sisters' girlhood, recounting the tales of long gone lives and the gossip about them. Eventually we learn that in the 1940s, after the
Mussman family had settled in Haifa, on the outskirts of Rovno, in
the Sosenki Forest, "among boughs, birds, mushrooms, currants,
and berries," the Nazis slaughtered more than twenty thousand
Jews, with submachine guns, in the space of two days.

Fania was, as Elon says, "an imaginative woman who told Amos
tales of faraway forests and snow-covered meadows teeming with
fantastic creatures and ghosts ..." Yet, "life in the miserable Kerem
Avraham quarter must have been especially hard on her. She had few
friends and was shut up at home for most of the time." Oz makes
clear that he was aware that his mother was adrift, that relations
between his parents had deteriorated. Fania suffered from chronic
bouts of depression that began with migraine headaches; as her mel-
ancholia grew alarmingly worse, she spent entire days and nights
staring out of a narrow apartment window, while her husband slept
fitfully in the fold-out bed, or migrated to his son's tiny bedroom in
order not to disturb his wife. Eventually she in turn moved to Amos's
bedroom, and the boy joined his father in the fold-out sofa in this
game of discordant unmusical beds.

As Oz told David Remnick, "Among the immediate reasons for
my mother's decline was the weight of history, the personal insult,
the traumas, and the fear for the future. My mother had premonitions all the time ... she might have sensed that what happened to
the Jews in her home town would sooner or later happen here, that
there would be a total massacre. This is not something she would
share with a little boy, except perhaps obliquely, through some of the
stories and fairy tales she told."

Fania gradually neglected housework, all but stopped eating, and
was tended by her husband and son like a child. It was the only time
when father and son became close, "like a pair of stretcher-bearers
carrying an injured person up a steep slope." The reader learns early
on in the story that Fania is doomed; at the end, she wanders the

streets of Tel Aviv in a downpour, the very streets Oz himself will retrace many years later, eventually taking her life with an overdose of
sedatives in January 1952. She was just thirty-eight years old; her
son was twelve-and-a-half, only a few months short of his bar mitzvah. A year after her death, Arieh remarried; there had long been
another woman in his life. Fania's family never spoke to him again.

A year later, at fifteen, Amos left home for good, joined the Hulda
kibbutz, and changed his name to Oz. "I killed my father," writes the
Oedipal son, "I killed him particularly by changing my name."

The porcelain-delicate portrait of the woman who was Oz's mother,
and her suicide, is the heart of the tale, a story that Oz approaches
again and again, from every angle, in the course of all the other object-
filled, talk-crowded, rescued memories in the multi-strands of his
book. Its telling is carefully balanced between the perspective of the
child and that of the man who has lived in the desert for half a century.
Very late in the book, recalling the days after the mourning period,
alone in the apartment with his father, Oz delivers his *cri de coeur*:

> We never talked about my mother. Not a single word. Or about
> ourselves. Or about anything that had the least thing to do with
> emotions. We talked about the Cold War. We talked about the
> assassination of King Abdullah and the threat of a second round
> of fighting. My father explained to me the difference between
> a symbol, a parable and an allegory, and the difference between
> a saga and a legend … And every morning, even on these grey,
> damp, misty January mornings, at first light there always came
> from the soggy bare branches outside the pitiful chirping of [a]
> frozen bird … but in the depth of this winter it did not repeat
> [its] song several times as it had done in the summer, but said
> what it had to say once, and fell silent. I have hardly ever spoken
> about my mother till now, till I came to write these pages. Not
> with my father, or my wife, or my children or with anybody else.

Oz adds, "From the day of my mother's death to the day of my
father's death, twenty years later, we did not talk about her once.
Not a word. As if she had never lived. As if her life was just a cen-
sured page torn from a Soviet encyclopedia." Critic John Leonard
rightly uses the term "lamentation" to describe Oz's book. In his estimate, Oz "makes up for that erasure with this indelible memoir,

circling so often around the wound, inching up and closing in, that finally Fania's furious son has no other ground to stand on."

2

Given that this is a writer's autobiography, there will in fact be other ground to stand on, both metaphoric and literal, although the latter will be primarily located in the desert. What anyone interested in reading about writers wants to know is how the precocious, secretive child, the eight-year-old writer of patriotic poems and a self-described "ceaseless, tireless talker," a boy, as David Remnick says, "confused by overheard news of death camps abroad and civil war at home ... who plots the history of a new country with toy soldiers and maps spread across the kitchen floor," will evolve into an author. This is the second great strand in Oz's *Tale*.

Right from the start, Oz tells us, "Books filled our home. My father could read in sixteen or seventeen languages, and could speak eleven (all with a Russian accent). My mother spoke four or five languages and read seven or eight. They conversed in Russian or Polish when they did not want me to understand. (Which was most of the time. When my mother referred to a stallion in Hebrew in my hearing my father rebuked her furiously in Russian: What's the matter with you? You can see the boy's just there!)" That the mere utterance of the word "stallion" could be considered risqué is but one of a thousand particulars by which Oz conjures up the lost world being recreated in this book. Elsewhere, Oz abjures us not to "underestimate those little details out of which, after all, the big picture is made up." Recalling the surfeit of available writing in his childhood home, Oz adds,

> The one thing we had plenty of was books. They were everywhere: from wall to laden wall, in the passage and the kitchen and the entrance and on every windowsill. Thousands of books, in every corner of the flat. I had the feeling that people might come and go, were born and died, but books went on forever. When I was little, my ambition was to grow up to be a book. Not a writer. People can be killed like ants. Writers are not hard to kill either. But not books: however systematically you try to destroy them, there is always a chance that a copy will survive and continue to enjoy a

shelf-life in some corner of an out-of-the-way library somewhere, in Reykjavik, Valladolid or Vancouver.

Since one can't, finally, *be* a book, perhaps the next best thing is to become a writer who makes books. Examples of such writers were close at hand. Oz's father was a minor scholar, constantly shuffling his index card notes at the table at night. There was the famous great uncle, Joseph Klausner, author of *Jesus the Jew* and *The History of the Second Temple*, whose home in the upscale suburban neighbourhood of Talpiot the poorer branch of the family would visit on Saturday afternoons, trekking on foot all the way across Jerusalem to get there, "in the same spirit that *shtetl* Jews would take the train to Warsaw to see the five-story buildings." At Uncle Joseph's afternoon salons, there were other writers, including the renowned poet Saul Tchernikhowsky.

In a passage about the vagaries of memory, Oz suddenly says, "Almost sixty years have gone by, and yet I can still remember his smell. I summon it and it returns to me, a slightly coarse, dusty, but strong and pleasant smell ... and it borders on the memory of the feel of his skin, his flowing locks, his thick moustache that rubbed against the skin of my cheek." It's a memory of Tchernikhowsky, who died in 1943, when Oz was little more than four years old, "so that this sensual recollection can only have survived by passing through several stages of transmission and amplification," as do many of the invoked memories of Oz's book.

For his parents, the story of the child sitting on the lap of the "giant of Hebrew poetry" is a cute anecdote of precocious banter and the benediction of the poet, "as if it had been Pushkin bending over and kissing the head of the little Tolstoy." Although it was Oz's childhood duty to confirm his parents' oft-told story ("Yes, it's true, I remember it very well."), the actual memory of the now elderly Oz about his early encounter with literary greatness is that he tripped and fell over at Uncle Joseph's home, and as he fell he bit his tongue and it bled a little. The poet, who was also a doctor, picked up the crying child, forced his mouth open and called for someone to fetch some ice. Inspecting the injury, he said something, "certainly not about handing on the crown of Pushkin to Tolstoy," but rather, "It's nothing, just a scratch, and as we are now weeping so shall we soon be laughing."

The distinction between the romanticized memory and the real recollection is among the writerly things that makes Oz's *Tale* one of the great books of the decade. As Oz says elsewhere, breaking into a story of meeting, a quarter century later, the teacher with whom he fell desperately in love at age eight, "Naturally I am reconstructing this morning and our conversation from memory – like trying to restore an ancient ruined building on the basis of seven or eight stones that are still left standing." And since the memory of their re-encounter is itself a quarter-century old, "In all these recollections, my task is a bit like that of someone trying to build something out of old stones that he is digging out of the ruins of something that was also, in its day, built out of stones from a ruin." Can there be a better definition of autobiographical writing than building in the ruins of ruins?

It is also a memory from the sensorium that returns Oz to Uncle Joseph. "The smell of my uncle's enormous library would accompany me all the days of my life: the dusty, enticing odour of seven hidden wisdoms, the smell of a silent, secluded life devoted to scholarship ... the severe silence of ghosts billowing up from the deepest wells of knowledge ... the cold caress of the desires of preceding generations." And then there's Uncle Joseph himself, curled up on a sofa in a foetal position, covered in a green and red tartan rug, who offered "a feeble wave of his translucent white hand ... and said something like this:"

'Come in, my dears, come in, come in,' (even though we were already in the room, standing right in front of him ... huddled together, my mother my father and myself, like a tiny flock that had strayed into a strange pasture) 'and please forgive me for not standing up to greet you ... for two nights and three days now I have not stirred from my desk or closed my eyes, ask Mrs. Klausner and she will testify on my behalf ... while I finish this article which when it is published will cause a great stir in this land of ours, and not only here, the whole cultural world is following this debate with bated breath ... And how about you? ... And dear little Amos? How are you? What is new in your world? Have you read a few pages from my *When a Nation Fights for Its Freedom* to dear little Amos yet? I believe, my dears, that of all that I have written there is nothing more suitable ... to serve as spiritual sustenance to dear Amos ... apart perhaps from the description of heroism and rebellion that are scattered through the pages of my *History of the Second Temple* ... Now, my dears, follow in Mrs. Klausner's footsteps and slake your thirst ...'

It's all there, the whole narcissistic aria of the famous old right-wing nationalist Uncle Joseph, rendered pitch-perfectly by Oz. But when it comes to sustenance, literary or other, the poorer relations of the Klausners would sneak across the street and secretly (because he and Uncle Joseph were great enemies), visit the neighbour on the other side of the road, the neighbour who is none other than the Hebrew novelist S.Y. Agnon, who would subsequently receive the Nobel Prize for Literature. Later in Oz's own life, it is Agnon whom the young writer would call on for advice and encouragement. But, in any case, there was no shortage of writerly role models.

In due course, the child takes the books into his own hands and teaches himself to read. "My parents were unable to separate me from books, from morning till evening and beyond":

They were the ones who had pushed me to read, and now they were the sorcerer's apprentice ... Just come and look, your son is sitting half-naked on the floor in the middle of the corridor, if you please, reading. The child is hiding under the table, reading. That crazy child has locked himself in the bathroom again and he's sitting on the toilet reading, if he hasn't fallen in, book and all, and drowned himself ...

Throughout, Oz discloses the wellsprings that led to his becoming a writer: his mother's strange forest fairy tales; or making up stories himself in the third grade to ward off bullies, until he "walked around in the playground during breaks like Rabbi Nauman with his flocks of students ... surrounded by a tight crush of listeners afraid of missing a single word, and among them there would sometimes be my leading persecutors, whom I would make a point of magnanimously inviting into the innermost circle'; or the occasional visits to literary cafés in Jerusalem, where his parents met with a small group of local writers. Because the perfectly-behaved child, Oz drolly remarks, was not only required to give "polite, intelligent answers to such difficult questions as how old I was," but to be otherwise invisible, and because "their café-talk lasted at least seventy hours," young Amos "developed a secret little game that I could play for hours on end without moving, without speaking, with no accessories, not even a pencil and paper."

The game consisted of looking at the strangers in the café and trying to guess "who they all were, where they came from, what they did." The child's game was never abandoned by the adult writer. Oz's 2007 novella, *Rhyming Life and Death*, is based on the conceit of a protagonist called "the Author," who in the course of an evening in which he gives a public reading, conjures up the lives of all his characters exactly as the boy in the café did.

In the middle of *Love and Darkness*, after recounting his infatuation at age eight with his teacher, a woman named Zelda, who later turned out to be a moderately well-known poet, Oz suddenly breaks into the chronological tale and gives us a chapter-long present-day account of his everyday life as a writer in remote Arad. It's not the story of how he became a writer (that comes later), but a portrait of being a writer.

> Every morning, a little before or a little after sunrise, I am in the habit of going out to discover what is new in the desert. The desert begins here in Arad at the end of our road ... I go down into the wadi and advance along a winding path to the edge of the cliff from which I have a view of the Dead Sea, nearly three thousand feet below, fifteen and a half miles away ... Now you can hear the full depths of the desert silence. It isn't the quiet before the storm, nor the silence of the end of the world, but a silence that covers another, even deeper, silence. I stand there for three or four minutes inhaling silence like a smell. Then I turn back.

He's ready for the day's work. On the way back there are barking dogs, sparrows "in noisy argument," the newspaper boy, a grumpy neighbour who wants to debate politics. Maybe Oz should write a newspaper article to explain to his out-of-sorts neighbour, a Mr Schmuelevich, "that getting out of the conquered territories will not weaken Israel but actually strengthen us. And that it's a mistake to see the Holocaust and Hitler ... everywhere."

But he decides to put off writing the article "because an unfinished chapter of this book is waiting for me on my desk in a heap of

scribbled drafts, crumpled notes and half-pages full of crossings-
out." It's a chapter in the book we've already read, about a teacher
at his very first school, who had an army of cats and a surprising
relationship to the young cashier at the cooperative store.

> I'm going to have to make some concessions there and delete
> some incidents about cats and about ... the cashier. They were
> quite amusing incidents, but they do not contribute anything to
> the progress of the story. Contribute? Progress? I don't know
> what can contribute to the progress of the story, because as yet
> I have no idea where this story wants to go, and in fact why
> it needs contributions. Or progress.

This story about being a writer in Arad turns out to be a story of
a dithering day, of getting distracted, of driving off to town to do a
few errands, of meeting acquaintances and strangers, of remembering the Arab workers who built his study, who laid the floor and
checked it with a spirit level, and now somebody passing the house
in a little red van is extracting the letters from the letter box on the
corner, and "somebody else has come to replace the broken kerb-
stone of the pavement opposite. I must find some way to thank them
all, the way a bar mitzvah boy publicly thanks everyone who has
helped him come this far."
     And right there, in the middle of his book, 300 pages in, 200 to go,
Oz pauses and recites a litany of thanks, acknowledging all of them,
from Aunt Sonia to the first teachers, to the man in the clothes store
who rescued five-year-old Amos when he got lost in a dark storage
closet, to Mr Agnon and politician Simon Peres "who went to talk to
Arafat again yesterday," right on down to "the turquoise bird that
sometimes visits my lemon tree. And the lemon tree itself. And especially the silence of the desert just before sunrise, that has more and
more silences wrapped up inside it." It's an extraordinary passage of
sheer gratefulness. Then Oz briskly adds, "That was my third coffee
this morning. That's enough. I put the empty mug down at the edge
of the table, taking particular care not to make the slightest noise
that would injure the silence that has not vanished yet. Now I shall
sit down and write." And you turn the page. There's the new chapter
about the childhood experience of visiting the home of a wealthy
merchant who had been helped by Amos's Uncle Staszek, who

worked at the post office ... and we're off, into the next adventure in the land of Oz.

Oz became a writer at Hulda kibbutz. He lived there for 30 years, fell in love with and married the daughter of the kibbutz librarian, a woman named Nily, to whom he's still married after half a century and with whom he has had three children (his eldest daughter, a historian, is named, not coincidentally, Fania). He became a writer in the back room of Herzl House, the cultural centre at the edge of the kibbutz.

> This is where I went every evening to read my book until nearly midnight, until my eyelids were stuck together. And this is also where I took up writing again, when no one was looking, feeling ashamed of myself, feeling base and worthless, full of self-loathing: surely I hadn't left Jerusalem for the kibbutz to write poems and stories but to be reborn, to turn my back on the piles of words, to be suntanned to the bone and become an agricultural worker, a tiller of the soil.

It's a classic story of you can take the boy out of the writing world, but you can't take the writer out of the boy. And anyway, writing poems might be a way for a shy kid to attract the attention of those mysterious creatures, girls. What's more, as he quickly discovers, these heroic suntanned Jews are as prone to reading books and endlessly arguing about politics as the pale, scholarly Jews back in Jerusalem. "The joke of it," Oz says, "is that what I found at the kibbutz was the same Jewish *shtetl*, milking cows and talking about Kropotkin at the same time, and disagreeing about Trotsky in a Talmudic way, picking apples and having a fierce disagreement about Rosa Luxemburg."

Oz is suitably self-deprecating about his ineptness as an agricultural labourer ("I was a disaster ... I became the joke of the kibbutz"), and eventually the people at the kibbutz ship him back to Jerusalem for a year or two to get an education at the university on Mount Scopus because the kibbutz could use a teacher of literature for its secondary school. Once Oz begins to get his footing as a promising young writer, the kibbutz re-arranges his workload, giving him a few days a week to write and a corresponding reduction of hours driving tractors, picking fruit, or patrolling the kibbutz perimeters, beyond which the jackals howl at night.

But there's a problem. "I almost gave up in despair," says Oz. For,

> surely to write like Remarque or Hemingway you had to get out
> of here into the real world, go to places where men were virile
> as a fist and women were tender as the night, where bridges
> spanned wide rivers and the evenings sparkled with the lights of
> bars where real life really happened. No one who lacked experi-
> ence of that world could get even half a temporary permit to
> write stories or novels. The place of a real writer was not here
> but out there, in the big wide world. Until I got out of here and
> lived in a real place there was not a hope that I could find any-
> thing to write about.

Then, the breakthrough. In the kibbutz library in 1959, Oz finds
the newly translated into Hebrew edition of Sherwood Anderson's
Winesburg, Ohio (1919).

> The whole of *Winesburg, Ohio* was a string of stories and epi-
> sodes that grew out of each other and were connected to each
> other, particularly because they all took place in a single, poor,
> God-forsaken provincial town. It was filled with small-time
> people: an old carpenter, an absent-minded young man, some
> hotel owner and a servant girl ... The stories in *Winesburg,
> Ohio* all revolved around trivial, everyday happenings, based on
> snatches of local gossip or on unfulfilled dreams ... So Sherwood
> Anderson's stories brought back what I had put behind me when
> I left Jerusalem, or rather the ground that my feet had trodden all
> through my childhood and that I had never bothered to touch.

Anderson's modest book hit young Oz "like a Copernican revolution in reverse." Whereas Copernicus showed that our world is not
the centre of the universe but just one planet among others, Anderson
showed that the written world "always revolves around the hand
that is writing wherever it happens to be writing: where you are is
the centre of the universe." It's not you who is the centre of the universe, but "where you are." For nearly "a whole summer night until
half past three in the morning I walked the paths of the kibbutz like
a drunken man, talking to myself, trembling like a love-sick swain,
singing and skipping ..." Literally: eureka! And then, at that early

hour when labour begins at the kibbutz, he put on his work clothes and boots and joined the work-party at the tractor shed, from where they set out for a field to weed the cotton. But now, after work, things were different:

> And so I chose myself a corner table in the deserted study room, and here every evening I opened my brown school exercise book on which was printed "utility" and also "forty pages." Next to it I laid out a ballpoint pen called Globus, a pencil with a rubber tip, printed with the name of the trade-union retail outlets, and a beige plastic cup of tapwater. And this was the centre of the universe.

From that day to the present one, all the rest is just a matter of listening to the silence, and hearing the voices that emerge from it. As Oz told a *Newsweek* interviewer who asked him how he plans his books, "I don't plan them. It's sudden. I hear some voices inside my head, voices of characters, voices of people" (Joanna Chen, "The Bitter Taste of Dreams Come True," *Newsweek*, Feb. 14, 2008). The interviewer wanted to know if he heard the voice of his mother. "Sometimes, yes," Oz replied. "I very often hear the voices of dead people." But what if a person doesn't want to hear the voices of dead people, the interviewer persisted.

> Not hearing those voices is missing part of yourself, part of your life. When I wrote *A Tale of Love and Darkness*, I was inviting the dead to my home for coffee. I said to them, "Sit down. Let's have a cup of coffee and talk. When you were alive we didn't talk much. We talked about politics and current affairs, but we didn't talk about things that matter... And after the talk and the coffee you'll go away. You're not staying to live in my home. But you are invited to drop by from time to time for a cup of coffee." This in my view is the right way to treat the dead.

3

It's almost impossible to have a sane conversation about Israel anywhere in the world. If you're in the company of conservatives and you offer a justifiable criticism of Israel's occupation of Palestine, of the ever-encroaching settlements outside the country's borders, of its over-violent response to violence, it's as likely as not that it will be suggested that you're an antisemite, and if you happen to be a Jew as well, a self-hating antisemite. If you're in the company of progressives and radicals of the left, and you so much as hint that the Palestinian leadership is something less than lovely and heroic, or that Israel should be regarded as a fact of *realpolitik*, someone will soon label you an imperialist Zionist lackey or worse. It hasn't been a good decade for genuine liberals to talk about the Middle East. Nor have the populations of Israel and Palestine, who seem to have a penchant for choosing extremists of various stripes to lead them, made it any easier.

Amos Oz, whose seventieth birthday in spring 2009 was marked in Israel by further awards, extensive media coverage, and academic conferences about his work, is a liberal Zionist. He's also one of the sanest persons in Israel.

The final strand of *A Tale of Love and Darkness* is, necessarily, the story of the founding of Israel, mostly as seen through a child's eyes. In a child's curious perspective, the battles and bombardments of the 1948 Arab-Israeli War are registered almost impartially by the death of a pet tortoise killed by shrapnel in the backyard or the sniper-shooting of a neighbour's child from down the street.

The Klausner family in which Oz grew up, particularly the boy's renowned Uncle Joseph, were conservatives, followers of the right-wing leader, sometime terrorist, and later prime minister Menachem Begin. Not only were the British, the Palestinians whom they had displaced, and the entire Arab world their enemies, but so were their socialistic, impious, kibbutz-supporting, Labour Party rivals, led by David Ben-Gurion.

Oz tells a long, funny story of accompanying his grandfather to a Begin public speech where the demagogic speaker, unfamiliar with the younger generation's use of Hebrew, repeatedly uses a verb he think means "to arm" which is actually used as an obscenity meaning sexual intercourse. Begin complains that the Egyptians are being armed, the Palestinians are being armed, everybody is being armed, but how come no one is arming us? The boy falls into helpless, convulsive laughter, to the embarrassment of his prominent Klausner grandfather and the other grandees sitting in the front rows, and has to be dragged by the ear out of the hall. Oz represents this as his initial break with the Israeli right. Later, on the kibbutz, while working in an orchard, one of the older and wiser heads points out to him that childish snickering over a faux-pas is not really a good basis for political judgments.

It was also on the kibbutz, during the time Oz was doing his military service, that he published a newspaper article that mildly challenged the philosophical musings of David Ben-Gurion, commander of the Israeli forces, and received a summons from the great man to come in for a chat at dawn. The ensuing encounter, like the Begin story, is a great set piece and offers a rather charming portrait of the vain, grandiose figure who was one of Israel's founders. Oz's aim in his *Tale* is to give us the flavour of the context of growing up in a land where "for us, history is interwoven with biography ... One can almost say history *is* biography," as he remarks in an essay from *In the Land of Israel* (reprinted in Nitza Ben-Dov, ed., *The Amos Oz Reader*, 2009). But he's not here to argue the case.

The arguments nonetheless emerge from his life. As Oz's daughter Fania, who teaches history at Haifa University, told David Remnick, *A Tale of Love and Darkness* can be read, in part, as an argument about the history of Zionism. Remnick reports, "The book, she said, portrays Zionism and the creation of Israel as a historical necessity for a people faced with the threat of extinction. It acknowledges the original sin of Israel – the displacement and the suffering of the Palestinians – but, at the same time, defends Zionism against some ... who challenge the state's claim to legitimacy even now, six decades after its founding."

That characterization of Israel's founding is close to Amos Oz's own views. He tells Remnick, "If there had been no Zionism, six and a half million would be dead rather than six million, and who would have cared? Israel was a life raft for a half-million Jews." In the long run, though, was Zionism a mistake? Remnick asks. "I don't think there was any real practical choice," Oz replies. "When antisemitism in Europe became unbearable, Jews might have preferred to go to the United States, but they had no chance in hell in the thirties of being admitted to America."

In his *Tale*, Oz tells the story of one of his grandfathers who was turned down for French, British, and Scandinavian visas, and was "so desperate that he even applied for German citizenship, eighteen months before Hitler came to power. Fortunately for me, he was turned down." Oz's point is that "the Jews had nowhere to go, and this is difficult to convey today. People now ask, Was it good to come here? Was it a mistake? Was Zionism a reasonable project? There was no place else."

While the Israelis can make an ancient claim to the Promised Land on the basis of Biblical myth as well as a contemporary claim based on historical necessity, there's also a legal fact of real politics. That legal fact is the two-thirds majority United Nations vote in November 1947 that declared the creation of a two-state partition of the British-ruled Palestinian protectorate. The night of that vote, as Oz recounts in his *Tale*, with all of the Kerem Avraham neighbourhood awake and huddled around a radio, was the only time he saw his father weep.

The declaration of the founding of the state of Israel came the following May, with the expiration of the British mandate. That night, Egypt, Syria, Jordan, Lebanon, and Iraq invaded. In books like *In the Land of Israel*, Oz clearly "harbors no illusions about that war," Remnick observes, "least of all about the displacement of more than seven hundred thousand Palestinian Arabs from their villages and cities and about their lives of misery in refugee camps throughout the region." At the same time, as Oz drily remarks, the Arabs were "under no obligation" to start a war in the wake of the U.N.-authorized partition plan. Again, Oz invokes historical necessity: "One minute after midnight we were told that Israel is being invaded by five regular Arab armies, and that there was shelling and bombardment by artillery batteries. There was nowhere to send the kids, nowhere to go."

Oz's political evolution, which isn't really a primary subject of his memoir, began with the kibbutz and military duty. In the late 1950s, while doing his military service, he was involved in skirmishes along the Syrian border. He served with a tank unit in Sinai during the 1967 war, and in the 1973 Yom Kippur War he was with a unit in the Golan Heights, on the Syrian border. Remnick asked why there's almost no mention in *A Tale of Love and Darkness* of Oz's participation in the army.

"It is difficult for me ... to talk about the experience of fighting," Oz replies. "I have never written about the battlefield because I don't think I could convey the experience of fighting to people who have not been on the battlefield. Battle consists first and foremost of a horrible stench. The battlefield stinks to high heaven ... This doesn't come across even in Tolstoy or Hemingway or Remarque. This stifling mixture of burning rubber and burning metal and burning human flesh and feces, everything burning. It is where everyone around you had shit their pants."

His experiences gave him a "gut hatred of war and fighting," he says in another interview, but "I am not a pacifist in terms of turning the other cheek. There is a difference between myself and some of the peace people in Europe: whereas they think that the ultimate evil in the world is war, I think the ultimate evil in the world is aggression, and aggression sometimes must be repelled by force" (Aida Edemariam, "A Life in Writing: Amos Oz," *The Guardian*, Feb. 14, 2009). Oz recalls a Holocaust survivor relative, later a peace activist herself, who said to him, "You know, we were liberated from the concentration camp not by peace demonstrators carrying placards but by American soldiers carrying submachine guns."

In fact, it was war that motivated Oz to become one of his own country's most prominent peace activists. Two months after the end of the 1967 war, he sent an article called "Land of the Forefathers," to a Labour newspaper, calling for the Israeli government to immediately begin negotiations with the Palestinians over the occupied West Bank and Gaza. "Even unavoidable occupation is a corrupting occupation," he wrote. He was one of the early advocates of a two-state solution, an end to occupation, and a secure division of Israel and Palestine. In 1978, Oz, along with other liberals and former Army officers and reservists, was a founder of the grassroots movement Peace Now.

Three decades later, the same intelligence is applied to the 2009 Israeli retaliatory invasion of Hamas-controlled Gaza. "I am outraged with both Hamas and the Israelis in this war," he told an interviewer, "it's an anger in both directions ... Israelis were genuinely infuriated, as was I, about the harassment ... and rocket attacks on Israeli towns and villages for years and years by Hamas from Gaza. And the public mood was 'Let's teach them a lesson.' Trouble is, this so-called lesson went completely out of proportion. There is no comparison between the suffering ... that Gaza inflicted on Israel for eight years, and the suffering, devastation and death Israel inflicted on Gaza in twenty days. No proportion at all," Oz laments, in the killing of 300 Palestinian children, the slaughter of hundreds of innocent civilians, the destruction of thousands of demolished homes, and the possible use of dirty bombs. "There is no justification. No way this could be justified."

Nor is Oz a sentimentalist about the eventual two-state solution, even though through most of the first decade of the new century it seemed a distant, if not dead, prospect. "It is the only possible solution," he said in 2009. "There is no other possible solution. And I would say more than that. Down below, the majority of Israeli Jews and the majority of Palestinian Arabs know that at the end of the day there will be two states. Are they happy about it? No, they are not. Will they be dancing in the streets of Israel and in Palestine when the two-state solution is implemented? No, they will not. But they know it."

Over the years, Oz has developed a formulation that he repeats like a mantra. The situation in the Middle East is "a clash between right and right – the Palestinians are in Palestine because they have no other place in the world. The Israeli Jews are in Israel for the same reason – they have no other place in the world. This provides for a perfect understanding and a terrible tragedy." Or, as Oz put it to another interviewer who wanted to know if there couldn't be a happy ending in the holy land: "No, I don't believe in a happy ending to this kind of tragic conflict ... Any compromise will mean concession; it will mean renouncing something which both parties very strongly regard as their own ... There are no happy compromises." Perhaps "no happy compromises" is a definition of liberalism, a liberalism that has received little hearing in times of unreason.

The story of the birth of Israel and the argument about politics is the least prominent strand in *A Tale of Love and Darkness*, a book primarily about grief and self-fashioning, but it's the context that permeates everything else in the story. There's also an epilogue to the publishing history of Oz's *Tale*. In 2004, George Khoury, a 20-year-old student at Hebrew University, the son of a prominent family of Palestinian lawyers, was shot to death from a passing car by a group of men who mistakenly thought he was a Jew. The Palestinian authorities personally apologised to the family, but the boy's father, Elias Khoury, rejected the overture. "Terrorism is blind," the father told Israeli radio. "It does not discriminate between Jews and Arabs, or between the good and the bad."

The family wanted to make a public gesture to demonstrate their feelings about the killing of George Khoury, something beyond their private grief, and through various friends, the boy's uncle met with Amos Oz. Although Oz's work has been translated into all the major languages of the world, few of his books have been translated into Arabic. It was suggested that the family read *A Tale of Love and Darkness* and consider underwriting its translation into Arabic. The dedication to the Arabic edition would be a tribute to the murdered boy, written by Oz. The Khoury family agreed to underwrite the translation, although both the family and the author recognized that readers would not somehow be converted by the book. But it might lead at least some to a recognition that there are many tales of love and darkness in the lands of Israel and Palestine.

7

Homeland Alone:
9/11, Afghanistan, Iraq

For the United States, and parts of the rest of the world, the "day of infamy" in the first decade of the 21st century was September 11, 2001, or "9/11," as it came to be known. On that morning four teams from an Islamist terrorist organization, al-Qaeda, based in Afghanistan, seized four U.S. commercial airplanes while in flight, crashed two of them into New York's World Trade Centre towers and another into the Pentagon in Washington, D.C. The fourth, intended probably for the White House, was crash-aborted in a Pennsylvania field when passengers and crew resisted the hijackers.

The terrorist attacks and plane crashes caused the deaths of more than 3,000 civilians, the largest mass murder in contemporary American history. They also ignited a military response by the United States that included an attack upon Afghanistan's Islamist Taliban regime, a search for the crime's ultimate perpetrator, al-Qaeda leader Osama bin Laden, and an ongoing war in Afghanistan that has lasted for all of the decade. And it led to a separate and highly controversial invasion and occupation of Iraq in spring 2003, which also continues to the present.

As the central political events of the beginning of the new century, 9/11 and the wars that followed it have inspired a profusion of books, from popular accounts to academic treatises, many of them sharply critical of the political ideology and actions of U.S. President George W. Bush and his administration. Both the terrorist attacks and the subsequent wars were horrific and the number of books may be the result of our need to understand the specifics of the events. In the context of the horrifying wars of the previous decade in the former Yugoslavia, Rwanda, and other parts of Africa, these chilling chronicles have the virtue of making us more aware of one particular horrifying episode in precise detail, as well as the reasons that lie behind both the terrorism and the subsequent wars.

The events of the decade brought to prominence a remarkably competent and talented generation of reporters, feature writers, and essayists, especially journalists working at the *New York Times*, the *Washington Post*, and the *New Yorker* magazine. In this chapter, I survey several of the important and, in many cases, prize-winning works that examine major political themes of the period. In some instances, such as Richard Clarke's *Against All Enemies* (2004), the book itself became something of a political event. Works like Steve Coll's *Ghost Wars* (2004) and Lawrence Wright's *The Looming Tower* (2006) are investigative reconstructions of bodies of background information that were heretofore generally unavailable to the public. George Packer's *The Assassins' Gate* (2005) and Rajiv Chandrasekaran's *Imperial Life in the Emerald City* (2006) offer revealing portraits of the American occupation of Iraq, while Ann Jones's *Kabul in Winter* (2006) provides an eyewitness narrative about the situation of women in Afghanistan. Alli Allawi's *The Occupation of Iraq* (2007) is a scholarly survey of events in that country by a former minister in Iraq's post-war government, and Dexter Filkins's *The Forever War* (2008) is a reporter's first-hand account of his years on the battlefields.

The title "Homeland Alone" of course plays on that of *Home Alone* (1990), an American comedy film about an eight-year-old boy, accidentally left behind while his family flies to France for Christmas, who has to defend his home against idiotic burglars. The patriotic-sounding term "homeland" was adopted by the American government shortly after 9/11, and a cabinet level agency for "homeland security" was created. Whether the American government was as negligent as the parental adults in the comedy film, or America's antagonists as myopic as the household intruders, is one of the issues that this discussion attempts to examine.

1. SMOKING GUNS

Like everyone else, excepting a few Washington, D.C. insiders, I'd never heard of former U.S. counter-terrorism adviser Richard Clarke until he stepped out of the shadows one Sunday evening in spring 2004 on the CBS TV news magazine *60 Minutes*.

The program's viewers quickly learned that Clarke was a civil servant with 30 years' tenure who began his Washington career during the Richard Nixon era in the Departments of Defense and State, and went on to serve in the White House as presidential adviser on counter-terrorism to Presidents George Bush Sr., Bill Clinton, and the then-incumbent, George W. Bush. In short, his non-partisan credentials were impeccable.

Clarke had resigned from government service the previous spring, in 2003, just as U.S. troops were launching a punitive expedition into Iraq to overthrow the dictatorship of Saddam Hussein. In the wake of his resignation, Clarke wrote *Against All Enemies: Inside America's War on Terror* (2004), one of the first important works of the decade to critique U.S. foreign policy. It would be followed by a number of comparable books that analyzed the wars in Afghanistan and Iraq, as well as the institutions of U.S. security and how they failed on 9/11. Together, these books are not only of high journalistic competence but the readable second draft, after the initial dispatches, of American history in the first decade of the 21st century. Their reassessment of conventional pieties about American values and actions provides one of the defining themes for writing in the decade.

Clarke's book was released the day after his television interview. The point of *60 Minutes'* thumbnail career resumé of Clarke was simply to establish that Clarke wasn't a flake, a liberal in the belly of the neo-conservative beast, or a partisan fundamentalist of any sort. He's probably best described as a non-party hawk, one of those Washington Jesuits obsessed with their specialty – in this case, counter-terrorism and crisis management. He was a sober Cold Warrior who didn't flinch from recommending political assassinations to presidents or seeking authorization for the military to launch missiles at targets from Afghanistan to Sudan. He had comfortably rubbed shoulders over the years with the likes of Vice-President Dick Cheney, Secretary of Defense Donald Rumsfeld, and his own most recent former boss, National Security Adviser Condaleezza Rice, as well as with countless CIA and FBI "spooks." Equally, he'd gotten on with Clinton, Vice-President Al Gore, and Clinton's security adviser, Sandy Berger – i.e., Clarke travelled well. From the moment the beefy, mid-50ish, white-haired, blue-suited bureaucrat popped up on the tube and began speaking in complete sentences – unlike some of his former employers – it was clear that this was a critic not to be dismissed lightly.

All of which made Clarke's sweeping charges against the Bush administration the more remarkable. Clarke presented his case in a variety of venues – on *60 Minutes*, in *Against All Enemies*, before the government's 9/11 commission, and on every TV forum available to him. The executive summary of Clarke's claims went like this:

First, the George Bush administration, notwithstanding its post 9/11 "War on Terror," had not paid a lot of attention to the threat of terrorism posed by Osama bin Laden and his al-Qaeda organization from January 2001, when the new president took office, to September 11, 2001. Furthermore, Clarke argued, Bush, Rumsfeld, Rice et al. hadn't made terrorism a priority, despite a series of warnings from the previous Clinton administration, the CIA, and Clarke himself. There was even a prescient e-mail from Clarke to Rice months before the attack, imagining "hundreds of dead in the streets of America" and asking, "What will you wish then that you had already done?" Within the bowels of the spy business, it was known that there were al-Qaeda agents resident in the U.S., that suspicious men were at U.S. flight schools learning to maneuver but not land airplanes, and that the eavesdropping on international electronic chatter indicated something "very, very, very big" was about to happen, maybe even in the U.S. itself. Some hints of the near-negligence of the Bush administration were already known. For instance, *Washington Post* editor Bob Woodward's *Bush at War* (2003) reported in passing Bush's concession that prior to 9/11 he was not "on point" on the al-Qaeda threat. But it was not until Clarke's extensive from-the-horse's-mouth revelations on *60 Minutes* and in his book that anything like the behind-closed-doors side of the story of 9/11 and subsequent events was available.

Now, it's true that even if all the available intelligence had made it to the White House and all the "principals" (as the top cabinet-level and agency people are known) had further "shaken the trees" and had their "hair on fire" (to use a couple of Clarke's favourite metaphors), it couldn't be claimed (by Clarke or anyone else) that events would have happened any differently. However, the Bush principals didn't formally discuss terrorism until Sept. 4, 2001. If they had done something earlier and more urgently, maybe, just maybe … is about as far as Clarke allows himself to dream. Despite the administration's subsequent self-congratulatory tone about its response to terrorism, Clarke makes a persuasive case that, prior to 9/11, the Bush regime was negligent. Instead of terrorism, the early focus of

Bush and his officials was on "Star Wars" missile defence schemes, and the dangers of China, Russia, North Korea, Iran, and Iraq.

It's the latter country that's important to Clarke's argument. That the Bush administration was obsessed with Iraq to the point of distraction is Clarke's second major claim in *Against All Enemies*. He offers unprecedented evidentiary support for his charge that the administration was determined to find a pretext for war with Saddam Hussein (more about this further on).

Finally and more broadly, Clarke argues that the war in Iraq was disastrous for the war on terrorism, diverting military and fiscal resources from the hunt for al-Qaeda to the adventurism of "regime change" in Iraq. Worse, it spawned the growth of terrorist recruitment and organization rather than diminishing it.

Against All Enemies begins, in the style of such international thriller fiction writers as Tom Clancy, with an eyewitness account of what happened inside the evacuated White House on September 11. The pop prose notwithstanding, it's a pretty riveting tale, and Clarke is the guy to tell the story, since he was, for all practical purposes, running the government of the United States from the West Wing of the White House that morning, while the president was visiting a kindergarten in Florida and Vice-President Cheney and NSA Rice were stashed in an East Wing emergency bunker.

Once the initial steps to secure the U.S. had been taken, talk immediately turned to the response, which would obviously involve going after al-Qaeda in Afghanistan and the fundamentalist Islamic Taliban government there that harboured the terrorist organization. But that wasn't the only target on the minds of U.S. leaders in the hours right after 9/11. Clarke was incredulous to discover that Secretary of Defense Rumsfeld "was talking about broadening the objectives of our response and 'getting Iraq,'" an initiative he and his deputy Paul Wolfowitz had pushed prior to 9/11. An astonished Clarke likened the idea to "invading Mexico after the Japanese attacked us at Pearl Harbor." But Rumsfeld didn't drop the notion. Instead, according to Clarke, the defense secretary "complained that there were no decent targets for bombing in Afghanistan and that we should consider bombing Iraq, which, he said, had better targets. At first I thought Rumsfeld was joking. But he was serious and the President did not reject out of hand the idea of attacking Iraq." This was on Sept. 12, 2001, a year-and-a-half before the Iraq war was launched.

If there is any doubt about this preoccupation, the most dramatic anecdote in Clarke's book (which he also related on *60 Minutes*) was his encounter with Bush on the evening of Sept. 12. "He grabbed a few of us and closed the door to the conference room. 'Look,' he told us ... 'See if Saddam did this. See if he's linked in any way ...' I was once again taken aback, incredulous, and it showed. 'But, Mr. President, al-Qaeda did this.'" Bush, however, was not to be put off, and insisted on checking the Saddam connection. Clarke replied: "'Absolutely, we will look ... again ... But, you know, we have looked several times for state sponsorship of al-Qaeda and not found any real linkages to Iraq. Iraq plays a little, as does Pakistan, and Saudi Arabia, Yemen.' 'Look into Iraq, Saddam,' the President said testily and left us."

The exchange is worth repeating not only for its glimpse into the Bush administration's thinking but also because it had an immediate role in the extraordinary counterattack on Clarke that the White House launched in the wake of Clarke's shocking revelations. The first hint came the night of Clarke's appearance on *60 Minutes*. Since it's standard practice for such programs to provide a semblance of "balance" by allowing for rebuttals to sensational accusations, *60 Minutes* looked for a White House respondent to Clarke's allegations. The best it could scare up on short notice was one of Condaleezza Rice's minions. Confronted by the story of Bush's order to Clarke to find an Iraq connection, Rice's staffer told *60 Minutes* reporter Lesley Stahl, "We have no record of that conversation in the White House." The implication was unsubtlely obvious: maybe Mr. Clarke is lying.

The veteran reporter cast a very cold eye on the messenger, and said words to the effect of, "Young man, perhaps you've never heard of *60 Minutes*, but we have a substantial budget to do fact-checking, and we have two sources to substantiate Mr Clarke's story of his conversation with the president and one of them is an eyewitness." The sub-text of her thrust was: Do you think we're so dumb as to let Clarke make a sensational claim like that without checking it? There was a nanosecond of silence in the perpetual white noise of television as the camera watched Rice's subordinate swallow his tongue before his brain clicked onto the inner mechanism that produces the requisite bureaucratic babble. The next day the White House allowed that perhaps such a conversation had taken place. The day after that, it was conceded that the president had asked Clarke to check for an Iraq connection in the interest of canvassing all options.

The connection (or absence of one) between Iraq and 9/11 mattered for two reasons. First, the suggestion that there was a link between the two was one of several pretexts, all of them false as it turned out, concocted by the Bush administration to justify the invasion of Iraq in 2003. Second, the administration succeeded at one point in getting more than half the American public, according to polls, to believe that Saddam Hussein had something to do with the terrorist attacks on America. As long as we're looking at manufactured gullibility, it should also be noted that more than half the international Muslim population, according to polls, came to believe that the 9/11 attacks were a Jewish plot, which tells us that inculcating ignorance is not limited by national boundaries or cultures.

From the moment I first saw and heard Clarke on *60 Minutes*, I had the sense that this was a smoking gun. In all of his subsequent appearances, Clarke was credible, consistent, unflappable. We had become accustomed to getting a lot of "spin" and not much substance from public rhetoric. This was unnervingly different. There might be some argument with the interpretation, but the facts weren't in dispute. For people who had seen the Watergate hearings in the 1970s, or the Iran-Contra scandal hearings in the mid-80s, Clarke's story, told over several days, in a variety of oral and printed forms, had much the same weight. But in a country that prides itself on gun ownership, perhaps smoking guns, especially metaphoric ones, are no longer surprising – or even revelatory. Clarke's *Against All Enemies* was published in spring 2004, in the midst of Bush's 2004 presidential re-election campaign, and it might be thought that the revelation that the Iraq invasion had been more an ideological concoction than a matter of national security would have had some effect on that campaign. As it turned out, it didn't.

But it was enough of a danger to mobilize the Bush White House. For about four or five days after the publication of *Against All Enemies*, not very much governing took place in the United States. That's because practically every major government official in the Bush administration had taken to the media hustings to denounce Dick Clarke. Cheney, Rumsfeld, Rice, and a legion of White House communications coordinators appeared on every available journalistic outlet to vilify the former counter-terrorism adviser as money-grubbing, disloyal, disgruntled, self-seeking, two-faced, and whatever other epithets they could hurl.

In the end, the reason to read Clarke, even though *Against All Enemies* is hardly deathless prose, is to get a sustained and expert sense of the story and the issues it raises. About the only ideological disposition required is an acceptance of the notion that, Yes, Virginia, there really are terrorists out there. And the story is, as Clarke puts it, "how, even after the attacks, America did not eliminate the al-Qaeda movement, which morphed into a distributed and elusive threat; how instead we launched the counter-productive Iraq fiasco; how the Bush administration politicized counter-terrorism as a way of ensuring electoral victories; how critical homeland security vulnerabilities remain; and how little is being done to address the ideological challenge from terrorists distorting Islam into a new ideology of hate." Clarke even has the savvy to devote a thought or two to the protection of civil liberties in the midst of excessive "Patriot Act" security measures. Though in subsequent years much of Clarke's story has simply assumed its place in American political history, many of the issues that he was among the first to address remain relevant to the present day.

2. WHO WERE THOSE GUYS?

While Richard Clarke presents much of the inside-the-White-House version of the momentous events at the beginning of the decade, the question of who the 9/11 terrorists and their sponsors were is addressed in two notable books. Steve Coll's *Ghost Wars: The Secret History of the CIA, Afghanistan and Bin Laden, from the Soviet Invasion to September 10, 2001* (2004), and Lawrence Wright's *The Looming Tower: Al-Qaeda's Road to 9/11* (2006) provide complex background stories, unknown to the general public until their publication. What's remarkable about both books – each won the Pulitzer Prize for its respective year of publication – is that Coll and Wright are able to piece together coherent narratives of the shadowy realm of would-be religious revolutionaries and institutional spies that exists behind the mundane scenery of everyday life. What's more, they do so while maintaining a high level of page-turning prose, even as they slog through innumerable interviews with secret agents of every political stripe. That they fashion plausible stories out of what must have looked like a scrambled jigsaw puzzle is no small achievement.

Coll focuses on the secret history of CIA involvement in Afghanistan and Pakistan from 1980 to the millennium, while Wright probes the ideological roots of the various Islamist movements and the developments that eventuated in the 9/11 attacks by al-Qaeda. Both books, somewhat overlapping in their content, offer an in-depth survey of Islamic proponents and anti-American antagonists.

The answer to the colloquial question, "Who were those guys?" quickly extends beyond the identification of Mohamed Atta, the Egyptian-born leader of the 19-man terrorist team and the hijacker pilot of American Airlines flight 11 that struck the World Trade Centre on September 11. Both Coll's and Wright's books provide an extensive roster of "principal characters." The *dramatis personnae* of Coll's story range from Osama bin Laden, his ideological mentor Ayman al-Zawahiri, and their adjutants in the al-Qaeda organization to the diverse Afghanistan warlords and mujahedin leaders during that country's more than twenty-year-long anti-colonial and civil wars, especially the two most prominent mujahedin commanders, Gulbuddin Hekmatyar and his chief rival, Ahmed Shah Massoud. Equally important, the principal characters in Coll's tale of "ghosts" include a wide range of clandestine personnel from the American, Pakistani, and Saudi Arabian intelligence agencies and their variably attentive political masters.

Coll's *Ghost Wars* begins with a harrowing, little-known tale of the November 1979 riot by 15,000 mostly Islamic students at the U.S. Embassy in Islamabad, Pakistan, that came within a hair's breadth of causing the deaths of some 150 American personnel. Coll's gripping minute-by-minute reconstruction of the situation inside a burning embassy during the riot and his account of the failure of Pakistani authorities to intervene establishes the stakes and sets the scene for a complex narrative of war, politics, and religion that will unfold over the succeeding two decades. The incident itself received little attention at the time because it was overshadowed by two contemporaneous upheavals.

The most prominent of these regional transformations was the Islamic revolution in Iran in 1979, which brought an exiled Iranian cleric, the Ayatollah Khomeini, and his religious confreres to power. One of the theological revolution's immediate side-effects was the seizure of 52 U.S. Embassy employees in Tehran as hostages and their imprisonment during much of the 1980 presidential transition in the U.S., in which the ultra-conservative government of Ronald Reagan and the Republican Party succeeded that of the more moderate Jimmy Carter, a Democrat.

The other major regional development in the same period was the revolt in Afghanistan by Islamic mujahedin militias, aidèd by Pakistan, Saudi Arabia, and the U.S., against the country's Soviet Union–inspired communist regime and eventually against Soviet troops themselves. To add to the geo-political complexity of the situation, within a year Iran's newly established theocratic state would be at war with its western neighbour, the Saddam Hussein-led dictatorship in Iraq, itself a predominantly Muslim country. The Iraqi-instigated war, which would last eight years, was fully supported by the U.S. The special Mideast envoy appointed by American president Ronald Reagan to deliver intelligence and logistic assurances to Saddam was Donald Rumsfeld, the same person who, two decades later, as U.S. secretary of Defense, would launch the American war on Saddam in 2003.

All of these events unfolded against an even broader Middle East background that included a near-permanent simmering state of war between Israel and a displaced Palestinian population, as well as internal tensions within countries like Egypt, Sudan, and Saudi Arabia, tensions connected to a widespread Islamist "revival." Each of the parties involved in the various conflicts brought to battlefields, mosques, countless back-room meetings, and occasional negotiating tables its own often shifting political agendas. The resulting Gordian knot of cross-purposes, motives, and actions yields a story, as one book blurb succinctly put it, "with a cast of few heroes, many villains, bags of cash and a tragic ending."

The perspective of a CIA operative, usually located somewhere on the Pakistan-Afghanistan border, is Coll's characteristic point of departure for each of the succeeding episodes in his chronicle of the mujahedin guerrilla war against Soviet Union troops occupying Afghanistan in the 1980s. The CIA perspective is quickly supplemented by that of Pakistan's notorious Inter-Services Intelligence (ISI) agency, its army, and its often shaky, and sporadic civilian regimes. As well, the views and actions of the Saudi Arabian intelligence agencies are thoroughly canvassed. Although the Soviet Union is the common target of various militias, spies, and governments, their opponents' motives and longer-range intentions are bewilderingly diverse and often in conflict. Perhaps the only constants are the international arms traffic and the increasingly large sums of money provided by the Americans, Saudis, international Muslim "charities," and independent political and religious entrepreneurs like Osama bin Laden.

By the end of the 1980s, the dying Soviet Union under the reform leadership of Mikhail Gorbachev was prepared to call it quits in Afghanistan and withdraw its troops. It was expected that the puppet communist regime in Kabul would rapidly fold, and the Pakistanis, Saudis, and Americans all began jockeying for position in support of their preferred Afghan warlord.

At which point, there was the first of a series of small surprises. The indigenous communist regime, led by a former secret police chief named Najibullah, didn't collapse, thanks in equal parts to its own shrewd maneuverings and to the bungling of its mujahedin opponents, despite the arms and money poured into their ranks. Not until three years later, in 1992, was the regime at last overthrown and Najibullah pulled from a United Nations sanctuary and summarily executed. But instead of creating a credible coalition government made up of former militia leaders and available Afghan exiles, as might be expected, the Afghan warlords entered into a brutal civil war, levelling much of the capital of Kabul in the process. It was this failure that, in the mid-90s, gave rise to an even more radical Islamic force, the Taliban, led by a previously obscure warrior-cleric, Mullah Omar, and backed by Pakistani intelligence agencies, who soon swept most resistance aside and installed a theocratic regime as extreme and puritanical as any in the Muslim world. After the Taliban takeover, bin Laden and Al-Zawahiri relocated to Afghanistan in the mid-1990s, joined forces under the banner of al-Qaeda and, as troublesome guests of the Taliban, launched a global jihad against the U.S. that eventuated in 9/11.

Those are the broad strokes that Steve Coll chronicles in his dense, blow-by-blow narrative. It's impossible to reprise all the details here, but readers can be assured that Coll demonstrates a sure-handed command of the voluminous body of facts that make up an extraordinary saga of war, politics, and theology. Though Coll doesn't spend an inordinate amount of time pondering the meaning of the events he narrates, the story of the Afghan wars raises some troubling questions that will eventually have to be addressed.

Before doing so, it's worth considering Lawrence Wright's *The Looming Tower*. Wright's book begins with a sketch of Sayyid Qutb (pronounced "kuh-tub") a mid-20th century Islamic thinker from Egypt. It's a beginning indicative of the direction Wright will take with the 9/11 story, placing more emphasis on al-Qaeda's ideological roots and, as much as possible, following developments from the perspective of those who launch the terrorist attack on the "the looming tower." The eponymous reference is to a verse in the Quran, allegedly cited repeatedly by Osama bin Laden at a wedding shortly before 9/11: "Wherever you are, death will find you, even in the looming tower."

From the outset, Wright immerses us in the theological politics of Islam as he tells the story of Qutb, a thinker, writer, and official in Egypt's Ministry of Education who went to the United States to study in 1948. The ideologue who would eventually give birth to modern Islamic fundamentalism arrived in a post–World War II New York that was booming, sexy, affluent, and shocking to the devout, if provincial, Muslim. His arrival coincided with the creation of Israel in the Middle East and the inception of the long-term American policy of support for the Jewish state.

Qutb, after a stint at a university in Greeley, Colorado, returned to a chaotic Egypt in 1950, in the wake of the first Arab-Israeli war. He had been radicalized by his sojourn in the sensually tempting West and was drawn to the doctrines of Egypt's Muslim Brotherhood, an organization founded in 1928 whose founder, Hasan al-Banna, had written, "It is the nature of Islam to dominate ... to impose its law on all nations, and to extend its power to the entire planet." When an army colonel, Gamal Abdul Nasser, the leader of a group of military plotters, seized control of the country and sent Egypt's King Farouk packing in a 1952 revolutionary coup, it was expected that Qutb, again working in the Ministry of Education, would ascend to the ruling Revolutionary Council. Instead, Qutb became a critic of the new regime for its failure to impose a sufficiently stringent Islamic dictatorship. When an assassination attempt was made on Nasser's life in 1954, Qutb was among the hundreds of Muslim Brothers suspected of orchestrating the plot who were jailed.

During the following decade, the imprisoned Qutb produced a multi-volume commentary on the Quran as well as a manifesto, *Milestones*, whose "ringing apocalyptic tone," Wright suggests, is the Islamic equivalent of such famous political pamphlets as Rousseau's *Social Contract* and Lenin's *What Is to Be Done?* Scarcely six months after Qutb left prison, he was again arrested for plotting against Nasser's regime, convicted, and executed by hanging in 1966, declaring shortly before his death, "Thank God, I performed jihad ... until I earned this martyrdom."

Wright offers a similarly extended portrait of Ayman al-Zawahiri, an Egyptian doctor who assumed Qutb's ideological mantle. Jailed in the wake of the 1981 assassination of Anwar al-Sadat, Nasser's successor, upon his release he worked as a physician in the Pakistan-Afghanistan border region during the mujahedin revolt against the Soviets. After a lengthy career along the winding road of would-be Islamic revolution, Zawahiri ended up back in Afghanistan in the mid-1990s, where he joined forces with the man who would orchestrate the 9/11 terrorist attack. Osama bin Laden, scion of a wealthy Saudi Arabian family in the construction business, is the subject of an equally compelling biographical portrait, which Wright develops at length in the context of an analysis of Saudi Arabian, Sudanese, and Pakistani political and theological developments.

By the time an exiled bin Laden "flew over the suckling supertankers docked beside the massive refineries lining the ports of the Persian Gulf," across the desert of southwestern Afghanistan that borders Iran, and into Kandahar, "surrounded by the ruins of its irrigation canals and pomegranate orchards," for his final relocation in 1996 within the mountainous Afghan outback, Wright has painted a broad canvas of the radical Islamist revival and set the scene for al-Qaeda's declaration of war against the United States, posted from a cave in Afghanistan.

Wright's panorama of Islamic thinkers and warriors is counterbalanced by a remarkable portrait of a driven, demon-haunted American FBI man, John O'Neill, a close friend of counterterrorism adviser Richard Clarke, who was one of a handful of U.S. intelligence agents engaged in an ultimately failed hunt for the leaders of al-Qaeda. The flamboyant and gruff O'Neill, with "the flashy suits, the gleaming fingernails" and a harem of girlfriends in addition to a wife and two children in New Jersey, "concealed a man of humble background and modest means" who was drowning in debt to support his extravagant lifestyle. In his way, O'Neill is as bizarre a figure as any of his jihadist opponents. And yet, before his death in the Twin Towers on Sept. 11, where he was head of the World Trade Centre's security force, O'Neill came cliffhanger-close to tracking down bin Laden in the caves of his mountain fastness. But for the senseless turf wars between American intelligence agencies, O'Neill and like-minded American agents might have prevented 9/11.

Though both Steve Coll and Wright employ novelistic techniques to tell their respective true stories, Wright's narrative is the more economical and benefits from emphasizing the background and perspective of its radical Islamist protagonists. Both books leave readers on the cusp of the 9/11 tragedy.

The first observation to be derived from both of these informative narratives is that during the Cold War the U.S. foreign policy establishment was so preoccupied with defeating the Soviet Union that it more or less completely missed the rise of Islamic fundamentalism and its terrorist strategy. Although Richard Clarke in *Against All Enemies* gives relatively high marks to President Bill Clinton's alertness to terrorism in the 1990s, in fact, during the triumphalist post-Soviet decade, the continuing civil war in Afghanistan was put on the American back burner as the administration attended to crises in the Balkans and Africa, and the accession of the Taliban regime was treated with relative indifference.

After 9/11, amid the rush to American military action in Afghanistan, a muted political discussion ensued in the U.S., in which leftists and liberals insisted on locating the "root causes" of the terrorist attack rather than accepting the simplistic account of the Bush administration that al-Qaeda hated American values of freedom and democracy. As the *New York Times'* lead critic Michiko Kakutani noted in her review of *The Looming Tower*, Wright's account suggests that bin Laden "is not opposed to the United States because of its culture or ideas but because of its political and military actions in the Islamic world" (Michiko Kakutani, "The Evolution of Al Qaeda," *The New York Times*, Aug. 1, 2006). Similarly, combat reporter Dexter Filkins, also writing about Wright's book, says, "Wright shows, correctly, that at the root of Islamic militancy – its anger, its antimodernity, its justifications for murder – lies a feeling of intense humiliation. Islam plays a role in this, with its straight-jacketed and all-encompassing worldview. But whether the militant hails from a middle-class family or an impoverished one, is intensely religious or a 'theological amateur' ... he springs almost invariably from an ossified society with an autocratic government" (Dexter Filkins, "The Plot Against America,"

The New York Times, Aug. 6, 2006). Worse, those autocratic regimes are often supported by American money and troops.

While the "root causes" argument, as it came to be called, certainly has some traction, the stretch from political criticism of the U.S. to suicide bombings of American civilians in their own country is considerable. Even after one has a grasp of "root causes," the question remains of whether the terrorists' program made any sense, in terms of politics, morality, or justice. Certainly, the harsh version of Islam they propagated, with its brutish theocracy, allegedly based on Islamic or *sharia* law, and its idiosyncratic declarations of who was and wasn't a legitimate Muslim, thereby justifying the murder of allegedly apostate members of their own faith, was unintelligible even to those sympathetic to religious claims. For some activists on the left, in North America, Europe, and elsewhere, whose political priorities opposed American imperialism and Zionism, and who viewed the Bush administration as not merely a period in American history but a permanent condition of U.S. politics, the "root causes" approach was persuasive. For the rest of us, though we might be critical of neoconservative American politics and administrations, the terrorists seemed as intellectually aberrant as the perpetrators of other secular mass murders.

The American-led coalition war in Afghanistan poses the question, retrospectively, of what should have been done. The options included a) more or less doing nothing and leaving the problem to international institutions, such as the United Nations; b) treating the terrorist attack as simply a criminal act and attempting to hunt down the perpetrators by "normal" police methods; and c) launching a full-scale assault against the fundamentalist Taliban regime because it "harboured" al-Qaeda and afterward attempting the reconstruction of the country on a democratic basis.

In the event, the last option was chosen as the only one that was feasible and would satisfy American public opinion. The war in Afghanistan, unlike the subsequent invasion of Iraq, was authorized by the UN, and an international military coalition was assembled, again in contrast to the subsequent and largely fallacious "coalition of the willing" that was cobbled together for the Iraq expedition. What's more, and again in contrast to the Iraq occupation, the coalition presence in Afghanistan, according to all reputable polling information, was largely supported by the Afghan public. So, while the question of "intervention," whether "humanitarian" or military, is arguable (as it was during previous interventions in the 1990s), there was a plausible basis for it in terms of legality, practicality, and democratic ideals. Further, the conditions in Afghanistan, whether those created by Taliban fundamentalism or by the deeper cultural structures of patriarchal tribalism, were such that a case could be made that the attempt to develop a democratic, independent Afghanistan could be seen as being in the liberal and leftist traditions of international "solidarity."

Still, while a strong theoretical case can be made for the war in Afghanistan, there is the further issue of assessing its actual operation. After a decade of war, with still no end in sight, international supporters of Afghan solidarity can point to the existence of a legally elected, albeit deeply corrupt, government; the end of Taliban restrictions on everyday life; and some improvement of conditions for women and children in the country. On the other hand, a Taliban force not only continues to exist but appears to be undefeated; the war and destruction continue (including the deaths of large numbers of civilians); the fractures within Afghan society remain deep; and the permeability of the Afghanistan-Pakistan border has meant that the dangers of Islamic fundamentalism have also increased in Pakistan and further endangered that country's very fragile, quasi-secular institutions. Further, it remains an open question as to *who*, exactly, the coalition is intervening on behalf of, and whether or not there really is a potentially unifiable state entity that can be called Afghanistan.

Finally, there is what has been awkwardly referred to as a "clash of civilizations" question. Here, the problem concerns democratic secular societies versus theocratic and/or tribal ones. The secular version of civilization is complicated by the fact that, at least in the United States, political institutions have been closely tied to a particular, limited form of capitalist economics (an unregulated, environmentally harmful, globalized economics, sometimes known as "cowboy capitalism") and a debased commercial culture driven by market priorities, as well as the U.S.'s own fundamentalist Christian "revival." Other more social democratic models of society on offer (in Europe, say) have received little consideration as roads to substantive reform.

Questions about theocratic and tribal cultures remain. For instance, it is possible to argue, not only about Islam and its various widely divergent forms but about Christianity, Judaism, and other faiths, that they are all based on fantastical tenets that ought to be challenged in any rational discussion. In the "west," there has been a debate about religion for at least two centuries that, in the last decade, has been conducted under the rubric of "the new atheism." That debate has not occurred within the Islamic world, and outsiders have remained chary about treading on what are deemed multicultural toes.

None of the above questions and observations is the primary subject of books like those of Steve Coll and Lawrence Wright, which have confined focuses. But their astute historical narratives provide a foundation for any of the necessary discussion that will take place in succeeding decades of the 21st century.

The other American-led military operation of the decade, the war in Iraq, offers a more cautionary and sadder story.

3. CONQUEST FOR DUMMIES

One Saturday morning in March 2003, a couple of years before the publication of George Packer's *The Assassins' Gate: America in Iraq* (2005), I was marching in the streets of downtown Vancouver, in the company of about 100,000-or-so like-minded people, to protest the impending American invasion of Iraq. Maybe "marching" puts it too strongly: it was more of a duty trudge, since the war was by then inevitable and we understood that our protestations were unlikely to have a significant impact. Similar protest marches were taking place in cities around the world. Even for those of us who had approved of the war in Afghanistan in late 2001, the upcoming Iraq war, a year and a half later, was disturbing.

For one thing, the proposed assault appeared to be frankly illegal. Rather than a response to directs acts of aggression, as could be argued in the case of Afghanistan, the punitive expedition against Saddam Hussein's Iraq was clearly a "pre-emptive" war, in defiance of international law and institutions. If the United States had been part of the International Court of Justice system (which it isn't), the American architects of the war would be prospective defendants at the war crimes tribunals in The Hague. (For those interested, the extended case against the illegality of the war is made in Philippe Sands's *Lawless World: Making and Breaking Global Rules*, 2006.)

Second, the claim that the anticipated war was justified by the possession of "Weapons of Mass Destruction" that the Iraqi regime intended to use within the foreseeable future was completely without substance, as was soon conclusively demonstrated. Iraq under Saddam was undoubtedly a totalitarian dictatorship, but hardly an imminent danger to its immediate neighbours, the U.S., or to "world peace," such as it is. It was a danger primarily to its own inhabitants, and even that threat had been somewhat curtailed in recent years. The regime had, for a decade, since its defeat in the Gulf War of 1991, been under United Nations' economic sanctions and was effectively hedged in militarily by "no-fly-zones" that covered large portions of the country, including the Kurdish north and the Shia Muslim south. Finally, and crucially, there was no evidence whatsoever that Iraq had connections with Osama bin Laden's al-Qaeda or with the "9/11" attack on the U.S., notwithstanding American propaganda to the contrary. What's more, with the occupation of Afghanistan, al-Qaeda and the Taliban both appeared to be on the run. Why not nail down the situation there rather than embarking on a dubious new venture?

That the venture was dubious soon became clear as the American occupation became hopelessly bogged down in an "insurgency" by Iraqi militants that killed scores of American soldiers every month and completely derailed American plans for reconstruction of the country. By 2005, with the U.S. wallowing in the third year of the war in Iraq, , no one could continue to reject "quagmire" as an appropriate description of the occupier's situation.

The day-to-day focus of the media predictably provided a combination of blood, spin, and "progress" reports. But more germane than the day's solemnly reported and always horrific body count and suicide bombing, or the occasional hostage rescue, is a deeper account of what in fact happened in Iraq. That's where *New Yorker* magazine writer George Packer comes in.

Packer's *Assassins' Gate* is his loosely connected but surprisingly coherent reportage-based narrative from Iraq and America. It was a Pulitzer Prize finalist, the winner of several lesser awards, and was named as one of ten best books of 2005 by the *New York Times*. The "gate" of the title is a high sandstone ceremonial arch that provides a "main point of entry into the vast and heavily fortified Green Zone along the west bank of the Tigris River, where the Coalition Provisional Authority (CPA) governs occupied Iraq." When Packer first arrived in Baghdad in summer 2003, he mistook the arch for one of the city's antique gates, built in medieval times to keep out would-be Persian invaders.

Later on, he learned that he'd been wrong about the Assassins' Gate. Far from being an ancient civic landmark, the gate had been constructed in recent years by Saddam in "grandiose imitation of Baghdad's classical entrances. It wasn't even the Assassins' Gate – not to the Iraqis." It had only acquired the nickname of "Assassins' Gate" from occupying American troops. "It was an American invention for an ersatz Iraqi monument, a misnomer for a mirage." The point of Packer's little introductory anecdote about the Iraqi supplicants he met there, who gathered at the gate each morning seeking admission to the CPA-controlled Green Zone with a variety of requests and petitions for the occupiers, is that so much of the American presence in Iraq was also a misnomer for a mirage.

Packer's opening chapters offer a thoughtful portrait of the neo-conservative administrators and ideologues who arrived in Washington thanks to the disputed election of George W. Bush in 2000. The leading neo-conservative figures – Vice-President Dick Cheney, Defense Secretary Donald Rumsfeld and their minions, Paul Wolfowitz, Richard Perle, and Douglas Feith, many of them dating back to the Reagan administration of the 1980s – were particularly contemptuous of former president Bill Clinton's tentative "humanitarian interventions" in Bosnia, Kosovo, and the Middle East in the 1990s and "saw Iraq as the test case for their ideas about American power and world leadership. Iraq represented the worst failure of the nineties and the first opportunity of the new American century." A mish-mash of motives, from control of oil to exercise of imperial power to some idealistic if naive musings about democracy, made Iraq a focal point of neo-conservative foreign policy ambitions as early as the mid-1990s, well before the younger Bush's presidency. As we learned from Richard Clarke's *Against All Enemies*, although the Bush administration was ill-prepared for the "9/11" attack, as soon as it occurred, it was made the fortuitous excuse to roll out plans for the already-contemplated war on Iraq.

The most poignant figure in *Assassins' Gate*, who periodically pops up throughout Packer's chronicle, is an Iraqi exile named Kanan Makiya. Packer first met him in Boston, where Makiya, an architect and an archivist, worked at Brandeis and Harvard universities. In 1989, under a pseudonym, Makiya had published a book about Iraq under Saddam Hussein called *Republic of Fear*. When the Gulf War of 1991 came along in the wake of Saddam's ill-judged attempt to annex oil-rich Kuwait, Makiya's book, which had languished in obscurity, became a minor bestseller among readers who wanted to know something about Iraq. In the aftermath of the war, as it became clear that Saddam's regime would not be toppled by the American-led coalition, Makiya went public and became one of a group of exiled spokesmen advocating forcible regime change in his homeland, writing two more books about the fate of Iraq.

Makiya is that all-too-rare bird, an Iraqi secular humanist. It's Makiya's brand of liberalism that leads a writer like Packer to his own initial, if ambivalent, support for the war. It was similar descriptions of the internal horror of the Saddam regime that drew so many strange left-of-centre intellectual bedfellows to this quixotic cause, including such well-known writers as Christopher Hitchens, Paul Berman, the *New Republic's* Leon Wieseltier, and Canada's Michael Ignatieff, among others. While ideas about "humanitarian intervention" that developed in the 1990s go some way to explaining how some liberals became hawkish enough to sign on to a neocon-inspired war (admittedly one that had some anti-totalitarian promise), it's still puzzling how they came to accept contravening international legal norms, one of the grounds of liberalism. In each of the previous interventionist cases – Afghanistan, Bosnia, Kosovo – there was a plausible and legal justificatory argument to support the incursion, as well as some form of international imprimatur from the United Nations. Packer, at least, is more conscientious than most in reassessing his position in light of the actual subsequent events on the ground.

When Makiya and Packer meet up again in Iraq in mid-2003, Makiya is engrossed in an effort to establish a "memory foundation" think tank to ensure that the regime's horrors will not be forgotten. "Ultimately and in the very long run," Makiya tells Packer, "it's about reshaping Iraqis' perceptions of themselves in such a way as to create the basis for a tolerant civil society that is capable of adjusting to liberal democratic culture." Although Makiya says all the right words, Packer sees his friend as drifting out of touch. "Makiya was consumed with thoughts about the past and the future," Packer explains. "I wanted him to acknowledge that the present was a disaster. Phrases like 'tolerant civil society' and 'liberal democratic culture' did not inspire me in Baghdad in the summer of 2003. They sounded abstract and glib amid the daily grinding chaos of the city, and they made me angry at him and myself – for I had had my own illusions."

Indeed, as Packer points out, Makiya and his counterparts pursued their own mirage. "The returned exiles in Baghdad lived in a world apart. They went to one another's dinner parties, they traveled easily in and out of the Green Zone ... they hatched plans and business schemes and visionary ideas for transforming Iraqi society. The event that had crashed like a bomb in the lives of other Iraqis, shattering the state and leaving them stunned in the smoke and debris, was to the exiles the opportunity of a lifetime." Increasingly, Makiya's arguments seem unconvincing to Packer, and his schemes sound more "like an excuse for all that he'd gotten wrong. Iraqis, it turned out, were not who he had thought they were" from the perspective of his long exile. "They were not Kanan Makiya."

Makiya makes later reappearances in Packer's chronicle. But the main story line is Makiya's ultimate irrelevance as a legitimate liberal as events unfold in Iraq. At the end, over a pot of Turkish coffee in Boston, Packer is still trying to sort out his feelings. "He was my friend and I loved him," Packer declares. "He had devoted his life to an idea of Iraq that I embraced. He had attached that idea to the machinery of war, and a lot of people had gotten killed. No idea remains intact once it's been bloodied by history, and history had not followed Makiya's blueprint. At times, his vision of Iraq had been so at odds with what I saw and heard there that dreaming began to seem irresponsible and dangerous."

Meanwhile, back on the ground, history had not followed the blueprint of the Bush administration either. That "blueprint," such as it was, was the product of the fantastical thinking of Donald Rumsfeld and his Defense Department, the dominant secretariat in the American government. Plan A called for the invasion of Iraq with minimal numbers of troops, joyous expressions of liberated gratefulness on the part of the Iraqis, troops out within three months or so, reconstruction of the country by American contractors paid for by Iraqi oil money, followed by democratic elections and a changed world. They had, it turned out, no Plan B.

Packer's book focuses on what happened after the swift American "shock and awe" invasion. It is the story of a disastrously misjudged occupation. The central and most important chapters of *Assassins' Gate* provide a useful and cautionary account of the bumbling bureaucrats led by the U.S. civilian administrator of the occupation, Paul ("Jerry") Bremer, and his entourage of youthful, inexperienced subordinates. Many of the young Bremer-crats, as they soon were called, rapidly became aware of the morass in which they found themselves.

As one investment banker who'd been sent to work on economic development told Packer, "First there was the arrogance phase, and then there was the hubris phase. The arrogance phase was going in undermanned, underplanned, underresourced, skim off the top layer of leadership, take control of a functioning state, and be out by six weeks and get the oil funds to pay for it. We all know for a variety of reasons that [this] didn't work. So then you switch over to the hubris phase: we've been slapped in the face, this is really much more serious than we thought, much more long-term, much more dangerous, much more costly. Therefore we'll attack it with everything we have, we'll throw the many billion dollars at it, and to make Iraq safe for the future we have to do a root-and-branch transformation of the country in our own image." The one thing the two disparate approaches had in common, the investment banker added, is that "they're very conceptual, very ideological. They're not pragmatic responses to a detailed understanding of facts on the ground."

The chief ideologue in-country was Bremer, about whom Packer offers a less than flattering profile. His "provisional authority" was housed in one of Saddam's main palaces, now safely barricaded within the Green Zone. "On the first floor of the palace, off the rotunda, past the metal detector and the bodyguards, Paul Bremer's long, high-ceilinged office was lined with bookshelves that were nearly bare when I visited. Rudolph Giuliani's *Leadership* stood on one shelf, and a book about the management of financial crises on another, near a box of raisin bran." As it turned out, Bremer's reading habits and breakfast food preferences provided suggestive clues to a man who arrived in Iraq in May 2003 knowing little about the country. When he left a year later, not much had improved. The occupation, as Packer says, "was launched with a hodgepodge of improvised moves that reflected no one agency's strategy, no considered strategy at all other than a belated assertion of American control." It soon gave way to a virulent insurgency and a descent toward possible civil war.

Though Packer's chronicle takes us only up to the beginning of 2005, the spectre of civil war was already apparent to observers on the ground in 2004, even though it didn't become a TV item for home consumption until many months later. As Packer says in a late chapter titled "Civil War?", "Iraq without the lid of totalitarianism clamped down became a place of roiling and contending ethnic claims ... It sometimes felt as if a civil war had already started." Packer notes that some analysts had "looked at the mess and decided that only a separation of Iraq into three autonomous regions could prevent civil war." (The proposal is taken up in more detail in Peter Galbraith's *The End of Iraq*, 2007.)

Packer's notion of a "mirage" is more fully depicted in Rajiv Chandrasekaran's *Imperial Life in the Emerald City: Inside Iraq's Green Zone* (2006), a brisk, readable account of the American occupation of Iraq in its initial years. Chandrasekaran, a *Washington Post* national editor and former Baghdad bureau chief, covers much of the same ground as Packer, focusing on the seven square mile enclave known as the Green Zone, home to the occupation's Coalition Provisional Authority. Chandrasekaran's book was nominated for a National Book Award and won several subsidiary prizes, such as the Samuel Johnson Prize, as well as receiving numerous "books of the year" citations. Its message of misguided mirages is signalled in the book's title reference to the Land of Oz's Emerald City. The American "viceroy," as Chandrasekaran dubs CPA head Paul Bremer, is devastatingly portrayed as resembling the Wizard of Oz, the fatuous old con man in L. Frank Baum's famous series of children's books.

Much of what Chandrasekaran wants to convey of the American mirage is present in his opening riff, a scene at the Green Zone's Republican Palace, or "Versailles on the Tigris," as Chandrasekaran dubs it: "In the back garden of the Republican Palace ... bronzed young men with rippling muscles and tattooed forearms plunged into the resort-size swimming pool. Others, clad in baggy trunks and wraparound sunglasses, lay sprawled on chaise lounges in the shadows of towering palms, munching Doritos and sipping iced tea. Off to the side, men in khakis and women in sundresses relaxed under a wooden gazebo. Some read pulp novels, others noshed from an all-you-can-eat buffet. A boom box thumped with hip-hop music. Now and then, a dozen lanky Iraqi men in identical blue shirts and trousers walked by on their way to sweep the deck, prune the shrubbery, or water the plants." The mirage is not one of romantic Middle East deserts but of an American holiday spa.

Even at the time of Chandrasekaran's opening bucolic sketch, June 2004, better than a year into the occupation, one of the countless CPA administrators confesses to the journalist, "I'm a neoconservative who's been mugged by reality," reversing the old rightwing boast that "a neoconservative is a liberal mugged by reality." Reality is beyond the bunkers, blast walls, and razor wire of the Green Zone, in the unremitting violence of Baghdad and the rest of the country. *Imperial Life in the Emerald City* sets out a step-by-step series of vignettes that detail the illusions and ideologically driven fantasies that were the substitute for a workable post-war plan in Iraq.

Much of Chandrasekaran's tale would be comic – a sort of Keystone-Cops-Meet-the-Sheik-of-Araby slapstick movie – were it not that it's so dishearteningly sad. The staff of Bremer's provisional authority was made up largely of rightwing neo-conservative ideologues, often youthful, unqualified, and inexperienced. They had been hired primarily on the basis of their Republican Party political credentials and, after their brief tour of duty, would return to jobs in President Bush's 2004 re-election campaign or to conservative think tanks. To make matters worse, in the internecine turf war within the Bush administration, the unabashedly neo-conservative Department of Defense under Secretary Donald Rumsfeld regularly trumped the more moderate Secretary of State, Colin Powell, when it came to personnel, policy, and fiscal allocation decisions, as Chandrasekaran persuasively documents.

The various schemes for reconstruction envisaged by Bremer and his superiors mostly came to naught. Notions of privatizing state-owned factories were purely ideologically driven and found no takers, other than looters. Quixotic plans to revamp the Baghdad Stock Exchange, establish an American-style traffic code, or renovate Iraq's destroyed and looted university system turned into fools' errands. Repeatedly, Chandrasekaran details fantasies of reform, both political and material, that collapsed in the face of Iraqi realities, leaving readers with a don't-know-whether-to-laugh-or-cry sense of absurdity. The really important reconstruction issues – the provision of electricity, water, and security to the population – were invariably fiscally short changed and either failed or limped along at less than pre-war levels.

To make matters worse, Bremer, inspired by Vice-President Cheney and Rumsfeld, made a series of political decisions that undercut the very goals he was attempting to achieve. Former government officials were turfed out of office on grounds of political loyalty and the former military and police structures were disbanded, depriving the dismantled state of the expertise and experience it desperately needed. A local firebrand Shia mullah, Muqtada al-Sadr, leader of Baghdad's largest Shiite section of Baghdad, Sadr City, which housed some two million people, was needlessly provoked and by spring 2004 his Mahdi army militia was in open revolt. As if that weren't enough, at the same time the U.S. military launched an ill-advised full-scale assault on the city of Falluja, a Sunni insurgent stronghold.

Within six months, insurgent rockets were falling on a besieged, locked-down Green Zone. Though a proto-governing council of Iraqi politicians, former exiles, and religious power brokers was cobbled together, it came nowhere close to cohesion or the ability to function. Nonetheless, it was to this body that Bremer handed over formal political authority a year after his arrival, in a contrived "sign of progress" ceremony made largely in the interests of President Bush's re-election campaign rather than as a reflection of the situation on the Iraqi ground. That ground, outside the Green Zone's partial sanctuary, was an inferno of insurgency, suicide bombings, ethnic cleansing, and mounting casualties.

There would be, over the remainder of the decade, oscillating levels of violence, elections of various sorts, an American troop "surge" late in the game, and a great deal of muddling through. While American casualties, over 4,000 dead, would be carefully counted, the number of Iraqi dead are unknown. Figures vary wildly, from a hundred thousand to a million, along with as many as two million people driven into exile. By 2009, there was also the promise by a new American president, Barack Obama, to "responsibly" withdraw American troops from combat in Iraq by decade's end, leaving the country to a still very uncertain fate. Many of these later developments would also be the subject of various books and reportage, but Chandrasekaran's *Imperial Life in the Emerald City* and Packer's *Assassins' Gate* stand as early, utterly damning, indictments of the American occupation of Iraq.

Meanwhile, Ann Jones's *Kabul in Winter: Life without Peace in Afghanistan* (2006) is devoid of Oz-like images or yellow brick roads to democracy. However, Jones strongly suggests that the entire project of constructing a democratic, secular nation out of a patchwork of battling tribes and theological disputes may also be little more than a deeply misguided fantasy. In her report of a three- year stint in Afghanistan as a foreign-aid education worker during the same period that U.S. troops were becoming progressively bogged down in Iraq, Kabul could hardly be mistaken for an Emerald City, either of the fictional variety or the contrived virtual version established in the U.S. enclave within Baghdad.

Instead, "Kabul in winter is the color of the dust, though the dust is no color at all. It's a fine particulate lifted by winds from old stone mountains and sifted over the city like flour. It lies in the streets and drifts over the sidewalks ... Rain and snowmelt make it mud. Mountain suns bake it. Cart wheels break it down. Winds lift it and leave it on every surface ... Dust fills the air and thickens it, hiding from view the mountains that stand all around. Dust fills the lungs, tightens the chest, lies in the eyes like gravel, so that you look out on this obscure drab landscape always through something like tears."

High-altitude Kabul "stands alone in the thin air, ringed by mountains." Above the broad deep bowl of the city, "lay a mass of black smog, dense and opaque: a tangle of twisted strands of oily soot and smoke, like a great pot-blackened Brillo pad." Once the plane bringing Jones to Afghanistan "descended into that soup and the lights dimmed," she's in a ruined capital whose main English guidebook promises little more than, "There is a lot to see in the city, even if most of it is wrecked."

Kabul in Winter is several things at once. As a political travelogue, Jones's well-written, keenly observed vignettes give readers a clear sense of the lives of the inhabitants of a blighted landscape, attempting to survive in hovels, supplied only with threadbare blankets and clothes and less than the bare necessities of life. Jones is there, in the back lanes and crowded dwellings, feeling awkward as her Afghan aid colleagues ask her to take snapshots of the impoverished recipients of the second-hand clothes that the aid workers are delivering in order to prove the NGO's legitimacy to the agency's donors.

As the author of a work of impassioned reportage, Jones pays particular attention to the condition of Afghan women, visiting them and talking with them in their homes, in schools, and in women's prisons. Not only is this the most powerful aspect of Jones's work, it is also the first available portrait of the lives of the most oppressed segment of the Afghan population. The story of their oppression makes for grim but necessary reading. It is a tale of beatings and deprivation of freedom, education, and work. Readers will recoil at the stories of young women, in despair at being married off to a man they fear or loathe, who pour gasoline on themselves and light a match. As Jones documents, the hospitals in Afghanistan are filled with such cases.

Much about the condition of Afghan women is encapsulated in Jones's sardonic remarks about the history of "veiling." "It's difficult to say with certainty just when and why Afghan women came to be clad in pleated polyester body bags," Jones notes. Some claim that veiling reached Afghanistan as a sign of class. "If such theories are correct – and who knows? – veiling seems originally to have been an affectation of the urban leisure class by which rich men publicly advertised that their wives did not have to work. (Who could work in such a getup?)" A more common explanation of body-length *burqas* is that they're necessary for "protection." But, asks Jones, "protection of whom? From what?" Opinions differ, but "many male commentators report that Allah endowed Muslim men with awesome sexual prowess and desire. Any man is likely to be aroused by the mere glimpse of an ankle or a wisp of hair escaping from beneath a scarf. Can he be responsible for what he then feels compelled to do? Of course not. So to protect women from the uncontrollable God-given appetites of men, women must keep themselves under wraps."

Other commentators on Islamic society, says Jones, "argue that veiling is prescribed to protect men from women. In this view, it's women, not men, who are thought to be endowed with an insatiable sexuality ... Women must be kept under wraps then to safeguard the whole community from the disruptive potency of their whopping erotic capacities." In any event, Jones's dripping sarcasm aside, it's a case of heads-men-win, tails-women-lose. The overarching point of Jones's excurses is that men not only covered up women, they "covered up women's history, too ... I tell you this long story so you'll know that the burqa didn't come from nowhere. That it has a history as hidden and as real as the history of the women who from time to time are forced to wear it." What's more, "what a Muslim woman wears is not just a matter of gender. She wears the whole weight of the Islamic world."

Among the distressing features of Afghan sexism that Jones emphasizes is the degree to which it is "internalized" by its victims. The society's patriarchal tribal mores are so deeply engraved in the Afghan psyche that even feminist lawyers that Jones worked with were timid in the advocacy of their clients' rights and frequently saw little wrong with the lopsided traditional arrangements under which women labour. Occasionally, Jones offers a moment of inadvertent comic relief, as when she's trying to explain the western concept of a "blind date" to her language students and one of them says, "Like my wedding."

As a feminist leftist, Jones's book is, unsurprisingly, a polemic, one that lashes out at American policy-makers, of whom she's sneeringly contemptuous. She's also critical of the entrenched Afghan patriarchy and its corrupt political structures. Finally, she directs some of her wrath at many of the foreign non-governmental aid organizations, their wasteful system of allocating funds and the ineffectiveness of their projects. In many cases, she says, their presence in Kabul has done little more than drive up the cost of living for ordinary Afghan residents. The polemic is perhaps the most arguable aspect of the book, and some commentators have faulted Jones for descending into diatribe. If so, it is, understandably, a diatribe of despair. A half-decade after the publication of *Kabul in Winter*, the limited signs of a springtime of hope that Jones pointed to have increased only marginally, if at all.

4. TERRIBLE SWIFT SWORDS

Like Chandrasekaran's *Imperial Life in the Emerald City*, much of what *New York Times* reporter Dexter Filkins has to say in his wide-ranging battlefield dispatches, *The Forever War* (2008), is laid out in a dramatic prologue. It's titled "Hells Bells" and provides an "embedded" journalist's eyewitness account of the second U.S. assault on Falluja, Iraq, in November 2004.

At 2 o'clock in the morning, as minarets "were flashing by the light of airstrikes and rockets were sailing on trails of sparks," a strange "dialogue" begins to unfold. "First came the voices from the mosques, rising above the thundery guns." A loudspeaker in a minaret howls, "The Holy War, the Holy War! Get up and fight for the city of mosques." As the "bullets poured without direction" overhead, a new sound can be heard, "violent, menacing and dire. I looked back over my shoulder to where we had come from, into the vacant field at Falluja's northern edge. A group of marines were standing at the foot of a gigantic loudspeaker, the kind used at rock concerts."

The sound blasting out of the loudspeaker is from AC/DC, an Australian heavy metal band. "I recognized the song immediately," Filkins says. "'Hells Bells,' the band's celebration of satanic power, had come to us on the battlefield. Behind the strains of the guitars, a church bell tolled thirteen times."

In the midst of this surrealistic but real-life *Apocalypse Now* moment, "The marines raised the volume on the speakers and the sound of gunfire began to recede. Airstrikes were pulverizing the houses in front of us. In a flash, a building vanished. The voices from the mosques were hysterical in their fury, and they echoed along the city's northern rim." Against AC/DC's ominous verses ("I won't take no prisoners, won't spare no lives"), the muezzins from the minarets cry out, "God is Great!"

After that, it's all bullets, mortars, air-strikes, and house-to-house urban warfare as the American troops attempt to dislodge the jihadist insurgents who for months had controlled Falluja. Filkins's reporting is a far cry from the exultant tones of the embedded correspondent in the early days of the Iraq invasion who cited Winston Churchill on camera: "There's nothing more exhilarating than being shot at and missed!"

In Filkins's more realistic dispatch, the picture looks like this: "The wind from the bullets brushed my neck. Marines were writhing in the street, tangles of blood and legs, while other marines were stooping and helping them and also getting shot. I kept running, pumping, flying toward the other side as fast I could with my seventy pounds of gear when I saw a pair of marines standing in a doorway and waving to me to come on, come on. I ran straight for them and I could see by the looks on their faces they weren't sure I was going to make it. They were holding their arms out like they wanted to save me, and I reached them and they grabbed me by my pack and threw me through the door. I lay on the floor for a minute as I regained my senses and thought I was nothing so much now as a child. A child in

his crib in the care of his parents, they nineteen and me forty-three."
It may be the first time but it won't be the last that we wonder what
in the world Filkins is doing there at all.

Filkins's book, which ranges from scenes of Taliban executions in
soccer stadiums in Afghanistan, to "Ground Zero" in New York on
9/11, to the battlefields and jogging paths of Iraq (Filkins is a dedicated runner), is an intentionally disjointed, jagged-edged assem-
blage of fog-of-war vignettes. It pointedly eschews analysis (which
Filkins, as readers of the *New York Times* know from his other articles, is perfectly capable of) in favour of the raw feel of war. *The
Forever War* is in the writing tradition of grim war reportage that
extends from Eric Maria Remarque's World War I novel, *All Quiet
on the Western Front*, to Michael Herr's *Dispatches* from the
Vietnam War. Filkins won the National Book Critics Circle Award
for non-fiction, and *Time Magazine* and the *New York Times*, among
others, put *The Forever War* on their ten best books of 2008 lists.

Among its virtues, Filkins's book repeatedly captures the self-delu-
sions of the Americans and the double lives of the Iraqis. "There
were always two conversations in Iraq," Filkins reports, "the one the
Iraqis were having with the Americans and the one they were having
among themselves. The one the Iraqis were having with us – that
was positive and predictable and boring, and it made the Americans
happy because it made them think they were winning … The conversation they were having with each other was the one that really mattered of course. That conversation was the chatter of a whole other
world, a parallel reality, which sometimes unfolded right next to the
Americans, even right in front of them. And we almost never saw it."

The conversation that the Iraqis "were having among themselves"
can be glimpsed in Ali Allawi's *The Occupation of Iraq: Winning the
War, Losing the Peace* (2007). Allawi, a former minister in the post-
war Iraqi governments (but no relation to former Iraqi prime minister Awad Allawi) was in Iraq for some two-and-a-half years, but he's
also one of those Iraqis who has mostly not been there, as a result of
several decades' enforced exile. Educated in the U.S., he worked
most of his career as a successful international banker based in
London and was politically active in the diaspora of Iraqi opposition, until he was called back to his native land in 2003.

For all the pyrotechnic virtues of Filkins's prose, one reads Allawi's
sober history of the occupation, fashioned in workman-like style,

almost with relief. Although Allawi lets us in on some of the Iraqi conversation, it is, for the most part, not a happy conversation, or even a hopeful one. It's a conversation of competing ambitions, squabbles about constitutional documents, and fine-grained dissections of sectarian disputes, both political and religious.

Allawi is sharply critical of the American occupiers (and particularly the blunders of Paul Bremer's Provisional Coalition Authority), nor he does not spare his Iraqi counterparts. Allawi's book lacks the laconic bravura of Filkins's writing, but it is as fair-minded and knowledgeable a chronicle of contemporary Iraq as we're likely to get. It comes from a courageous participant who "steadfastly refused to move to the relative safety of the Green Zone, not because of any heroics, but because I felt then – and still do – that the Green Zone is the symbol of all that has gone wrong in Iraq since the occupation. A marooned political class living cheek by jowl with the foreign contingent, both cut off from the terrible, daily anguish of Iraqis." Not living in the mirage of the Emerald City had its costs. "My convoy was ambushed twice; the second time was a near-run thing. The sound of the heavy machine guns of my security detail firing back at the assailants still reverberates in my ears." Later, while Allawi's bodyguards were having lunch at a local restaurant, a suicide bomber struck. Three men perished, another half-dozen were wounded.

Writing at the end of 2006, Allawi sadly observes that "the backdrop to the crisis in Iraq began to change" – for the worse. "Death squads and the infiltrated police force began to match – and exceed – the insurgents in the scale and viciousness of their attacks on civilians ... The cynicism and anger of the populace were palpable, as public services deteriorated further. Gasoline queues, power shortages, insecurity, lawlessness, car bombs, internal exile – Iraq appeared to be nearing total bedlam."

In the end, says Allawi, "The Iraqi political class that inherited the mantle of the state ... was manifestly culpable in presiding over the deterioration of the conditions of the country. The absence of leadership on a national scale was glaring." At the time of Allawi's departure from Iraq, "there was no national vision for anything, just a series of deals to push forward a political process, the end state of which was indeterminate." By decade's end, though there had been periodic surges and ebbs in the vortex of violence, the end state was still indeterminate.

I suppose there's bound to be a certain sense of helplessness attendant on having watched the Afghanistan and Iraq wars from a (safe) distance for most of a decade. What one can do is fairly limited. One can, if it's appropriate, march in protest, though that seemed increasingly futile as events unfolded. What's more, the insistence of the anti-war march organizers on rolling all engagements – Iraq, Afghanistan, Haiti, Darfur, god-knows-where-else – into one anti-war-everywhere mirage made the prospect of marching less appetizing to those, like me, who are unwilling to endorse such a blanket policy. Alternatively, one could decide to "critically support" the occupation and try to figure out better ways to make it work than the present administrators have. However, most of those who have taken that course find themselves as befuddled and lost as those who claimed to possess the roadmaps.

One can, minimally, "keep up" with the situation by reading books like those written by Coll, Wright, Packer, Chandrasekaran, Jones, Allawi, and Filkins, which are, I think, among the most informative and poignant of the crop of volumes that have appeared about the failures and minimal successes of the wars in Afghanistan and Iraq. I guess that's been my own almost instinctive response, given my predilection for reading and reviewing. And one can, I suppose, hope that history will take another turn, especially in light of the election of Barack Obama in 2008, and his goal of changes in American foreign policy. Looking at the recent past, however, I'm amazed, as are many of the authors I've discussed, by the sheer incompetence of those who so confidently, just yesterday it seems, declared how the world would go under their exercise of power. Well, it hasn't, and I suspect that history will continue to be astonished that the United States invaded hapless nations without even a slightly realistic plan for how to administer their transformation.

8

Lost and Found: Daniel Mendelsohn

No one of Jewish descent growing up in America just after World War II could be entirely unaffected by the Holocaust. In my family, Uncle Walter and Aunt Holla were presented to us (I'm tempted to say, "exhibited" to us) in the early 1950s as our "survivor" relatives. They had managed "to make it out just in time," I was repeatedly told, in what became the recitation of a family legend, a story whose moral concerned the dangers of procrastination and the vagaries of luck.

Yes, Uncle Walter and Aunt Holla, now placidly seated on a sofa across from us in a relative's large living room in Chicago, had sailed on "the last boat out of Europe" in 1939. As a ten-year-old, I somewhat confusedly tried to imagine a Europe out of which no more boats sailed.

It would be some time before I would have even an inkling of what had happened. The singularity of the Holocaust in the 20th century, in which six million Jews were murdered by the Nazis, is pinpointed by cultural critic George Steiner in his *Grammars of Creation* (2001). The *Shoah* (as the Holocaust is known in Hebrew) was underwritten, says Steiner, by the unique principle that "a category of persons, down to infancy, was proclaimed *guilty of being*. Their crime was existence, the mere claim to life." Not until years later – years of schooling, conversation, and the reading of a dozen or more key books – would it become clear to me what had happened to Jews in Europe, or the "Old Country," as it was called in the Yiddish-inflected English of my and many other Jewish immigrant families.

Things were not all that different in Daniel Mendelsohn's family when he was growing up two decades later, in the late 1960s and early 1970s. As he says at the beginning of *The Lost: A Search for*

Six of Six Million (2006), "Some time ago, when I was six or seven or eight years old, it would occasionally happen that I'd walk into a room and certain people would begin to cry." The rooms that the Long Island, New York–born Mendelsohn entered were those of aging Jewish relatives now living in Miami Beach, Florida, whom the Mendelsohns visited during holidays. And what made those elderly Jews weep was the boy's striking resemblance to his dead great-uncle Shmiel Jaeger, who, with his wife and four daughters, had been killed by the Nazis in the 1940s in the small town of what was then Bolechow, Poland (now a part of Ukraine).

That phrase, "killed by the Nazis," was all that Mendelsohn knew of his lost great-uncle. It was "the unwritten caption on the few photographs that we had of him and his family ... a prosperous-looking businessman of perhaps fifty-five, standing proprietarily in front of a truck next to two uniformed drivers; a family gathered around a table, the parents, four small girls ...; two young men in World War I uniforms, one of whom I knew to be the twenty-one-year-old Shmiel." The phrase "killed by the Nazis" was the extent of what Mendelsohn's grandfather, Abraham Jaeger, one of Schmiel's several siblings, would permit himself to say about his long-lost brother.

Out of those scant sources – a chilling phrase, some few photographs, and years of conversation with his otherwise loquacious and elegant grandfather – Mendelsohn embarked on an Odysseyan search for his lost relatives. By the time his multi-continent quest reached its almost obsessive heights in the late 1990s and early 2000s, the boy who made elder Jewish relatives cry at the very sight of him was now a man in his 40s.

Mendelsohn is a humanities professor at Bard College, the author of work in his scholarly field about the Greeks and Romans, as well as a memoir about gay identity, *The Elusive Embrace* (1999), and an array of remarkably wide-ranging and well-written essays that appear regularly in the *New York Review of Books* – writings that persuade some readers (including me) that he's the best American essayist since Gore Vidal. His cultural criticism is collected in *How Beautiful It Is and How Easily It Can Be Broken* (2008). He's also translated, in two volumes, the collected poems of the 20th century Alexandrian Greek poet C.P. Cavafy (2009). But it's as the author of an extraordinary family memoir that he commands our attention here.

There are multiple reasons that Mendelsohn's Holocaust tale, *The Lost*, won the National Book Critics Circle Award and a host of "best book of the year" mentions in 2006. For one thing, it is likely one of the last Holocaust stories to be based on living witnesses. Already, at the end of his book, Mendelsohn lists *in memoriam* ten or so of the people he interviewed, then in their 70s and 80s, and now gone. Second, it's a terrific page-turning tale of detection, filled with astonishing coincidences, last-minute discoveries, and seeming dead ends that turn into heart-thudding findings about the fate of the perished.

Third, it's brilliantly written. From the story's very beginning, the vignette about the boy who makes old relatives cry, to its conclusion, Mendelsohn conjures up entire lost sub-cultures, from the Jewish diasporas of New York, Miami Beach, Europe, and Australia to the almost forgotten *shtetl*-life of now-gone Jewish communities, as well as the living culture of Israeli habitations and émigré outposts. He captures the strange sounds of disappearing languages like Yiddish and revived ones such as Hebrew and, best of all, he brings to life a remarkable cast of people, beginning with his grandfather Abraham and extending to mentors, guides, interviewees, and witnesses. Mendelsohn writes with almost Proustian intensity, or perhaps I should say with the wealth of detail one finds in Israeli author Amos Oz's *A Tale of Love and Darkness*, a work to which Mendelsohn's bears some resemblance, just as the boy's appearance reminds his relatives of his lost great-uncle.

Beyond all that, which would be sufficient to make *The Lost* memorable in any case, Mendelsohn succeeds in doing several novel things with what can easily become a tired genre, the genealogical quest for Jewish relatives lost in the Nazi genocide of World War II. In the necessary Jewish insistence on remembering the Holocaust, there's the danger of a kind of misuse of memory, a nagging for attention for sentimental or political reasons. I like the brutal Jewish quip criticizing the excesses of exploitation of Holocaust memories cited by Jacobo Timerman in his book *The Longest War* (1972), "There's no business like *Shoah*-business." After all, 20th century politics has produced so many millions of other deaths, driven by various comparably evil principles, that the Holocaust claim of uniqueness need not be an appropriation of exclusivity with regard to suffering. Mendelsohn avoids all the pitfalls.

In a work in which one of the themes must be judgment, Mendelsohn is strikingly non-judgmental and without bitterness, although necessarily sorrowful. One phrase, uttered by many survivors referring to the killings in the multi-ethnic town of Bolechow, that echoes in Mendelsohn's ears throughout his search is, "The Germans were bad, the Poles were worse, and the Ukrainians were worst of all." Yet Mendelsohn's guide to Bolechow over a period of years is his Ukrainian friend, the historian Alex Danai, who, in Mendelsohn's vivid portrait of him, demonstrates an emotional and intellectual courage that undercuts all easy generalizations.

What is striking about Mendelsohn's stance is the way he cautions against quick judgments and instead leaves us with the question, What would you have done?, irrespective of who the "you" might be, Jew, or Pole or Ukrainian. Yes, there are countless stories of the inexplicable betrayal of ethnic neighbours with whom one had lived in peace for generations, but there are also stories of Ukrainians who hid Jews, or the Polish boy who was in love with one of Shmiel's daughters, who died for their actions.

There are two "framing" devices and one textual theme that elevates *The Lost* above most other attempts to recover the past. In the Jewish tradition there is a prescribed list of weekly readings from the Torah, the core books of the Hebrew Bible, that raise themes of creation, destruction, sacrifice, fratracide, conquest, and covenants. There is also a long tradition of commentary on the Torah known as the Talmud, added to over the centuries by rabbis, scholars, and other writers.

In *The Lost*, Mendelsohn interleaves his narrative with his own Talmudic commentaries, which relate the Biblical themes to the issues provoked by his quest. Once Mendelsohn does it, it seems like a perfectly obvious thing to do, but I don't know of any similar works that utilized this mode before Mendelsohn's. When I very briefly spoke to him at a talk he gave in Berlin in 2008, he confirmed that his Talmudic commentaries were a relatively late add-on in the composition of the book. They work very well, giving the project an additional layer of meditative depth. What's more, I like Mendelsohn's attitude to the biblical texts, which makes no theological claims for their veracity but rather treats them as the thematic myths that he has inherited. One can't help reflecting, however, that it's a very strange and destructive God that has "chosen" this tribal people.

A second, equally effective, framing device is the photographs scattered through the book, some from family collections and others, of people encountered on the search, taken by Mendelsohn's younger brother, Matt. This illustrative notion was introduced, in recent writing, by the émigré German writer W.G. Sebald and it's used here as both an homage to Sebald and something more. After a long introductory lead-up in which Mendelsohn's great-uncle Shmiel gradually assumes written form, it's startling to come upon a full-page battered old photo of a strikingly handsome young man in a World War I uniform, gazing out at us through time. This is the man for whom we're searching.

In presenting Matt Mendelsohn's photos, Daniel Mendelsohn talks frankly and autobiographically about the tensions of sibling relationships, a subject that has some point not only because there are questions about the relationships of the lost but because Mendelsohn dragged most of his kin into his occasionally obsessive quest, *schlepping* them, as he would say, halfway around the world. Not entirely coincidentally, the subject of sibling relationships is one the themes of his Talmudic commentary, since the murderous tale of Cain and Abel is one of the founding myths of this particular tribe and resonates in the stories of relatives and neighbours who turn upon each other.

Finally, the narrative is filled with reflections on the nature of story itself, in this case a story about loss. "How easy it is for someone to become lost, forever unknown," Mendelsohn reflects. "At night, I think about these things. I'm pleased with what I know, but now I think much more about everything I could have known, which was so much more than anything I can learn now and which is gone forever." This is a truism that clearly applies not only to those lost in the Holocaust but to those all of us have lost.

Well along in reconstructing something of the life and death of Shmiel, his wife, Ester, and their four daughters, but with the story still incomplete, Mendelsohn asks himself, "For whose benefit, exactly, is the wholeness that I want so desperately? The dead need no stories; that is the fantasy of the living …" At this point Mendelsohn had met and interviewed many of the living survivors of Bolechow – out of some 6,000 Jews who lived there when World War II started, perhaps 50 escaped with their lives; a half-century later a dozen of them were still alive, scattered around the globe – and various elderly residents of the town who might remember some priceless detail. So, Mendelsohn could tell himself that there was now more of a story than there had been when he set out, and "surely that counted for something, if as some people think the dead need to be appeased." That's not good enough for this intrepid searcher.

"But of course, I don't believe this," he says. "The dead lie in their graves, in the cemeteries or forests or roadside ditches, and all this is of no interest to them, since they have, now, no interests of any kind at all. It is we, the living, who need the details, the stories, because what the dead no longer care about, mere fragments, a picture that will never be whole, will drive the living mad." The need for the story is not a sentimentality, but a matter of survival.

Mendelsohn's methods, described in considerable detail, which range from scouring genealogical Internet sites to jet lag–inducing distant journeys, amount to what I think of as "following the story to make the story." In a sense, there is no intrinsic story. The story of Shmiel and his family could have remained no more than the phrase "killed by the Nazis." Mendelsohn and the rest of us would have been none the wiser, although we would have been considerably worse off, as we can see from the results. What "following the story" amounts to is pursuing various faint clues, paying attention to unexpected encounters, going back to a seeming dead end one more time, just to be sure. And if something happens, new trails open up, to be followed further. What unfolds is the story (what happened in Bolechow in those years) and the story of the story.

Near the end of his journey, a recollection of one of the women he had interviewed stays in Mendelsohn's mind: "It was like what she was interested in was not so much the story of her grandmother but how to tell the story of her grandmother ... How to be the storyteller."

Mendelsohn reiterates the point again, and more explicitly, just after a last-minute coincidental encounter leads him to go back to a previously examined site one more time and to discover something startling and unexpected that helps the story click into place. "I did and do believe, after all that I've seen and done, that if you project yourself into the mass of things," he says, "if you look for things, if you search, you will, by the very act of searching, make something happen that would not otherwise have happened, you will find *something*, even something small, something that will certainly be more than if you hadn't gone looking in the first place, if you hadn't asked your grandfather anything at all."

Mendelsohn's justifiably large book in search of a very few people, people seemingly insignificant and irrevocably lost, is a testament to an investigative idea that succeeds in breaking through the abstraction of the Holocaust, a catastrophe "so big, the scale of it so gigantic, so enormous, that it becomes easy to think of it as something mechanical. Anonymous." Of course it isn't anonymous, as we well know, but we are tempted to forget. As Mendelsohn says, "Everything that happened, happened because someone made a decision. To pull a trigger, to flip a switch, to close a cattle car door, to hide, to betray." At the highest Nazi bureaucratic levels, there may have been, as Hannah Arendt famously put it in her *Eichmann in Jerusalem* (1963), a "banality of evil," but on the ground, as Mendelsohn demonstrates in *The Lost*, what we need to know are the exact details of evil, if we are not to succumb to forgetting, the "forgetting of being," as one philosopher phrased it.

9

Walking, Seeing, Shelving

In thinking about the books that have appeared in the decade 2000–2009, what I've been recurrently struck by is not so much those few books that can make an arguable claim for "greatness," or the prize winners, or even the annual lists of the "Top Ten" books of the year, but the fact of the abundance of good books. That abundance is partially recognized in such extensive listings as the *New York Times'* "Notable Books of the Year," or *The Globe and Mail's* "100" list. I'm cheered by the fact that every year, in every culture, every language, every national literature, there's a profusion of readable, interesting, intelligent books that propose slightly new ways of seeing and understanding the world and ourselves.

In a period marked by a decline in book reading, and a muffling or dispersal of the critical discussion necessary to a lively culture, these "good" books all too often receive insufficient attention and are too quickly forgotten. What follows is a sort of demonstration "sampler" about three exceptionally good books published in one year in one country (Canada) by writers I know personally and whose work extends the boundaries of the themes I identify as marking the decade. These books didn't necessarily make the best-seller lists or win any major literary prizes, but they're as good as or better than many books that did. What's more, I could produce such a sampler for any other given year in the decade, and for any other given country, and in every case such a sampler would only scratch the surface of what's available. There are more good books than I, or any single reader, can read. If that's a cause for despair (what am I missing?), it's also a recognition that's both humbling and reassuring.

I. WALKING

As I was re-reading the title chapter of Terry Glavin's *Waiting for the Macaws* (2006), which recounts an episode that takes place in the forests of Costa Rica, a blackbird landed in the feedbox on the balcony of my apartment in Berlin and began poking around for the last crumbs of yesterday's bread. The feedbox, an unused planter hanging from the balcony railing, is also periodically visited by neighbourhood sparrows, fat greedy pigeons, and the occasional starling or magpie. The blackbirds wake up just before dawn and carry on a chattering conversation through much of the day that sounds at least as intelligent as people talking on cellphones. They're my favourites. The balcony, which faces onto a narrow, closed courtyard with two maples and one ash tree, is about as close as I get (or want to get) to the Great Outdoors.

Whereas my ventures into nature are decidedly timid, in Terry Glavin's wonderfully intelligent and beautifully written book of "stories from the age of extinctions," the adventures are spectacular. The intrepid Glavin can not only be found half-snoozing in a Costa Rican wildlife refuge, awaiting the always-startling arrival of the big scarlet macaws of the book's title, but he's also up in the almost inpenetrable Himalayan mountains of Nagaland along the Indian-Burmese border, where the locals in a longhouse are shyly displaying a cache of the skulls of former enemies from the next tribe over and wondering if the sight of them would help or harm the possibilities of tourism. Or he's aboard a Norwegian whaling vessel drifting at the edge of the mythic but also real Maelstrom, the swirling ocean pool that drags sailors to the depths. And sometimes Glavin is just in an abandoned apple orchard on Mayne Island, B.C., his home base, where his kids are engaged in the honourable art of stealing apples, local species of apples whose taste is otherwise unknown on the planet.

The commanding image of Glavin's book is that of taking a "long walk." The walk begins quite a ways from Glavin's Mayne Island, but nonetheless close to "home" of another sort. It's an actual, rather than metaphoric, walk through the local "rolling hills, bogs and woods" around his mother's ancestral family farm in Coolreagh, Clare County, Ireland. He'd just begun working on the book we now have before us, going over some of his notes before starting out on "a long walk."

There are two items of interest in his notebooks, he reports. One is an Old Testament passage from the prophet Hosea that *the land will mourn, and everyone that dwelleth therein shall languish … yea, the fishes of the sea also shall be taken away*. The other is a recent newspaper article about the not-so-distant future in which 1100 scientists forecast the destruction of two-thirds of the natural world within decades, along with the "mass extinction of species, and the collapse of human society."

With those bleak thoughts in mind, Glavin sets off on his walk in the countryside around Coolreagh. Immediately, he makes the first crucial move in how he's going to position himself in fashioning this account. In Glavin's view, the landscape is not just rolling hills, Irish bogs, woods, fields, and mountains in the near distance, it's also a veritable storybook.

For example, Glavin finds himself "beside a field called the Castle Field, which takes its name from a craggy and vine-covered rock in the middle of it, the remnant of a stone fort built by local tribesmen loyal to Brian Boru, the great warrior-chief who defeated the Vikings at Clontarf in 1014. In the Castle Field you will notice the ground beginning to rise gently, and if you walk that way, up Blackguard's Hill, you'll find yourself heading through Ballyvaughan into the Slieve Bernagh mountains." But,

> if you walk in the other direction, northward, you will eventually find yourself in the townland of Fossamore, and the ground begins to rise there, too, into the Slieve Aughty mountains. It's wilder up that way. Above Fossamore is Powlagower, the Goat's Hole, and Tabernagat, the Well of the Cats. There is the Struthanalunacht, the Stream of New Milk, which once ran white with milk but long ago it turned to water, they say, when a woman washed her feet in it. There are people who live at Cloonusker who say that at the end of the world, the final battle of the last war will be fought up there, above Gortaderra, in a place called the Valley of the Black Pig, and on that last day of battle the Stream of New Milk will turn to blood.

And it's not just the old people at Cloonusker who brood on that prophecy. William Butler Yeats, Glavin notes, "was haunted by these things, and just as the world was carrying the great weight of dread and foreboding in his apocalyptic poem, 'The Valley of the Black Pig'" – with its *clash of fallen horsemen and cries of unknown perishing armies* – "so it was when I began writing this book."

Along with the recognition that we, too, are living in strangely apocalyptic times, what especially interests me, in the extended passage I've quoted above and throughout his book, is Glavin's strategy in approaching his subject. It's something he's done consistently ever since his first book, *A Death Feast in Dimlahamid* (1991), about aboriginal people, landscapes, and stories in northwestern British Columbia, and the perspective has been maintained in subsequent work: *A Ghost in the Water* (1994), about the disappearance of ancient sturgeon from our rivers, *Dead Reckoning* (1996), on the crisis in the Pacific fisheries, *This Ragged Place* (1996), and *The Last Great Sea* (2000). Once you get the point of his narrative "strategy," what Glavin is broadly up to becomes quite clear.

Wherever he goes, Glavin takes in not only the mundane features of the world but also its place names and their histories, and the stories that people tell ("long ago it turned to water, they say, when a woman washed her feet in it") about how the world got to be the way it is and how it might become ("there are people ... who say that at the end of the world, the final battle of the last war will be fought up there ... in a place called the Valley of the Black Pig"). Glavin gives a kind of equal, almost impartial, weight to all this information and telling. He doesn't bog us down by asking, Now, was there actually a woman who washed her feet in the Stream of New Milk, and if so, when exactly, and what are the chemical transformations required to establish the fact of that story, if, indeed, it is a fact? Nor does he worry about the relation of myth to the mundane. Rather, he simply passes on the tale, requiring no more than that casual, elegant folk attribution of, *they say*. The effect is a kind of *magical naturalism* which insists that all of the material – names, etymologies, the sounds of various languages, historical events, myths, poems, stories resting on the authority of *they say* – must be vividly co-present if we're to have a sense of reality sufficient to focus our attention. Otherwise, the world will be mere "scenery." Glavin's remarkable art as a writer is founded in that highly charged *way of seeing*, to recall John Berger's phrase, and it informs just about every passage, argument, claim, and meditative reflection in *Waiting for the Macaws*.

"This is a book about extinctions," Glavin declares at the outset, pointing out that "roughly 34,000 plants, or 12.5 percent of all the plants known to science, are threatened with extinction." Ditto for one in eight bird species (maybe including those poking around in my balcony feedbox), one in four mammals, four of every ten turtles, and half of all the surveyed fish species in the world's waters. Facts and figures of this sort punctuate the text, even if they "constitute only the most crude sort of barometer of the great unravelling of the living world." But equally distressing, extinction is taking place outside the categories of animals and plants. "It is happening down where the true measure of life's diversity is found. Extinction is taking away the subspecies, the local population, the particular, the neighbourhood, the singular, and the specific. And it is not confining itself to the 'wild' things of the world."

Glavin is talking not just about "nature," and I put that word in quotes, because what is natural and cultural, what is "inside" and "outside," is one of the things that this book puts in question. "Humanity's diversity," says Glavin, "is similarly withering. Though the world population has surpassed six billion, it is as though some savage ethnic cleansing is underway. The world is losing an entire language every two weeks. Fully half of the world's 5000 languages are expected to be gone, with all their songs and sagas, by the middle of this century. We are losing religious and intellectual traditions, entire bodies of literature, taxonomies, pharmacopias, and all those ways of seeing, knowing and being that have made humanity so resilient and successful a species for so long ... We are not gaining knowledge with every human generation – we are losing it."

My first serious apprehension of that loss of memory, imagination, and investigation that Glavin's book is about was awakened more than two decades ago when I read Brian Fawcett's *Cambodia: Stories for People Who Find Television Too Slow* (1986). So, Glavin's message here is not a new one, but it is powerfully and effectively delivered. One of Glavin's several concerns is how to express that message. And here he makes another important move.

He says, "A dark and gathering sameness is descending upon the world, and the language of environmentalism is wholly inadequate to the task of describing the thing. It can't even come close. It isn't that environmentalism exaggerates the phenomenon," an accusation frequently levelled against it, say, in the debates about global warming. Rather, it's that environmentalist discourse "just doesn't have the words for it." Ever since his journalistic days as a reporter for the *Vancouver Sun*, when he was reporting on and arguing with his editors about getting adequate space for stories about the political struggles of Haida native people in the Queen Charlotte Islands, Glavin has been regarded as an environmentalist writer, so his declaration of its inadequacy as a vocabulary may be taken by some as a betrayal of commitments, though of course it's not. He charges that the environmentalist discourse is burdened with "language that draws arbitrary distinctions between 'wilderness' and everything else and that places 'nature' outside of culture." And that will no longer do.

The method that Glavin adopts in *Waiting for the Macaws* is a culturally more traditional one, but one that is also more risky than discourse that rests on scientific authority. As he says, "To make sense of the world, people tell stories. This is a book of stories, not only because as novelist Doris Lessing says, 'our brains are patterned for storytelling.' It is also because at a time when the world is filled with dread and foreboding, and when the great master narratives we've relied on to understand things are collapsing all around us, there should be some virtue in going for a walk through the hills and coming back at the end of the day with an account – a story – of what's out there."

As much as "nature" in its conventional sense is imperilled, so too are our stories. "For all its splendid, flourishing, and elaborately interconnected profusions of life, the earth is also a tomb, and the dead breathe their stories out of the ground," Glavin observes. "But those very stories, all over the world, are vanishing just as certainly as all those birds, languages, turtles, songs and apples. They are also vanishing just as quickly." So, this is a book about the extinction of vital cultural practices as much as it is about the extinction of nature, both in and out of quote-marks.

This act of repositioning in terms of how to deliver a message may seem rather modest, but if one of the cultural practices threatened with diminishment if not extinction is narrative itself, Glavin's commitment to story is more significant than it may appear at first. In terms of modes of language adequate to the situation being described, I'd be tempted to go even further and suggest that perhaps we need *poetry* to get an understanding of what needs to be understood, but I'm realist enough to recognize that poetry in our time has been relegated to very specialized laboratories of language-users. I'll settle for good storytellers, and Glavin is definitely one of them.

Finally, in terms of the strategies, methods and repositionings of this book, one of the interesting things about *Macaws* is that it's not a doom-and-gloom environmentalist jeremiad, though it provides the full complement of apocalyptic prospects without flinching. "After a fairly thorough reconnaissance of the extinctions at work in the world," Glavin declares, "I found absolutely no evidence that any of this is what humanity really wants. That is good news. I can also confidently report that the roads and boreens that wind their way through the East Clare hills do not lead inevitably northward beyond Fossamore into the Valley of the Black Pig."

Even the recent newspaper article about portending extinctions doesn't "describe one inescapable fate." The article is based on a United Nations Environment Programme report that actually out-lines "four roads through the hills," only two of which head toward the Black Pig. The "security first" and "markets first" approaches of-fer dire prospects in which "the powerful and wealthy end up gating themselves into enclaves leaving the masses of poor to survive as best they can in the collapsing environment outside the walls," and the state loses its capacity to regulate human affairs and is subsumed to faith in market forces, further globalization, and greater trade libe-ralization. Margaret Atwood's dystopian novel, *Oryx and Crake* (2004), imagines the more extreme outcomes likely to result from travelling such roads.

The "policy first" and "sustainability first" approaches, by contrast, "lead to a different sort of countryside altogether," one that focu-ses on local and coordinated responses to environmental disrup-tion and poverty, and in which "new institutions make room for radical changes in the way people interact with one another and with the living, breathing world." Along these latter roads, "we all muddle through."

Glavin concedes that the present extinctions, unlike previous ages of extinction, can all "be reliably attributed, in one way or another, to a single species: *Homo sapiens*." He adds, "But it is not a simple story, with human beings as the cruel villain of the piece. In the case against humanity, this book is offered as evidence for the defence." What Glavin relies on is a sense that "deep within the human consciousness is an ancient and abiding desire to be in the presence of flourishing, abundant, and diverse forms of life. Like the desire for narrative, enchantment with the beauty, utility and diversity of living things is an inescapable aspect of human nature."

Glavin's concept of "humanity" is of course to be distinguished from particular human regimes, social classes, corporate cabals, and the rest. Still, humanity presents a puzzling dynamic. Perhaps the best we can claim is that there's "the wisdom of the people," which really does exist, *and* there's popular ignorance, even wilful human stupidity. The important term in the dynamic is "and."

Everything I've reprised is found in the opening chapter of *Waiting for the Macaws*, which provides a framework for understanding Glavin's subsequent experiences as well as a brief demonstration of his magical naturalist method while walking in the hills of East Clare. After that, in a sense it's all downhill, or downhill, uphill, over hill and dale, onto the ocean's bounteous blue, and from home to the middle of nowhere and back to the apple orchards of Mayne Island.

In each of the stories that follow – stories about tigers and the simulacra of safaris in Singapore, to cougar attacks on Vancouver Island, to the shrine of Kali in Calcutta which shimmers at story's end – the story is sustained by Glavin's cosmopolitan intelligence, a sense of curiosity that is at once precisely local, but that simultaneously measures the local in terms of the worldly. In Glavin's case, his intelligence is motivated by passion (the heated charm of an Irish temperament) and unrestrained by ideological prejudice or pre-judgement. That is, he approaches experience without over-determined preconceptions, though of course he comes to each scene, like all of us, with ideas. But the ideas do not feel imposed on the landscape. Rather, the adventure (and this is a book of adventures) is refracted through the prism of the reality Glavin encounters, and that reality is permitted to test, shape, and rewrite whatever notions Glavin brings to the scene.

While Glavin's locations seem exotic to me, given my natural habitats, what you learn from reading his stories is that the locales he arrives at are not really exotic, they're simply other places where people have ways of living, ways of telling, that are ultimately recognizable to us. My "natural habitats" tend to be classrooms, urban streets, libraries (public and personal), cafes, and the occasional balcony where blackbirds make social calls. What *Waiting for the*

Macaws does for a reader like me is to sharpen my attention toward the disappearances, losses, and extinctions of cultural practices taking place in my own backyard: letter-writing has been
replaced by qualitatively diminished electronic messages, teaching
is becoming an almost lost art in the face of overcrowded university
lecture theatres, and sometimes I wonder if conversation and books
themselves are not also disappearing. Glavin's book not only awak-
ens memory and inspires investigation, but it's that rare thing, a
narrative that stays in mind. It says that it's time for all of us to take
"a long walk."

2. BLIND MAN'S BLUFF

Ryan Knighton is my first blind guy. His *Cockeyed: A Memoir* (2006)
is my first book about blindness.

He's mid-30ish, has a shaved head, frequently wears a black pork-
pie hat, has a gym-developed hard-body, sports some this-generation
tattoos, teaches English at Capilano University in North Vancouver,
British Columbia (which is where I also work), and taps around the
universe with a long white cane. Knighton has retinitis pigmentosa
(RP), a genetic eye disease that's progressively reduced his sight over
the last fifteen years to about one per cent in one eye. Eventually, it'll
be all gone.

Since we both teach early morning classes, I frequently pick him
up for the ride to work. My one-liner is: "We're a carpool, but I
don't let him drive very often." On the road, in between literary gossip and my running description of the traffic pattern ("Oh no, we're
sandwiched between two 18-wheelers ... Hey, you SUV pig! Get a
bigger vehicle! How 'bout a Hummer with a machine-gun mount?"
etc.), we occasionally refer to his obvious, but unseeing "condition"
or "situation" or whatever you call it – how about blindness? I have
a one-liner for that, too: "You've got two choices: irony or suicide."

Since there are about 300,000 blind Canadians (about 1 per cent
of the population), I guess it's just the luck of the draw that Knighton
is "my first blind person." Pretty good luck, I'd say. And more or less
like with my first Jew, or first poet, or first lesbian, one of the side-
benefits of knowing an identifiable Other of any sort is that you
quickly become sensitized to a bunch of things you otherwise might
not have noticed.

At work, as we're heading off to the coffee kiosk through a maze of stairwells, doors, and student-crowded corridors, I confine myself to occasional warnings in the jargon of World War II fighter pilots, like, "Bogie at 3 o'clock," to indicate some major obstacle that I don't think his white stick will fully appreciate.

But let's get back to choices, since deciding what to do about blindness is one of any blind person's big decisions, and is one of the things that Knighton's brilliant, funny, crisply written, and serious-but-not-over-serious memoir, *Cockeyed*, is all about. As he notes, there are actually more than two choices on offer. In addition to irony, there's also cynicism, victimhood, and possibly something resembling serenity, although the latter is pretty much out of reach, given Knighton's mildly angst-ridden temperament. Suicide, too, is presumably not an option. Or, well, of course it's an option, and it's silly not to face it, but it doesn't seem like an especially good one. Knighton, like most writers, prefers writing to suicide. So did Jorge Luis Borges, who also had RP, and possibly even such other famous scribes as John Milton and, who knows, mythic Homer himself.

Cockeyed is an episodic rather than a one-damned-thing-after-another sort of memoir, though it's roughly chronological. Written under an epigraph from Ovid's *Metamorphoses* – "My purpose is to tell of bodies which have been transformed into shapes of a different kind ..." – the bodily changes in Knighton's life first registered in early adolescence around a family dinner-table in Langley, B.C., when Uncle Brad remarked, "Look at his face. Ryan's got a squint or something. See? He's kind of cockeyed." The squint persisted and the kid found himself "trying to focus through a problem I couldn't see. Not yet."

Things become even less clear in his mid-teens when young Knighton scores a summer warehouse job that includes driving a forklift. That's when he starts "missing" things in his field of vision. There's an effort to pass it off as mere bumbling, but it's more than klutziness. He'd imagined a "summer of fortune" for himself, thanks to his great job, but "instead of wealth, I found another fortune, the kind that is told. Somehow I'd bumbled into my fate as a blind man before it was upon me." In hindsight, it's like Pozzo's line in Samuel Beckett's *Waiting for Godot*, which Knighton cites: "I woke up one fine day as blind as Fortune." Actually, it's not until he's 18, after he drives the family car in a slow-motion nightmare into a ditch on a foggy night, that he gets the full monty RP diagnosis. And after that, he's dealing with the "situation."

What makes *Cockeyed* unique among tales of encroaching darkness is that Knighton mostly treats blindness as a kind of surrealism. It's a brilliant move that allows him to write a series of very funny set-pieces about everyday mishaps and worse that are unfailingly presented with perfect pitch and timing.

There's the woman in the pub who asks him why he's staring at her when he isn't staring at her. He decides to "pass" as sighted; she eventually presses a note with her address into his hand; hours later, he's stumbling around in a cul-de-sac, accidentally busting into someone's house and discovering that things go bump in the night-blindness. Much later, well past his sowing-wild-punk-oats period, there's the trip to Ikea with his wife, Tracy, to buy a couch. All he sees are brownish blurs and blobs, but it occasions a discourse on "Ikealism," the ideology of classless furniture, and taut domestic relationships. Then there's the problem of asking a waitress where the bathroom is and being told it's "over there," but "indexicals," as such site-specific terms are known, aren't much help to a blind guy. And finally there's the story about the decision to come out of the blindness closet by learning to navigate with a long white stick.

If that was all there is to *Cockeyed*, it would still be pretty good. Think humourist David Sedaris, with added oomph. But there's way more to Knighton's book. The crux chapter of *Cockeyed* is called "Missing." It's about a family tragedy, whose details I won't reveal, but it's the moment where blindness moves beyond the slapstick of surrealism. "I had been a young man in denial, one who resisted his diagnosis and its future at every turn," Knighton reflects. "I'd mocked blindness, ignored it, camouflaged it, even accepted it, to a very minor degree." The family tragedy, however, "left a space, and that space demanded I become the kind of person I wanted to be: resolved, selfless, capable, any number of adjectives I'd let my blindness disfigure in me ... If I'd been at war, it was more or less over. Whatever I'd been fighting didn't matter to me anymore. It was just too small."

In the elegies required for tragedies, familial and otherwise, Knighton sees that "seeing itself is touched with elegy. Reality seems to press its light into us, it is happening, but that's not the way things are. The eye can process only so many images per second, taking in sights the way a camera takes a series of stills ... We think we are seeing life as it happens, but pictures are missing. Moments disappear between the stills and make up our unwitnessed lives. To see is to miss things. Loss is always with us."

The other place in *Cockeyed* where we're well beyond the surreal is in Knighton's accounts of his relationship to his spouse, Tracy, who is the undeniable hero of the tale of our Knighton-errant. People often ask him how they live together and what it's like to build blindness into an otherwise normal middle-class life. "The truth is, it's hard to see," he says. "Blindness for us is mostly made up of many small things. I reach for a glass but can't find it. I continue to talk to you over the table, looking for the glass with my hand. The moment I give up, Tracy nudges the glass to my fingers. It's so casual, the allowance she gives me to try and to fail, and it is so reflexive, her help when I need it," but not *before* he needs it. "From where you sit," he adds, "our way might not catch your eye. The exchange is so fluid and quick, like one of those moments in between the stills."

The reason for quoting the text at some length here is to underscore one of the more important points about *Cockeyed*. Ryan Knighton is a writer, not a blind-writer, and his book is a work of writing, not a self-help, disease-of-the-week, or triumph-over-disability handbook.

Although Knighton's publishers have done their best to position and market the book as hip and other than a "conventional confessional," the public is so conditioned to psychologizing suffering that the point might still be missed. Knighton even includes a prefatory note that twits author James Frey about truth-in-telling in order to make clear that his book isn't just one of those "misery memoir" knockoffs: "Should a reader determine that the author is not disabled, please contact the appropriate authorities. He would gladly delete his blindness from any further memoirs." Irony instead of suicide, sentimentality, cynicism, right?

At 30-something, Knighton is writing about blindness because writers have to work through whatever situation the world has handed them. When he gets done working through blindness as a writer, I expect he'll write about other stuff. That he's written about this stuff with such grace and moxy is a sign of what's to come.

For readers, what you get out of *Cockeyed* is to become sensitized to what you see: "indexicals," "Bogies at 3 o'clock," the missing stills, and such literary references as Vladimir's question in *Godot*, "When did this happen to you?", and Pozzo's haunting reply, "I don't know … The blind know nothing of time." Such gifts, of course, are the whole point of, pardon a final pun, insightful writing.

3. SHELF LIFE

At night, Alberto Manguel tells us in *The Library at Night* (2006), his book-length meditation on the nature of libraries, memory, and perhaps much more, "when the library lamps are lit, the outside world disappears and nothing but this space of books remains in existence … In the dark, with the windows lit and the rows of books glittering, the library is a closed space, a universe of self-serving rules that pretend to replace or translate those of the shapeless universe beyond."

The library in question is located in a tiny French village south of the Loire River. It was built by and belongs to Manguel, a well-known, multi-lingual anthologist, translator, critic, biographer, and novelist, to house some 30,000 volumes he has collected during a peripatetic literary lifetime. *The Library at Night* begins with Manguel's autobiographical account of how this idiosyncratic building project, almost a classic "folly," took shape out of the stone-wall ruins of a 15th century barn, adjacent to a presbytery, or priest's house, where Manguel now lives.

Although officially a Canadian (that most fluid of national identities), Manguel was born an Argentinian, partially raised in Israel (where one of his parents was in the diplomatic corps), and schooled in Buenos Aires, where the teenager became an acolyte of the great Jorge Luis Borges, about whom Manguel would later write extensively and perceptively. In truth, the well-travelled Manguel is not so much a burgher of a nation-state as a full-fledged citizen of the Republic of Letters.

His autobibliographical tale is only the first of dozens of stories Manguel tells about libraries, stories that range from the vast, almost mythical, destroyed library of Alexandria, Egypt, one of the real wonders of the Ancient World, to the eight-book children's library in Block 31 of the Birkenau concentration camp during World War II, a library whose readers were all exterminated.

His often magical, always literally bookish tales include the "Biblioburro" program in rural Colombia, where donkeys haul book bags up to remote mountain villages. The only book the scrupulous peasant library borrowers didn't want to return, reports Manguel, was Homer's *Iliad*. As the librarian, who eventually made a gift of the book to them, told Manguel, the villagers "explained that Homer's story exactly reflected their own: it told of a war-torn country in which mad gods wilfully decide the fate of humans who never know exactly what the fighting is about, or when they will be killed."

Much the same could be said of what Manguel tells us about the looting of the National Library of Baghdad in 2003, a grim account of how "sometimes a library is wilfully allowed to vanish." While a conquering Anglo-American army stood by, "in a few hours, much of the earliest recorded history of humankind was lost to oblivion," including the 6,000-year-old first surviving examples of writing.

Manguel's stories are told with appropriate gravitas, but also always with a genuine lightness of touch that other writers strive for, often only to fail to transcend the trivial. At one end of sophistication, there's a rapturous description of the Laurentian Library built by Michelangelo at the San Lorenzo Monastery in Italy. At the other end, there are the oasis towns in the desert of Adrar in central Mauritania, obligatory stopping points on the route to Mecca, which still "house dozens of age-old libraries whose very existence is due to the whims of passing caravans laden with spices, pilgrims, salt and books."

A story is told in Ouadane, one such oasis city, of a silent 15th century beggar who settled into one of the libraries and only seemed to care for "spending long hours among the books of Ouadane, reading in complete silence." After months of such mysterious behaviour, the local imam reminded the reader that "it is written that he who keeps knowledge to himself shall not be made welcome in the Kingdom of Heaven. Each reader is but one chapter in the life of a book, and unless he passes his knowledge on to others, it is as if he condemned the book to be buried alive." At which point, Manguel tells us, "the man opened his mouth and gave a lengthy and marvellous commentary on the sacred text he happened to have before him. The imam realized that his visitor was a certain celebrated scholar who, despairing of the deafness of the world, had promised to hold his tongue until he came to a place where learning was truly honoured."

Manguel's personal library, both during the day and at night, inter-mittently re-appears throughout the book, as he considers various as-pects of the library: as myth, as order, as mind, as survival, and so on. The autobiographical foundation of his book immediately lets us know that this will not be a "tidy succession of dates and names" and that Manguel's intention is not "to compile another history of libraries nor to add another tome to the alarmingly extensive collection of bib-liotechnology, but merely to give an account of my astonishment."

Beneath the astonishment conveyed in this brilliantly conceived, elegantly written, elegiac, and celebratory meditation, there's some-thing philosophically deeper. The very big question that Alberto Manguel poses at the outset of *The Library at Night* sets the tone for the intellectual quest-story that follows. The question is about the meaning of the dynamic relationship between chaos and order that we find everywhere, from the greatest magnitudes – "the starry heav-ens," as the philosopher Immanuel Kant called them – to the smallest particulars of our lives.

"Outside theology and fantastic literature," Manguel says, "few can doubt that the main features of our universe are its dearth of meaning and lack of discernible purpose." That is, unless you believe in God or Middle-Earth and Mordor, neither the universe nor the evolutionary process propose an answer to the riddle of human life. "And yet, with bewildering optimism, we continue to assemble whatever scraps of information we can gather in scrolls and books and computer chips, on shelf after library shelf, whether material, virtual or otherwise, pathetically intent on lending the world a sem-blance of sense and order, while knowing perfectly well that, how-ever much we'd like to believe the contrary, our pursuits are sadly doomed to failure. Why then do we do it?"

The Library at Night is the fourth in a decade-long series of books which Manguel began in 1996 with his best-selling *A History of Reading*, followed by *Reading Pictures* (2000) and *A Reading Diary* (2004). It is an invaluable serial contemplation of the practices and institutions of civilization itself, a structure of life that seems as much in peril today as at any previous time. Unsurprisingly, the lat-est instalment in the series is tinged with Manguel's sense that he might be writing an elegy.

If there are always two kinds of people in the world, in this in-stance they are readers and non-readers. "Libraries are not, never will be, used by everyone," Manguel notes. "In Mesopotamia as in Greece, in Buenos Aires as in Toronto, readers and non-readers have existed side by side, and the non-readers have always constituted the majority ... the number of those for whom reading books is of the essence is very small. What varies is not the proportions of these two groups of humanity but the way in which different societies regard the book and the art of reading." The news these days is not so good.

"Our society," he says, "accepts the book as a given, but the act of reading – once considered useful and important, as well as potentially dangerous and subversive – is now condescendingly accepted as a pastime, a slow pastime that lacks efficiency and does not contribute to the common good ... In our society, reading is nothing but an ancillary act, and the great repository of our memory and experience, the library, is considered less a living entity than an inconvenient storage room." The shelves gather dust.

As for the promise of that universal cyberlibrary, the Internet or Web, which "occupies no time except the nightmare of a constant present," Manguel recognizes that it's simply an instrument, but has his doubts about its uses. It stresses "velocity over reflection and brevity over complexity." It prefers "snippets of news and bytes of facts over lengthy discussions." Worse, it dilutes "informed opinion with reams of inane babble, ineffectual advice, inaccurate facts and trivial information, made attractive with brand names and manipulated statistics."

Of course, the fault lies not in our instruments or the stars. "We alone, and not our technologies, are responsible for our losses, and we alone are to blame when we deliberately choose oblivion over recollection," Manguel says, adding, "We are, however, adroit at making excuses and dreaming up reasons for our poor choices."

One of the better choices that readers can make is Manguel's wondrous *Library at Night*, a glowing patch of civility in the dark chaos around us.

The Gods That Failed: Richard Dawkins

I

One of the most striking intellectual developments of the past decade is the renewed advocacy of atheism. It's inspired a profusion of books, reviews, newspaper columns, blog comments, and websites discussing and debating the rejection of theism. More important, increasing numbers of scientists, philosophers, and other intellectuals, perhaps disturbed by the consequences of Christian and Islamic fundamentalist religious beliefs in the first decade of the 21st century, have decided to "come out" and declare that as far as they know God doesn't exist.

Books taking this view in the decade 2000–2009 include Julian Baggini's *Atheism: A Very Short Introduction* (2003), Sam Harris's *The End of Faith* (2004) and *Letter to a Christian Nation* (2006), Lewis Wolpert's *Six Impossible Things before Breakfast: The Evolutionary Origins of Belief* (2006), Daniel Dennett's *Breaking the Spell: Religion as a Natural Phenomenon* (2006), Christopher Hitchens's *God Is Not Great: How Religion Poisons Everything* (2007), and pre-eminently, Richard Dawkins's *The God Delusion* (2006).

Commentary on the New Atheism has reached Biblical Deluge proportions. Leaving aside the predictable negative reactions from "faith-heads" (as Dawkins dismissively calls them), serious criticism ranges from such scholars as Marxist literary critic Terry Eagleton in the *London Review of Books*, Nobel prize-winning physicist Steven Weinberg in the *TLS*, philosopher Thomas Nagel in the *New Republic*, biologist Allen Orr in the *New York Review of Books*, and philosopher Dan Dennett in *Free Inquiry*. *Time* magazine carried a cover story on the phenomenon, one of the first since its renowned obituary-black cover asked "Is God Dead?" back in the 1960s. Though the discussion may not have reached such day-time television venues as *Oprah*, Dennett and Dawkins have been popping up on the tube (and YouTube) with some regularity.

The tipping point in all the current soul-searching is clearly *The God Delusion* by biologist and Oxford Professor for the Public Understanding of Science Richard Dawkins, author of several widely praised studies of evolution, including *The Selfish Gene* and *The Blind Watchmaker*. Dawkins's book was on the *New York Times'* bestseller list for a year, and in Canada was at the top of the *Globe and Mail's* list.

The revived discussion of atheism, like periodic religious revivals and manias, has occurred several times before in history, usually in periods of scientific breakthrough and political upheaval. Atheistic speculation, for example, followed closely on the heels of the scientific discoveries of the 17th century astronomers. The Roman Catholic Church's demands for Galileo's recantation in the post-Reformation 1630s registered early religious unease about science's displacement of the earth from the centre of the universe, where God had allegedly located his greatest creation. The very name of philosopher Baruch Spinoza became almost a synonym for atheism in the mid-17th century and afterwards, as Richard Israel documents in *Radical Enlightenment: Philosophy and the Making of Modernity, 1650–1750* (2001), even though Spinoza was more probably a sort of Pantheist, someone who believes that God is in everything or that God is Nature.

Leaders of the French and American revolutions in the following century were almost all, if not outright atheists, the next best thing. The cosmic beliefs of a Thomas Jefferson, say, embraced something known as Deism, a sort of belief in a Higher Something or Other, but unlike the familiar Judeo-Catholic-Protestant-Islamic versions of God, the Deist higher power was utterly impersonal, indescribable, and unknowable. Perhaps the major impetus for questioning the existence of God came in the wake of Charles Darwin's 1859 publication of *The Origin of Species* and was renewed in the present decade, which marked the 150th anniversary of the appearance of that book. Whatever else Darwin's "dangerous idea" (as Dennett calls it in a 1995 book of that title) demonstrated about evolution, it has been reasonably clear ever since that human beings are not a special and separate creation but have evolved from previous forms of life. At best, God might be thought to have "kick started" the universe, unleashing a relatively undesigned evolutionary process that gave rise to life on earth, life that included dinosaurs and all sorts of other creatures that went extinct, as well as thousands of species of still-living termites, beetles, butterflies, rodents, and, oh yes, us.

Periodic bursts of atheistic questioning occurred throughout the 20th century, often in conjunction with various catastrophes and developments. The cataclysms included World War I, Freudianism, and Einsteinian and quantum physics in the first three decades of the century. The global upheavals of the 1960s and a failed U.S. war in Vietnam were accompanied by a proposed New Age spiritualism in place of the familiar deities. And now there's *this*, at the beginning of the 21st century, a period featuring terrorism and retaliatory war, computer technology breakthroughs, religious extremism, and the prospect of planetary destruction in the form of global warming.

2

Dawkins's book is meant to be a provocative, lively, popular work, aimed at a readership of ordinary, literate people, an intention occasionally forgotten by its more scholarly critics.

His aim, as he puts in the preface, is "consciousness-raising." Dawkins says, "I suspect – well, I am sure – that there are lots of people out there who have been brought up in some religion or other, are unhappy in it, don't believe it, or are worried about the evils that are done in its name; people who feel vague yearnings to leave their parents' religion and wish they could, but just don't realize that leaving is an option. If you are one of them, this book is for you." Dawkins doesn't say it, but it's likely also true that a lot of his readers are already non-believers and want their views confirmed and their arguments buttressed. Thus Dawkins, in addition to addressing the wavering, is also preaching to the existing choir of non-believers. But the main aim is to challenge the doubters. The book, he emphasizes, "is intended to raise consciousness to the fact that to be an atheist is a realistic aspiration, and a brave and splendid one. You can be an atheist who is happy, balanced, moral, and intellectually fulfilled."

Second, Dawkins wants people to become aware that natural selection and other scientific theories are far superior to the widely held but implausible "God hypothesis" in explaining both the world we live in and the distant cosmos. He takes up these issues in a series of chapters critiquing the belief in God, examining the classic arguments for God's existence, and putting forward his own position on "Why there almost certainly is no God."

A third aim of Dawkins's polemic is to argue against the indoctrination of children with religious beliefs, a practice that Dawkins views as akin to child abuse. Along the way, although it's not presented as a programmatic aim, Dawkins makes it clear that he's not opposing merely extreme or fundamentalist religion, but all religion, even the seemingly mild-mannered, reasonable sort. Finally, he hopes to instil "atheist pride" among non-believers.

Apart from consciousness-raising goals, Dawkins takes up a few other important items. He defends the use of the term "delusion" in his title, offering a dictionary meaning of it as "a persistent false belief in the face of strong contradictory evidence." He cites Robert Persig's quip, "When one person suffers from a delusion, it is called insanity. When many people suffer from a delusion, it is called religion." Dawkins also seeks to explain the ubiquity of religion, both historically and geographically, and to address the question of whether one can be moral without religious belief. In both cases, he offers a set of speculations based on an evolutionary account of religious beliefs and natural morality. Along the way he anticipates and responds to – how persuasively is a matter of debate – the objection that if religion in power has caused considerable harm, atheism in power has been equally monstrous. First and last, Dawkins offers an explanation of "how a proper understanding of the magnificence of the real world, while never becoming a religion, can fill the inspirational role that religion has historically –and inadequately – usurped."

If all goes well, religious readers who open his book "will be atheists when they put it down." Then Dawkins snorts self-derisively, "What presumptuous optimism!" More seriously, he recognizes that "dyed-in-the-wool faith-heads are immune to argument, their resistance built up over years of childhood indoctrination using methods that took centuries to mature. Among the more effective immunological devices is a dire warning to avoid even opening a book like this, which is surely a work of Satan." But the people Dawkins is seeking are more open-minded, "people whose childhood indoctrination was not too insidious, or for other reasons didn't 'take,' or whose native intelligence is strong enough to overcome it. Such free spirits should need only a little encouragement to break free of the vice of religion altogether." I cite this early passage in the book because it also suggests Dawkins' uncompromising, contentious, sometimes derisive tone, which may account for some of the fuss that his book has quite intendedly kicked up.

The opening lines of Dawkins' chapter about the "God Hypothesis," probably the most widely quoted passage in the reviews, gives an even stronger sense of the flavour: "The God of the Old Testament is arguably the most unpleasant character in all fiction: jealous and proud of it; a petty, unjust, unforgiving control-freak; a vindictive, bloodthirsty ethnic cleanser; a misogynistic, homophobic, racist, infanticidal, genocidal, filicidal, pestilential, megalomaniacal, sadomasochistic, capriciously malevolent bully."

Dawkins then pretends to relent,

> It is unfair to attack such an easy target. The God Hypothesis
> should not stand or fall with its most unlovely instantiation ...
> Instead I shall define the God Hypothesis more defensibly: *there*
> *exists a superhuman, supernatural intelligence who deliberately*
> *designed and created the universe and everything in it, including*
> *us.* This book will advocate an alternative view: *any creative*
> *intelligence, of sufficient complexity to design anything, comes*
> *into existence only as the end product of an extended process*
> *of gradual evolution.* Creative intelligences, being evolved,
> necessarily arrive late in the universe, and therefore cannot
> be responsible for designing it. God, in the sense defined, is
> a delusion ... a pernicious delusion.

Dawkins will later lean heavily on the old chestnut response to the claim that God created the universe: Yeah? Then who created God?

Here, however, I'm merely pointing to Dawkins's polemic strategy, which has come in for criticism. The claim above about Yahweh, which is fairly characteristic of the book's rhetorical heights, is intentionally over the top because Dawkins wants to emphasize exactly how strange so many religious beliefs are, whether it's the Old

Testament God, labyrinthine conceptions of a Trinity, fanciful prospects of paradise for suicide-bombers, or cult-like beliefs about
blood transfusions. It's only after arguing for recognition that believers have to take responsibility for their own over-the-top notions
that Dawkins is willing to say, okay, let's more reasonably consider
claims and counter-claims. That is, there is a strategy to Dawkins's
approach; it's not just uncontrolled venting against "the vice of religion." Again, I mention this because some of his critics seem to be
unaware of Dawkins's intentions.

3

Most of the reviewers of *The God Delusion* – and here I'm thinking
only of those who are or who might be expected to share Dawkins's
basic views – wish that Dawkins's book were better, as do I. The
criticisms range from the reasonable to the strange, and it's worthwhile to provide a sampling.

   Perhaps the most energetic of the critiques is that of Terry Eagleton,
who charges Dawkins with being a theological vulgarian, if not worse
(Terry Eagleton, "Lunging, Flailing, Mispunching," *London Review
of Books*, Oct. 19, 2006). "Imagine someone holding forth on biology," Eagleton begins, "whose only knowledge of the subject is the
Book of British Birds, and you have a rough idea of what it feels like
to read Richard Dawkins on theology." Dawkins's "vulgar carica-
tures of religious faith … would make a first-year theology student
wince," he says. "What, one wonders, are Dawkins's views on the
epistemological differences between Aquinas and Duns Scotus? Has
he read Erigena on subjectivity, Rahner on grace or Moltmann on
hope? Has he even heard of them?" Well, maybe not. Dawkins makes
no claims for sophistication when it comes to examining theology,
but he does examine various Biblical claims, Anselm's and Aquinas's
"proofs" for the existence of God, and sundry other bits of religious
thinking. More important, one wants to ask, is Eagleton claiming
that a more sophisticated knowledge of theology would give us good
reasons for believing in God (or the God Hypothesis), or is he simply
saying that a better grasp of theology by Dawkins would go some
way to satisfying intellectual standards?

   It's hard to tell. Eagleton scoffs at Dawkins for knocking down a
straw-man God, "if not exactly [one] with a white beard, then at

least some kind of *chap*, however supersized." Rather than such a caricature, claims Eagleton,

> for Judeo-Christianity, God is not a person … Nor is he a principle, an entity, or 'existent': in one sense of that word it would be perfectly coherent for religious types to claim that God does not in fact exist. He is, rather, the condition of possibility of any entity whatsoever, including ourselves. He is the answer to why there is something rather than nothing … This, not some super-manufacturing, is what is traditionally meant by the claim that God is Creator. He is what sustains all things in being by his love; and this would still be the case even if the universe had no beginning.

If Dawkins is cheerfully vulgarian about theology – he tends to airily reply that after all he doesn't believe in fairies, and no one demands that he master the fine points of fairy-ology – it's possible that Eagleton is a teensy bit over-sophisticated about it. He insists at several points that his God, whom it would be "perfectly coherent" to claim "does not in fact exist," and who is "the condition of possibility of any entity whatsoever," is in accord with the "traditional" understanding of God. He repeatedly chides Dawkins for understanding "nothing of these traditional doctrines." He complains that Dawkins seeks to grab "a victory on the cheap by savaging [theology] as so much garbage and gobbledygook"; though he concedes that "the mainstream theology I have just outlined may well not be true," he insists that "anyone who holds it is in my view to be respected." He is particularly incensed, and this may be his main objection, that Dawkins lumps together "the huge number of believers who hold something like the theology I outlined" with the "rednecks who murder abortionists and malign homosexuals."

I understand Eagleton's complaint about Dawkins' derisiveness, but what puzzles me is his claim that his own account represents "traditional" or "mainstream" theology, or the implication that it provides a good reason for believing in God. Which mainstream, traditional theology? I want to ask. Perhaps 17th century mainstream Deism? But of course there was no "mainstream" Deism. Nor, I suspect, are there a "huge number" of believers who share Eagleton's idea of "traditional" theology. There are, by my observation, fairly huge numbers of Catholics, Protestants, Islamists, Hindus, and even Jews who adhere to some form of the sort of vulgar theologies at which Dawkins directs his barbs. There are also sizeable denominations, like the United Church of Canada, to take a local example, whose theology is closer to, if not quite as ethereal as, that of Eagleton, and it is Dawkins's failure to pay much attention to them that leads other critics besides Eagleton to complain about that particular point.

In the end, though, Eagleton doesn't say much to refute Dawkins, and his own high-faluting theology reeks of obscurantism. Eagleton extends his critique of Dawkins (and Christopher Hitchens, melding the two into an imaginary creature he calls "Ditchkins") in his Terry Lectures at Yale University, *Reason, Faith and Revolution: Reflections on the God Debate* (2009). The lectures are, characteristically of Eagleton, witty, charming, and intelligent. He has interesting things to say about reason and revolution, and his polemic is shrewdly judged. He finds Dawkins vulgar with respect not only to theology but in matters of secular thought as well. Most of the latter complaint seems to be that Dawkins is a middlebrow liberal rather than a highbrow Marxist like Eagleton. But on the question of faith, Eagleton merely reiterates his earlier remarks about Dawkins and isn't, in my view, any more persuasive than before. While some forms of theism are not, *contra* Dawkins, simply "irrational" or delusional, they nonetheless hardly offer grounds for strong belief.

University of Rochester biology professor Allen Orr is free of Eagleton's pretensions, but his objections to Dawkins, if more plain-spoken, are just as wide-ranging (Allen Orr, "A Mission to Convert," *The New York Review of Books*, Jan. 11, 2007). "*The God Delusion* seems to me badly flawed," he says. Its most disappointing feature is "Dawkins's failure to engage religious thought in any serious way ... The result is a book that never squarely faces its opponents." Like Eagleton, Orr complains that there's no serious examination of theology, "no attempt to follow philosophical debates about the nature of religious propositions," no interest in Church-science history, and "no attempt to understand even the simplest of religious attitudes. Instead, Dawkins has written a book that's distinctly, even defiantly, middlebrow." Why the last is an objection is unclear, since "middlebrow" is precisely the readership Dawkins is seeking, unless Orr means that middlebrow by definition means shoddy goods.

What follows is a cogent litany of criticisms that range from the substance of Dawkins's claims to matters of style and approach. Orr's main complaint is that Dawkins is indiscriminate about lumping together different religious beliefs and further, he distorts the historical record of human evil when judging the results of religion and atheism when held by those in public office. Dawkins suffers from, Orr suggests, "a failure of metaphysical imagination. When thinking of those vast matters that make up religion – matters of ultimate meaning that stand at the edge of intelligibility and that are among the most difficult to articulate – he sees only black and white. Despite some attempts at subtlety, Dawkins almost reflexively identifies religion with right-wing fundamentalism and biblical literalism. Other, more nuanced possibilities – varieties of deism, mysticism, or nondenominational spirituality – have a harder time holding his attention. It may be that Dawkins can't imagine these possibilities vividly enough to worry over them in a serious way." I don't have a problem with Orr's criticisms of Dawkins; I share many of them. What I notice, however, is that Orr (and others) say very little about the core thesis Dawkins presents, namely, that there aren't any good reasons to believe in a God, apart from wishful thinking, psychological self-comfort, and delusion. Given the enormous extent of unlikely religious beliefs abroad, I'm surprised that such critics aren't prepared to cut Dawkins a bit more slack.

Physicist Steven Weinberg, himself a long-time public advocate of atheism, who has regularly cautioned fellow scientists about cavalierly talking about "the mind of God," offers a far more sympathetic reading of Dawkins (Steven Weinberg, "A Deadly Certitude," *Times Literary Supplement*, Jan. 17, 2007). Weinberg notes the harsh tenor of many of the reviews of Dawkins, remarking that he finds it disturbing that Thomas Nagel dismisses Dawkins as an "amateur philosopher" while Eagleton "sneers at Dawkins for his lack of theological training." Weinberg asks, "Are we to conclude that opinions on matters of philosophy or religion are only to be expressed by experts, not mere scientists or other common folks?" Weinberg's own criticisms tend to be offered as augmentations of or turns on Dawkins's interpretations.

Weinberg, for instance, takes up Dawkins's rejection of the classic "proofs" of the existence of God, saying, "I agree with Dawkins in his rejection of these proofs, but I would have answered them a little differently." While the "cosmological proof" – which posits God as a First Cause in a universe governed by cause-and-effect – is not much better logically than other proofs, "it does have a certain appeal for physicists," Weinberg admits. Since this is a discussion to which Dawkins gives especially short shrift, Weinberg is worth citing here:

> In essence, [the cosmological proof] argues that everything has a cause, and since this chain of causality cannot go on forever, it must terminate in a first cause, which we call God. The idea of an ultimate cause is deeply attractive and indeed the dream of elementary particle physics is to find the final theory at the root of all chains of explanation of what we see in nature. The trouble is that such a mathematical final theory would hardly be what anyone means by God. Who prays to quantum mechanics? The believer may justly argue that no theory of physics can be a first cause, since we would still wonder why nature is governed by that theory rather than some other. Yet, in the same sense, God cannot be a first cause either, for whatever our conception of God we could still wonder why the world is governed by that sort of God, rather than some other.

While the arguments from design and the ontological argument strike me as fairly decisively refuted, the cosmological argument, although it doesn't provide much reason to think there's a God, is still in play because our explanations of the origin of everything are still unsettled. Here, if anywhere, we're close to what Allen Orr calls "matters of ultimate meaning that stand at the edge of intelligibility and that are among the most difficult to articulate."

The other point where Weinberg differs with Dawkins is the respective weight to be given to the intransigence of Islam compared to Christianity. Weinberg sees considerable "weakening of religious certitude in the Christian West," much of which can be laid at the door of science, "but this has not happened to anything like the same extent in the world of Islam. One finds in Islamic countries not only religious opposition to specific scientific theories, as occasionally in the West, but a widespread religious hostility to science itself … In the areas of science I know best, though there are talented scientists of Muslim origin working productively in the West, for forty years I have not seen a single paper by a physicist or astronomer in a Muslim country worth reading. This is despite the fact that in the ninth century, when science barely existed in Europe, the greatest centre of scientific research in the world was the House of Wisdom in Baghdad."

Weinberg observes that "Dawkins treats Islam as just another deplorable religion, but there is a difference. The difference lies in the extent to which religious certitude lingers in the Islamic world, and in the harm it does. Richard Dawkins's even-handedness is well-intentioned, but it is misplaced. I share his lack of respect for all religions, but in our times it is folly to disrespect them all equally."

One of the most interesting of the reviews of *The God Delusion*, certainly the most interesting philosophically, is that of Thomas Nagel ("The Problem with Atheism," *New Republic*, Oct. 23, 2006). Nagel is the well-respected author of *The View from Nowhere*, an introductory philosophy primer called *What Does It All Mean?* and several collections of essays. He takes Dawkins's blunt polemic pretty much in stride. Dawkins, he notes, "attacks religion with all the weapons at his disposal, and as a result the book is a very uneven collection of scriptural ridicule, amateur philosophy, historical and contemporary horror stories, anthropological speculations, and cosmological argument." The various pyrotechnics "will certainly serve to attract attention," Nagel notes, "but they are not what make the book interesting."

Rather, "the important message is a theoretical one, about the reach of a certain kind of scientific explanation." At the core of the book, "Dawkins sets out with care his position on a question of which the importance cannot be exaggerated: the question of what explains the existence and character of the astounding natural order we can observe in the universe we inhabit." Nagel then traces out Dawkins's refutation of the standard arguments for belief in God, concentrating on the "design" argument, and offering his own sophisticated critique of it, which I won't attempt to reprise fully here. There are two parts to the reply to design. The positive part offers the theory of evolution by natural selection as one capable of explaining the existence of complex organisms like eyes. The negative part of the argument, Nagel says, "asserts that the hypothesis of design by God is useless ... because it just pushes the problem back one step. In other words: who made God?"

It's in this part of the debate about design that Nagel thinks Dawkins has made a mistake. "If the argument is supposed to show that a supremely adept and intelligent natural being, with a super-body and a super-brain, is responsible for the design and the creation of life on earth, then of course this 'explanation' is no advance on the phenomenon to be explained: if the existence of plants, animals and people requires an explanation, then the existence of such a super-being would require explanation for exactly the same reason."

But this is not what the concept of God entails, Nagel argues. "God, whatever he may be, is not a complex physical inhabitant of the natural world. The explanation of his existence as a chance concatenation of atoms is not a possibility for which we must find an alternative, because that is not what anybody means by God," says Nagel. Leave aside Nagel's loose use of "anybody" here. Obviously, lots of people mean lots of things when they refer to God, including a substantial, personalized version, who answers his cell phone, even late at night. Matters are further complicated when we take aboard Christianity's Jesus, who was a "concatenation of atoms." But Nagel's point is this: "If the God hypothesis makes sense at all, it offers a different kind of explanation from those of physical science: purpose or intention of a mind without a body, capable nevertheless of creating and forming the entire physical world. The point of the hypothesis is to claim that not all explanation is physical, and that there is a mental, purposive or intentional explanation more fundamental than the basic laws of physics, because it explains even them." If there is a God, it has to be the sort of thing outside of space and time whose existence can't be explained by causation.

Nagel pushes on from there, and his thinking is fascinating. A much more extended version of it than his review of Dawkins is available online in an earlier essay: Thomas Nagel, "Secular Philosophy and the Religious Temperament," Sept. 11, 2005. I'm not sure that the arguments that Nagel explores there are the sort that would be of interest to the readers at whom Dawkins is aiming, but of course it would be reassuring to other readers if Dawkins indicated that he was aware of such intellectual currents. Nagel's argument is not a God hypothesis argument, but it is a challenge to and a consideration of the limits of scientific arguments. As a by-the-way, I should also note that a not dissimilar case from the science side is made by geneticist Francis Collins, who led the Human Genome Project. Collins's views are available in his book *The Language of God: A Scientist Presents Evidence for Belief* (2006) and in his debate with Dawkins in *Time* magazine (the latter is available online).

4

Like many of Dawkins's critics, friendly and hostile, I wish that *The God Delusion* were a better book, and I'll explain in what ways I would want it better below, but the point I want to emphasize first is that it may be a good enough book for the moment. Dawkins, with his polemical approach and roughshod ways, has succeeded in putting atheism on the agenda in the public forum (even if only a "middle-brow" public forum) for the first time in years. And that's important.

If hundreds of millions of people subscribe with certitude to beliefs that are likely false, and those beliefs have public consequences (for politics, morality, and other aspects of social life), then the act of challenging such beliefs is a public service. Though Steven Weinberg may be right that the degree of certitude about religious beliefs is weaker in the West than in the realm of Islam, nonetheless the most recent polls I've seen report that more than 80 per cent of Americans claim to believe in God without any doubts. Further, polls about evolutionary theory suggest that only about 35 per cent of U.S. citizens believe that it is a sound scientific theory. I don't know if that adds up to delusionary thinking, but it certainly strikes me as cause for worry about the public mentality. But when Weinberg says, "I share [Dawkins'] lack of respect for all religions, but in our times it is folly to disrespect them all equally," he has a point. In the response to Islam in discussions in the West, there has been a lot of tip-toeing, distinguishing our respect for the vaster portion of "good" Islam from our objection to the small minority of extremist "bad" Islam. This attitude results in a distorted reading of majoritarian Islam, I think, and avoids challenging the tenets of Islam at all.

In wishing that Dawkins had written a better book, I should note that better books about atheism already exist. British philosopher Julian Baggini's *Atheism: A Very Short Introduction* is one of them. Part of Oxford's "very short introductions" series, Baggini's book is more modest, temperate, brief, and philosophically sound than *The God Delusion*. But Baggini doesn't command the public attention or star-power of Dawkins, his book is an even-tempered pamphlet rather than a blockbuster wrapped in a silver jacket, and accordingly it has sold modestly, rather than cracking best-seller lists.

The better book I'd like to see would be less about atheism and more about a-theism. That is, instead of insisting on atheism, I would put more emphasis on the argument that there aren't any good reasons for believing in God, and there are lots of good reasons for withholding our belief in the supernatural. Let me be quick to point out that I'm not arguing for a third position, agnosticism, the view that it's equally impossible to determine whether there is or isn't a God and therefore one should suspend all judgment. It seems to me that the preponderance of evidence and conceptual thinking suggests that God is unlikely.

Generally, there are five arguments for believing in a God: 1) personal experience, 2) authority, 3) logic or the "ontological argument," 4) design or the "teleological argument," and 5) the "cosmological argument." The briefest replies to those arguments are as follows:

1 Personal experiences of supernatural beings are notoriously unreliable, and many "religious experiences" can be reproduced by natural means in laboratories.
2 Authority can mean beliefs acquired through cultural indoctrination, but more often refers to documents like the Bible, Koran, or the Book of Mormon. All of these works are pre- or anti-scientific, produced by marginalised credulous groups, and unsubstantiated by any other evidence. They also contain, as Dawkins takes some pleasure in pointing out, a host of wacky assertions.
3 The ontological argument, invented by St. Anselm in medieval times, is a logical or semantic tongue-twister that says that the most perfect being we can conceive of must exist or else it wouldn't be the most perfect being, therefore God exists. A fellow monk of Anselm's pointed out that by that reasoning then there must also be a perfect island or a perfect whatever you can think of (say, a perfect hockey team). Others have pointed to the argument's circularity – that in order to get to belief in a God in this way you pretty much have to start out with such a belief.
4 The design argument is the one that has garnered most contemporary attention because of the debate in the U.S. over teaching "Intelligent Design" theories alongside evolution in schools. But the real argument over design, that God designed life on earth (and the rest of the universe) was first successfully refuted by Darwin's *Origin of Species* in 1859, and everything we've learned since from geology, archeology, and biology in the last century and a half supports Darwin's theory. Evolution, with

its extinctions, monstrosities, and quirky mutations, seems to demonstrate, as Dawkins has vigorously argued in his previous books, that life doesn't appear to start out with neat design, but with development of life forms by natural selection in relation to specific environments, and that design is a late arrival on the set.

5 The classic cosmological argument, advanced by Thomas Aquinas in the 13th century, is largely a conceptual argument about causation, and it runs into, as Dawkins insists, the problem of what caused the First Cause. This is the only form of the argument that Dawkins attends to, but there are more modern forms of cosmological investigation that are more interesting and relevant, of the sort that interest Steven Weinberg. I think this is where, if anywhere, we can satisfy demands like those of Allen Orr to "engage religious thought in [a] serious way" and address "matters of ultimate meaning." It's also the place where Nagel's challenge to "physical explanations" becomes pertinent.

The modern version of scientific cosmology focuses on the Big Bang theory of the origins of the universe. As writers such as Simon Singh in *Big Bang* (2004) and physicist Brian Greene in *The Fabric of the Cosmos* (2004) explain, we have a fairly good, albeit weird, evolutionary account of the universe since its inception about 14 billion years ago. An infinitesimal "something" explodes, initiating both time and space (and eventually, us). The temptation, however, is to ask, What caused the Big Bang, or, What was there before the Big Bang? The technical answer is either Nothing, or We Don't Know. But more important, can we even sensibly ask such a question? How can you ask about "before" when there is no time prior to the singular event that also "creates" time, and how can you ask about "there" or "where" before you have "space"?

In the inability to answer questions about the origin of the Big Bang or to even conceptualize questions about the origination of the "laws of nature," there's a conceptual opening. I don't know if it's an opening for a God, and if it is, it doesn't, as Weinberg points out, seem much like the God of the major monotheisms or even the God who is often effusively praised by wide receivers in football games, but it's an opening for "something." In the vastness of time and space, and in light of the recognition of our relative insignificance and mortal conclusion, you can see how someone might be tempted by such a "something," and might further be tempted to think of it as a "Higher Something." I don't think such thinking yields anything more than 17th and 18th century Deism, but Deism is at least the most rational and least offensive of the theisms.

It's this sort of thinking that leads to suggestions like that of Thomas Nagel when he says, "If the God hypothesis makes sense at all, it offers a different kind of explanation from those of physical science: purpose or intention of a mind without a body, capable nevertheless of creating and forming the entire physical world." The problem with such a hypothesis is that there's not any substantial evidence or any good reason to think that it might be true. Sure, it's possible that "not all explanation is physical, and that there is a mental, purposive or intentional explanation more fundamental than the basic laws of physics, because it explains even them," but what gives us grounds for thinking so other than our inability to explain ultimate matters?

Although Dawkins touches on the case for atheism, I find Baggini's account to be more satisfyingly explicit. The bottom line of the argument against theism is that there simply isn't strong evidence for a God or anything else supernatural, and in fact, there's quite a bit of what might be called "negative" evidence suggesting the absence of evidence for God, or simply the non-existence of God. On the positive side of Baggini's case for atheism, there's overwhelming evidence for the existence of the natural world and the mortality of human beings, and no evidence for anything else. For example, everything we know about consciousness suggests that minds, thoughts, sentences, and even "selves" are produced by material, finite brains, and nothing leads us to think that minds are a feature of souls that continue to exist after our deaths.

A lot of the debate, pro and con, as the paragraph above suggests, hinges on notions of evidence, a philosophic issue that Dawkins doesn't explicitly address. What constitutes evidence, and especially good evidence, Baggini admits, "is a big issue, but the key general principle is that evidence is stronger if it is available to inspection by more people on repeated occasions; and worse if it is confined to the testimony of a small number of people on limited occasions." Baggini argues that "all the strong evidence tells in favour of atheism, and only weak evidence tells against it. In any ordinary case, this would be enough to establish that atheism is true. The situation is comparable to that of water freezing at zero degrees centigrade; all the strong evidence suggests it does. Only the weak evidence of anecdote, myth, hearsay, and illusionists tells against it." In the case of theism, the concrete evidence is uniformly weak: it ranges from miraculously weeping statues of saints and the textual claims of biblical books, to near-death experiences and psychics who claim to be able to contact the dead. What evidence there is for God, the afterlife, heaven, and miracles is all far from "strong evidence" available to inspection by everybody on repeated occasions.

One sort of argument frequently heard in theistic debates concerns the inconvenient refusal of God to make a definitive appearance. The theistic reply to this rude fact is often the invocation of the principle that "absence of evidence is not evidence of absence." Sometimes this is couched in the form of a challenge: "Well, you can't prove that God doesn't exist, can you?" The answer to that is, No, you can't *prove* that God doesn't exist, but people who don't believe God exists don't have to prove God doesn't exist; the burden of proof for the existence of something as extraordinary as God rests with the claimant. Or, as Baggini puts it, "Indeed, it is hard to see what other evidence there could be for something *not* being there other than the failure to find any evidence that it *is* there. Something which does not exist leaves no mark, so it can only be an absence of marks of its existence that can provide evidence for its non-existence." Further, this sort of absence "really is strong evidence for absence." Admittedly, this discussion of evidence doesn't deal with Nagel's idea of explanations beyond our ordinary notions of evidence and reasons, but frankly, I don't know what to do about that sort of claim except to shrug and admit, almost anything is possible.

It's not completely fair to say that Dawkins refuses to engage religion in a serious way, but I understand what his critics are pointing at. Dawkins does talk about the natural universe, in both his opening and concluding chapters, evoking the wonder and beauty of it all, but he insists that our appreciation of it can't be supported by prosthetic deities, and he's not inclined to engage in the minute or transcendental claims of theology. I think a more modest and temperate argument, one that emphasizes that there aren't any good reasons for believing in God, ought to be more sympathetic to the spiritual impulse.

Though I don't agree with believers, I have considerable empathy for their yearnings. The prospect of living in a purposeless universe as a self-conscious animal whose end is mere mortality strikes me as a scary proposition. If belief in God entails weird propositions, it should also be admitted that evolution and Big Bang physics, although we have good reason to think both are true, are also very weird truths. It's easy to see why people would want to believe in a deity, even as one is arguing that there aren't any good reasons to believe in God. I don't see why we wouldn't want to make that admission; resistance to doing so strikes me as a kind of inhuman coldness. Or, as the novelist Julian Barnes expresses this sentiment in the opening line of his meditation on death, *Nothing To Be Frightened Of* (2008), "I don't believe in God, but I miss Him."

Similarly, the historical ubiquity of religion strikes me as fairly natural for the kind of evolving creatures we are. Dawkins has a substantial chapter on the "roots of religion" in which he offers a rather complicated account based on evolutionary psychology. I think the answer is evolutionary, but simpler. Given the kind of beings we've evolved to be, it seems reasonable that our hypothesizing would go beyond what might be just beyond the immediate horizon (food, mates, predators) and extend to a natural desire to want to understand "what it all means," and that in the course of the development of our intelligence religious explanations would come into play. As we know more, it also seems reasonable that at a certain historical point, atheistic explanations would come into play.

In addition to discussing religion's spread over time and geography, Dawkins has a similar chapter about whether we can be moral without God, and again he offers a complex account rooted in evolutionary psychology, an interesting but still speculative sub-discipline. Once more, this over-complicates matters. I think the ethical issue is relatively straightforward. It's simply not the case that if there isn't a God, social chaos will ensue. Humans are social animals who prefer to live with each other and are likely, in the course of evolution, to recognize that in order to do so, whether or not there's a God, they have to devise some rules, such as not arbitrarily killing each other, and institutions to support those rules. The reason we can be moral without God is that we are capable of moral discourse. Of course, there's no guarantee that people, left to their own devices, will produce a democratic, egalitarian moral order, but then, people left to God's devices have produced more than their share of moral tyrannies.

At the outset of his book, Dawkins offers a little pep talk about how to be a happy atheist. So do other advocates of atheism. Baggini, for instance, devotes a chapter of his book to meaningful meanings of life for atheists. But I think that's only part of the story. Both Dawkins and Baggini do their best to put a good face on the prospect of life in a universe without a pre-ordained purpose, life which ends in death. I'm more inclined to think, as other philosophers have put it, that there's also a "tragic sense" to life. The tragedy of death can be mitigated by various experiences, in art, eros, mountain-climbing, the creation of non-violent civil arrangements and much more, all of which might add up to a "good life," but I see no good reason to deny that it all occurs within a context of senseless mortality. Given that we've become more self-conscious about the absurdity of death in recent centuries, I suppose that ought to incline us to be more sympathetic to various efforts to extend life, if not necessarily to embark upon the sort of immortality project that futurist Ray Kurzweil describes in his book, *The Singularity Is Near: When Humans Transcend Biology* (2005).

Finally, there are a couple of issues where I find Dawkins's intransigence puzzling. There's the matter of the political record of theism and atheism in power. Dawkins is dodgy on this issue. He's vehement in discussing the harms that religion has caused. But when it comes to accounting for tyrants who happened not to be believers, such as Hitler or Stalin, Dawkins tends to twist and turn. Well, they weren't really atheists, or they weren't atheists when they were being murderous tyrants, or whatever. I think it would be a lot more straightforward to admit that both faith-based politicians and anti-clerical or atheistic politicians have been tyrants. Being an atheist political leader or an atheist society doesn't guarantee good government. What produces good government is good politics, and what good politics are and how we decide is another argument altogether.

The other puzzling issue is the one Weinberg flags, that of Dawkins's blanket condemnation of all religions without discrimination. I don't see either the intellectual point of his move here, or its strategic purpose. It's true that the religions to be castigated are not merely those with the most bizarre, cult-like beliefs. Broad swaths of Roman Catholicism and mainstream American Protestantism as well as much of Islam deserve vigorous challenge. But at the same time, there are denominations whose beliefs are intellectually substantial and whose public consequences are not harmful. Why insist that such believers are equally delusional?

Well, that's my idea of a better book about atheism. But I'm moved by Richard Dawkins's public avowal and his success in putting the subject on the public agenda. Certainly, there are a surfeit of lies and delusions in which our lives are immersed. The lies range from the trivial but incessant pounding of commercial advertisements to the familiar mid-level political chicanery to the vastest transcendental claims of religion. In all the noise, both white and dark, it's almost impossible to think. In its way, the value of Dawkins's campaign is to encourage us, borrowing Vaclav Havel's phrase, to attempt to "live in truth."

11

Exit Strategies:
Said, Coetzee, Saramago, Roth

I

It's fitting, I suppose, that I only belatedly read Edward Said's posthumously published *On Late Style: Music and Literature Against the
Grain* (2006). The multi-talented Said, who died in 2003 of leukemia,
at age 67, was a long-time Columbia University literature professor;
a cultural critic; the author of the groundbreaking if tendentious
Orientalism, as well as *Culture and Imperialism*; a Palestinian political activist; the subtle memoirist of *Out of Place*; and a non-profes-
sional but accomplished pianist. In *On Late Style*, Said is interested,
"for obvious personal reasons" – i.e., his own medical condition – in
"the last or late period of life, the decay of the body, the onset of ill
health or other factors that … bring on the possibility of an untimely
end." He proposes to "focus on great artists and how, near the end of
their lives, their work and thought acquires a new idiom, what I shall
be calling a late style."

   As literary critic Michael Wood, who edited and introduces this
final volume of Said's writing, says about one of the two key terms
in *On Late Style*, "It's worth pausing over the delicately shifting
meanings of the word *late*, ranging from missed appointments
through the cycles of nature to vanished life. Most frequently perhaps *late* just means 'too late,' later than we should be, not on time.
But late evenings, late blossoms, and late autumns are perfectly
punctual … Dead persons have certainly got themselves beyond
time, but then what difficult temporal longing lurks in our calling
them 'late'? Lateness doesn't name a single relation to time, but it
always brings time in its wake."

Said's notion of late style carries a particular twist. As he says, we're all familiar with "last works that reflect a special maturity, a new spirit of reconciliation and serenity often expressed in terms of a miraculous transfiguration of common reality," such as Shakespeare's *The Tempest*. "Each of us can readly supply evidence of how it is that late works crown a lifetime of aesthetic endeavour," Said says, then asks, "But what of artistic lateness not as harmony and resolution but as intransigence, difficulty, and unresolved contradictions?" Troubled lateness is what Said seeks to explore, what he describes as "late style that involves a non-harmonious, non-serene tension, and above all, a sort of deliberately unproductive productiveness going *against* ..." (ellipsis in the original).

Said's idea of "late style" is directly inspired by Theodor Adorno, the Frankfurt School critical theorist, who first broached the concept in an essay in 1937 on "Beethoven's Late Style." In Said's essays on the subject of late style, he takes up, among his examples, Beethoven, Adorno's reading of that composer as well as Adorno himself, and a diverse array of other musicians, writers, filmmakers, and performers ranging from Mozart to pianist Glenn Gould, with Jean Genet, Giuseppe Tomasi di Lampedusa, Thomas Mann, and Constantine Cavafy included along the way. While the individual judgments may be contestable, the scope and context of Said's discussion are consistently stimulating.

At the very outset, under the heading of "timeliness and lateness," Said's initial contention is that "all of us, by virtue of the simple fact of being conscious, are involved in constantly thinking about and making something of our lives, self-making being one of the bases of history ..." The important distinction for Said "is that between the realm of nature on the one hand and secular human history on the other." The body, in all its conditions, belongs "to the order of nature; what we *understand* of that nature, however, how we see and live it in our consciousness, how we create a sense of our life individually and collectively, subjectively as well as socially, how we divide it into periods, belongs roughly speaking to the order of history." Our reflections on our selves are part of the process of making those selves.

"I have for years been studying this self-making process through three great problematics," Said notes, briefly reprising his investigations of beginnings and mid-life continuities, "the exfoliation from a beginning" toward "youth, reproductive generation, maturity."

In the passages of human life, "there is assumed to be a generally abiding *timeliness*," meaning "that what is appropriate to earlier life is not appropriate to later stages." Those "later stages" of life are the third problematic and the focus of Said's book. It's at this point, at the end of one's time, that Said raises the possibility not of *timeliness* – "the accepted notion of age and wisdom in some last works that reflect ... a new spirit of reconciliation and serenity" – but its obverse, *lateness*. For Said, the artistic lateness of most interest is not that of "harmony and resolution" but "intransigence, difficulty, and unresolved contradictions." Said doesn't exactly say why he's so fascinated with this this "sort of deliberately unproductive productiveness going *against* ... ," but perhaps it lies in Said's self-description as a "profoundly secular person." For someone who doesn't allow him- or herself metaphysical consolation, perhaps the prospect of death ought to provoke not reconciliation but unresolved contradiction. Anything else would be, in the existentialist sense, "bad faith."

It is here that Said turns to Adorno on Beethoven's late works: the last piano sonatas and bagatelles, the Ninth Symphony, and the last half-dozen string quartets. "For Adorno, far more than for anyone else who has spoken of Beethoven's last works," Said says, "those compositions ... constitute an event in the history of modern culture: a moment when the artist who is fully in command of his medium nevertheless abandons communication with the established social order of which he is part and achieves a contradictory, alienated relationship with it. His late works constitute a form of exile." In Beethoven, and in Adorno's reading of him, Said says, "Late style is what happens if art does not abdicate its rights in favour of reality."

He adds, "The reason Beethoven's late style so gripped Adorno throughout his writing is that, in a completely paradoxical way, Beethoven's immobilized and socially resistant final works are at the core of what is new in modern music of our own time." Here, we must recall that these are hardly judgments from the sidelines: Adorno, as an occasional composer and pianist himself, and the musically competent Said are both speaking from the keyboard and not merely from a lectern.

Said then addresses Adorno's own "lateness" and finds in his "astonishingly bold and bleak ruminations on the position of the aging artist" something close to what seems, for Adorno, to be "*the* fundamental aspect of aesthetics and of his own work as critical theorist

and philosopher." Said is quick to admit that "no one needs to be reminded that Adorno is exceptionally difficult to read, whether in his
original German or in any number of translations." Adorno's prose
style, says Said, "violates various norms: he assumes little community
of understanding between himself and his audience; he is slow, un-
journalistic, unpackageable, unskimmable. Even an autobiographical
text like *Minima Moralia* is an assault on biography, narrative, or
anecdotal community; its form exactly replicates its subtitle –
Reflections from damaged life – a cascading series of discontinuous
fragments, all of them in some way assaulting suspicious 'wholes.'"

Perhaps this is a sufficient tracking of Said's text to suggest the
richness of his writing and thought. In each of the essays, no matter
how unpromising the subject may seem at the outset, I found some
observation of Said's, some thought, worth underlining in order to
return to it again, later. Even when I'm not sure if Said establishes his
case for a particular work as an example of late style, he makes even
a skeptical reader interested in taking another look at whatever it is
that's engaged his attention.

In a summary moment in his not quite completed final book, Said
says, "Each of the figures I have discussed here makes of lateness or
untimeliness, and a vulnerable maturity, a platform for alternative
and unregimented modes of subjectivity, at the same time that each
– like the late Beethoven – has a lifetime of technical effort and preparation." All of them, from Adorno to Glenn Gould, says Said, "play
off the great totalizing codes" of their culture and times. "It is as if
having achieved age, they want none of its supposed serenity or maturity, or any of its amiability or official ingratiation. Yet in none of
them is mortality denied or evaded, but keeps coming back as the
theme of death which undermines, and strangely elevates their uses
of language and the aesthetic."

2

Although Said's concept of late-work-against-the-grain is provocative, my own interest in this subject is rather more orthodox. Lately
(pun inevitable), like most critics of "a certain age," I've become more
focused on writers of pensionable vintage. Not only are they age
mates of mine, but the first decade of the 21st century marks the ending of generations of writers, born mostly in the 1920s, 30s, and 40s,

whose careers shaped the literary landscape of the second half of the preceding century. My attention is not so much on artists whose late works "constitute a form of exile," as Said describes them, but simply with how various writers have dealt/are dealing with their old age in terms of productivity and subject matter, as well as style.

My focus is more on what might be called "exit strategies," in Thomas Hobbes's blunt sense of seeking "a hole to crawl out of this world from." Of course, as the English novelist Margaret Drabble observes about the "gloomy reflections" in her memoir, *The Pattern in the Carpet: A Personal History with Jigsaws* (2009), they are "fitting for one in her seventieth year, an age at which we are obliged to work out survival strategies." So exit strategies are simultaneously tactics for going on. In some instances, such as those of John Updike, Norman Mailer, and possibly Kurt Vonnegut, all of whom died in the first decade of the 21st century, while their last years were more or less prolific (Updike, more; Vonnegut less), their late writings don't strike me as crucial to their body of work, either in terms of resistance or resolution. Something similar can be said about the later works of V.S. Naipaul, Gore Vidal, and perhaps Doris Lessing, at least to date. (I hesitate about Vonnegut because his final novel, *Timequake* (1997), written a decade before his death, seems to me a masterpiece, though that's not a view shared by most critics. Similarly, I hesitate about Lessing because of how taken I am with the title novella of her *The Grandmothers: Four Short Novels* (2003), a wicked adult fairy tale about pederastic love that she published in her mid-80s.)

It also seems to me that whether or not a writer produces memorable late works should not be regarded as a crucial measure of that writer's oeuvre. If a writer does, that provides an additional dimension to our understanding of the work; if not, then not. That is, I don't want to overburden the idea of late work. But with writers like Saul Bellow, Czeslaw Milosz, Ryszard Kapuscinski, J.M. Coetzee, Jose Saramago, and Philip Roth, the exit strategies have been explicit and profoundly interesting. There are no doubt many others who might be considered – Gunter Grass, Nadine Gordimer, and Gabriel Garcia Marquez come to mind – but let's refrain from an infinite list or else, as Coetzee says, We'll be here all afternoon.

Bellow, who died in 2005 at age 89, opened the new century with an elegiac yet surprisingly buoyant last novel written in his mid-80s,

Ravelstein (2000). It's a portrait of his late friend and sometime intellectual mentor Allan Bloom, the conservative thinker and author of *The Closing of the American Mind*, who died of AIDS in the early 1990s. I don't know if *Ravelstein* exhibits late style in Said's sense, but then again, none of the eponymous protagonists of Bellow's earlier novels, *The Adventures of Augie March, Herzog,* or *Humboldt's Gift,* can be said to bask in "a new spirit of reconciliation and serenity."

Certainly, there's a noticeable stylistic difference between Bellow's first major novel, *Augie March* (1953), and his last one, and the source of the difference is to be found in the constrictions of old age. Compared to the full-bodied impasto oil portraits and detailed scenes of his early work, *Ravelstein* offers looser, sketched-in, watercolour-like backgrounds. Instead of every object receiving equally impartial attention, Bellow picks out a luminescent, surrealistic detail, like the appearance of flocks of wild green parrots on the South Side of Chicago who built "their long sac-like nests in the lake-front park and later colonized the alleys ... in bird tenements that hung from utility poles." Various characters can be casually limned; Bellow only needs to etch with Dureresque precision the figure of Ravelstein who "with his bald powerful head, was at ease with large statements, big issues, and famous men," but whose "Japanese kimono fell away from legs paler than milk ... the calves of a sedentary man – the shinbone long and the calf muscle abrupt, without roundness." It's as if Bellow no longer has time to fill in the whole of the picture, but of necessity now has to practice what Philip Roth calls "compression." And perhaps also as a function of age, he views the fuzzier whole with more compassion.

Bellow's fond portrait of his friend Bloom cuts plenty of slack for a man who might be read as dogmatic, bullying, fiscally wasteful, and painfully self-indulgent. But as Bellow's narrator Chick says, "In my trade you have to make more allowances, taking all sorts of ambiguities into account – to avoid hard-edged judgments. All this refraining may resemble naiveté. But it isn't quite that. In art you become familiar with due process. You can't simply write people off or send them to hell."

The debt that instigates Bellow's short novel, tinged with death on all sides (including an account of the author's own near-death from food poisoning), as well as the always surprising flare-up of desire, is the duty of friendship. The narrator reports that "Ravelstein would

frequently say to me, 'There's something in the way you tell anecdotes that gets to me, Chick. But you need a real subject. I'd like you
to write me up, after I'm gone ...'"

"It depends, doesn't it," Chick replies, "on who beats whom to
the barn?"

The unsentimental Ravelstein brushes off the protocols. "Let's
not have any bullshit about it. You know perfectly well that I'm
about to die ..."

"Of course I knew it. Indeed I did," Chick admits to himself.

"You could do a really fine memoir," Ravelstein tells him, adding,
"It's not just a request. I'm laying this on you as an obligation. Do it
in your after-supper-reminiscence manner, when you've had a few
glasses of wine and you're laid back and making remarks ... I've often
thought how well you deal with a story when you're laid back."

"There was no way I could refuse to do this," Bellow recognizes.

And if *Ravelstein* is wonderfully laid-back, it's also the case that,
as Bellow says, "You don't easily give up a creature like Ravelstein
to death."

3

Each of the writers whose "exit strategies" interest me turns the
prism, through which the refractions of suffering, desire, sickness,
old age and death are seen, in his own distinctive way. The late work
of the Nobel Prize-winning Polish poet Czeslaw Milosz and his journalistic countryman Ryszard Kapuscinski is probably closer to
Edward Said's notion of "serene maturity." As Milosz, who died in
2004 at age 93, says in the poem "Late Ripeness,"

Not soon, as late as the approach of my ninetieth year,
I felt a door opening in me and I entered the clarity of early
morning

But in *Milosz's ABC's* (1997-98; English translation, 2001), in a
passage on "Adam and Eve" and our enduring fascination with the
story of the expulsion from the Garden of Eden, Milosz says, "In our
deepest convictions, reaching into the very depths of our being, we
deserve to live forever. We experience our transitoriness and mortality as an act of violence perpetrated against us."

That unreconciled tone is undergirded with melancholy resignation in a late prose poem, "Pity," which appeared in *Road-side Dog* (1997):

> In the ninth decade of my life, the feeling which rises in me is pity, useless. A multitude, an immense number of faces, shapes, fates of particular beings, and a sort of merging with them from inside, but at the same time my awareness that I will not find anymore the means to offer a home in my poems to these guests of mine, for it is too late.

A similar mixture of maturity and metaphysical unease is also found in the late work of Milosz's compatriot Ryszard Kapuscinski (1932–2007). After a turbulent half-century of incessant wandering around the world as a foreign correspondent, the renowned "literary journalist" and author of many books, including *The Emperor: The Downfall of an Autocrat* (1978), his account of the fall of the regime of Emperor Haile Selassie of Ethiopia, wrote a remarkable last work. Kapuscinski's *Travels with Herodotus* (2004; translated by Klara Glowczewska, 2007) is a memoir about the nature and purpose of investigative reportage.

In it, he recalls that as a young reporter in post–World War II communist-controlled Poland, upon receiving his first international assignment to India, his editor gave her novice foreign correspondent a gift that would last a lifetime. It was a book. Herodotus's *The Histories*, written in Greek 2500 years ago in the 5th century BCE, is regarded as the first work of its kind, and its author, Herodotus of Halicarnassus (in what is now Turkey), is often called "the father of history." Wherever Kapuscinski traveled, he tells us, he carried Herodotus's book in his luggage, across the most improbable borders during a half-century of following stories in Asia, Africa, the Middle East, and elsewhere.

Travels with Herodotus is a memoir of Kapuscinski's career as a writer, written with mature simplicity and filled with lonely and baffling moments in the seeming infinity of India and China, as well as death-defying episodes in various countries of Africa. It is also a close and re-peated "reading" of Herodotus and his book. In a sense, all of Kapuscinski's work is a meditation on the opening lines of *The Histories*:

> Here are presented the results of the enquiry carried out by Herodotus of Halicarnassus. The purpose is to prevent the traces

of human events from being erased by time, and to preserve the fame and remarkable achievements produced by both our own and other peoples, and more particularly, to show how they came into conflict.

In short, Herodotus seeks to preserve memory about both the accomplishments of culture and the causes of war, specifically the conflict between Greeks and Persians at the beginning of the 5th century BCE, shortly before the historian's birth. Herodotus, says Kapuscinski, "was obsessed with memory, fearful on its behalf. He felt that memory is something defective, fragile, impermanent – illusory even. That whatever it contains, whatever it is storing, can evaporate, simply vanish without a trace. His whole generation, everyone living on earth at that time, was possessed by that same fear." Without memory, Kapuscinski argues, we cannot live intelligently; memory tells us who and where we are, yet it is also "unreliable, elusive, treacherous." He adds,

In the world of Herodotus, the only real repository of memory was the individual. In order to find out that which has been remembered, one must reach this person. If he lives far away, one has to go to him, to set out on a journey. And after finally encountering him, one must sit down and listen to what he has to say – to listen, remember, perhaps write it down. That is how reportage begins; of such circumstances it is born.

If Herodotus is known as "the father of history" (the Greek verb from which we derive the word "history" means "to tell stories"), he was also called "the father of lies." Kapuscinski's work, too, especially after his death, was subject to criticism, about whether he got his facts right, as well as his interpretations. His famous book about Haile Selassie consisted of a collage of clandestine testimonies by former officials and servants of the Ethiopian emperor's court. *The Emperor* was read internationally as an example of the innovative "new journalism" of the era and in Kapuscinski's Polish homeland as a sort of Aesop's fable about the autocracy of the ruling Polish communist party. Later, critics questioned Kapuscinski's often unidentified sources and wondered whether the testimonies were strictly factual or partly invented. Herodotus's investigations, wide-ranging and circuitous as they were ("Digressions are part of my plan," Herodotus said), were similarly criticized. While contemporary journalism and non-fiction, although often oblivious to implicit ideological perspectives, insist on sharper boundaries between fact and fancy, in *Travels with Herodotus*, Kapuscinski offers a beautifully written defence of the methods of both his literary ancestor and himself.

Two other prominent senior writers at work throughout the century's first decade, the transplanted-to-Australia, South African-born J.M. Coetzee and Portugal's Jose Saramago, both, like Bellow and Milosz, Nobel Prize winners, make an equally engaging pairing. Coetzee, approaching 70 at the end of the first decade of the 21st century, is often described as reclusive, coldly dour, and decidedly unreconciled (in Said's sense), with a seldom-smiling spare visage and a temperament that puts me in mind of the great and eccentric Austrian novelist Thomas Bernhard. And yet in three novels written in the last decade, *Elizabeth Costello* (2003), *Slow Man* (2005), and *Diary of a Bad Year* (2007), Coetzee ranks with the very best of writers who have unflinchingly faced the grotesqueries of late life and who have remained committed to technical innovation in fiction. Perhaps I should say that Coetzee "arguably" ranks with the best, since there is a fairly long line of critics prepared to argue the worth of his late strategy.

Elizabeth Costello: Eight Lessons is, I think, not only unarguably readable and engaging but also one of the major novels of the decade. The framing device that Coetzee comes up with is that each "lesson" is a little story about a lecture given, often reluctantly, by an aging and famous Australian woman novelist, the title character. Several of these stories, especially those about the pain we inflict on other animals, were delivered as actual lectures by Coetzee. Right from the opening line of the first story, "Realism," there is, in addition to Costello and her son John, who is accompanying his aged mother, an unnamed narrator who offers observations or instructions about the storymaking in which he is engaged. Sometimes it's no more than a blunt stage direction to get on with it: "There is a scene in a restaurant, mainly dialogue, which we will skip." Or, having described Elizabeth Costello preparing herself for an evening out, the narrator intervenes:

The blue costume, the greasy hair, are details, signs of a moderate realism. Supply the particulars, allow the significations to emerge

of themselves. A procedure pioneered by Daniel Defoe. Robinson
Crusoe, cast up on the beach, looks around for his shipmates.
But there are none. "I never saw them afterwards, or any sign of
them," says he, "except three of their hats, one cap, and two
shoes that were not fellows." Two shoes, not fellows: by not being fellows, the shoes have ceased to be footwear and become
proofs of death, torn by the foaming seas off the feet of drowning men and tossed ashore. No large words, no despair, just hats
and caps and shoes.

Costello is presented with an award, prior to giving an acceptance
speech, titled "What is Realism?" But first Coetzee steps in: "The
presentation scene itself we skip. It is not a good idea to interrupt the
narrative too often, since storytelling works by lulling the reader or
listener into a dreamlike state in which the time and space of the real
world fade away, suspended by the time and space of the fiction."
Coetzee admits that breaking into the narrative "plays havoc with
the realist illusion." However, unless he skips, "we will be here all
afternoon," he says, mock-impatiently. In any case, "the skips are
not part of the text, they are part of the performance." I suppose
postmodern critics would describe all this as "destabilizing the text,"
but whatever it is Coetzee is doing in this virtuoso performance, it's
surprisingly compelling. At which point, Elizabeth Costello dons her
reading glasses and commences her lecture, which is about Kafka's
"A Report to an Academy," a story in which an ape gives a lecture to
a learned society about his former life as an ape. Costello says, "We
don't know and will never know, with certainty, what is really going
on in this story." Then she adds,

> There used to be a time when we knew. We used to believe that
> when the text said, "On the table stood a glass of water," there
> was indeed a table, and a glass of water on it, and we had only
> to look in the word-mirror of the text to see them.
>   But all that has ended. The word-mirror is broken, irrepara-
> bly, it seems. About what is really going on in the lecture hall
> your guess is as good as mine: men and men, men and apes,
> apes and men, apes and apes ... The words on the page will
> no longer stand up and be counted, each proclaiming "I mean
> what I mean!"

Each of the stories has a similar literally eccentric, off-centre, character about it. The story about "Realism," which centres on a surrealistic Kafka tale of metamorphosis, is a good example of Coetzee's oddness, given that the realistic details of the ape's report to a learned academy are what make the surrealist basis of the story believable. Each of the stories says something about art, about aging, about the world, and, at the end, about waiting "at the gate," a Kafkaesque gate on whose far side might or might not be another world.

Coetzee's subsequent novels, *Slow Man* and *Diary of a Bad Year*, are far more contested "performances," to put it gently, than the innovative *Elizabeth Costello*. One critic, the novelist Francine Prose, was practically driven up the wall by *Slow Man*, the story of an aging Australian photographer hit by a car while bicycling and his lengthy recuperation after the amputation of part of his leg. "My mixed feelings about Coetzee's earlier work hardly prepared me for, or explained, the strong emotions – feelings that ranged from impatience to a dull rage to a sort of despairing boredom – that overcame me ..." (Francine Prose, ".The Plot Doesn't Thicken," www.slate. com, Sept. 14, 2005).

Another reviewer, Robert MacFarlane, in the London *Sunday Times*, who wittily describes Coetzee as "one of the great novelists of omission ... He has always eschewed more than he has bitten off," judged that *Slow Man* "is not only unmistakably Coetzee's least accomplished work, it is also, by more general standards, a mediocre novel." Few critics were much kinder, and most of them were appalled that in the middle of the novel, almost out of nowhere, Elizabeth Costello, the protagonist of Coetzee's previous novel, turns up at the Slow Man's door in order to try to speed him up. The critics resented getting halfway into a book only to be met by the possibility that the protagonist was merely the creature of a story being written by a fictional author.

Yet, isn't Coetzee's *Slow Man* an example of Edward Said's notion of late style? The elderly Nobel Prize winner declines all notions of reconciliation and serenity, instead giving us characters filled with "intransigence, difficulty, and unresolved contradiction" and, to make matters worse, a narrative of tottering uncertainty. Despite it all, including *longeurs* in the text that made me at one point fantasize about what it would be like if Coetzee suddenly decided to turn the Slow Man's tale into Rocket Man pornography, there is something there, something about the struggle, not necessarily successful, against stasis and silence in our diminishing existence.

Coetzee's more recent *Diary of a Bad Year* fared better with the critics. In it, Coetzee tells the story of an aging, prominent South African novelist now resident in Australia, who bears more than a passing resemblance to J.M. Coetzee, as he writes a series of op-ed pieces under the heading "Strong Opinions," and at the same time is "uselessly afflicted with desire" (as critic James Wood puts it) for a young woman neighbour named Anya who lives in his apartment building and whom he hires to type his writing. Coetzee divides the printed page into three parts: at the top is the "strong opinion" piece he's writing, in the middle his account of his infatuation with the young woman, and at the bottom, her view of the awkward relationship, although there are occasional variations.

The exit strategy here is a weaving of worldly reflections with a tale of not entirely futile desire in late life. The opinions wander across a wide range of topics: democracy, terrorism, Guantanamo Bay prison camp, pedophilia, the fate of animals (as always), intelligent design, Bach, aging, and, inevitably, the writing life. About the latter, Coetzee or his alter ego says,

> During the years I spent as a professor of literature, conducting young people on tours of books that would always mean more to me than to them, I would cheer myself up by telling myself that at heart I was not a teacher but a novelist. And indeed, it was as a novelist rather than as a teacher that I won a modest reputation.
>
> But now the critics voice a new refrain. At heart he is not a novelist after all, they say, but a pedant who dabbles in fiction. And I have reached a stage in my life when I begin to wonder whether they are not right – whether, all the time I thought I was going about in disguise, I was in fact naked.

Meanwhile, down in the apartment tower's basement laundry room (and at the bottom of the page), "As I watched her an ache, a metaphysical ache, crept over me that I did nothing to stem. And in an intuitive way she knew about it, knew that in the old man in the plastic chair there was something personal going on, something to do with age and regret and the tears of things."

So, that's the way it is. We have, as long as we're able, something to say about the world, and we recognize, as the poet Robin Blaser put it, that "the love I never conquered when young / will end as such" as we prepare to "pay death's duty."

4

At the far end of the emotional spectrum from Coetzee are the late works of Jose Saramago, the author of an extraordinary series of a half-dozen or more playfully grim "what if" fables. The Portuguese master, who died in June 2010, at 87, was productive to the end, writing in his final decade not only several more parable-like novels but even a year-long internet blog in 2009, which was promptly made available in book form as *The Notebook* (2010).

The best known of Saramago's speculative fictions is *Blindness* (1995), in which a city is struck by a mysterious and contagious plague of sightlessness and soon reduced to conditions of barbarism. Both before and after that landmark novel, there are equally innovative fantasies: in one, the Iberian landmass is detached from Europe and sails the oceans as *The Stone Raft* (1986); in another, a lonely proof reader wilfully changes a single word in a text about *The History of the Siege of Lisbon* (1989) in an effort to alter the course of history. Saramago's imagination remained fertile throughout the first decade of the century. In his mid-80s, Saramago proposed, in *Death with Interruptions* (2006; English translation by Margaret Jull Costa, 2008), that death herself (but only lower-case "death," she insists) takes a sort of romantic holiday, leaving in her wake social chaos.

In a sense, all of Saramago's writings are late works, considering that he had such an unusually belated beginning, only becoming a full-time writer in his mid-50s. Born in 1922 to a family of impoverished peasants, Saramago was educated and worked as a mechanic, and only gradually and tentatively, by way of journalism, made his way to the literary trade. After an initial attempt at writing, Saramago fell into a sort of artistic silence for some three decades, finally emerging in the late 1970s with something equivalent to a "first novel." Only in his mid-60s did he write what is consensually regarded as a masterpiece, *The Year of the Death of Ricardo Reis* (1986), a meditation on the greatest writer in 20th century Portugal, Fernando

Pessoa, and the conditions of life under the Iberian dictatorships of the 1930s. To make matters more personally difficult, Saramago became and remained an unrepentant communist, to the dismay of some of his admirers. As the American literary scholar Harold Bloom puts it, "Saramago's novels are endlessly inventive, endlessly good-natured, endlessly skillful, but it baffles me why the man can't grow up politically."

In Saramago's mordantly comic *Death with Interruptions*, on New Year's Eve, people in an unnamed landlocked country of 10 million inhabitants, one equipped with the usual institutional accoutrements of modern society, suddenly stop dying. Though some may object to the immaturity of Saramago's leftist politics, his political satire on church, government, media, "maphia," and various branches of the funeral industry (now reduced to burying cats and dogs) will strike most readers as "deadly" accurate in this depiction of the effects of temporary immortality.

From the outset, the pace is simultaneously brisk but leisurely, and the tone is mock-dry:

> The following day, no one died. This fact, being absolutely contrary to life's rules, provoked enormous and, in the circumstances, perfectly justifiable anxiety in people's minds, for we have only to consider that in the entire forty volumes of universal history there is no mention, not even one exemplary case, of such a phenomenon ever having occurred, for a whole day to go by, with its generous allowance of twenty-four hours, diurnal and nocturnal, matutinal and vespertine, without one death from an illness, a fatal fall, or a successful suicide, not one, not a single one. Not even from a car accident, so frequent on festive occasions, when blithe irresponsibility and an excess of alcohol jockey for position on the roads to decide who will reach death first.

At first ordinary people are thrilled, at last in possession of "humanity's greatest dream since the beginning of time." But cooler, more calculating minds, those of authority, soon prevail. All the major institutions of power quickly come to view the end of death as a calamity. If people live forever, what will happen to the pension system? Funeral homes and life insurance companies will be driven out of business. The initial good news threatens to turn into a social catastrophe. "If we don't start dying again, we have no future," the prime minister tells the king.

All of this is delivered with Saramago's trademark eccentric punctuation. His tales are constructed in long run-on sentences marked only by commas, in which the characters' thoughts and dialogue, as well as the observations of the narrator, are undifferentiated. And who is the presiding narrative personality of this and other fictions? Saramago adopts the wry tone of the Portuguese peasant he was as a youth.

Then, halfway through, after we've pretty much got the absurdist picture, and just as death has suspended the "moratorium" on death as a botched experiment, there's a surprising turn in the tale. The surprise is for the title character, that shrouded rack of bones with only a scythe for companionship, who nonetheless has the shape-shifting power to become a corporeal being, say, an attractive young woman in her 30s. In the course of her professional duties, death runs into a cellist. Not a great cellist like Rostropovich, perhaps, but one good enough to perform the occasional solo when it's called for by the symphony orchestra that employs him. He's a rather lonely cellist of 50, with a dog, whose amusements are as modest as walks in the park, and whose evening repast is as humble as cellophane-wrapped sandwiches. Something about this cellist, not to put too fine a pun on it, strikes a chord in death.

What makes this late work of Saramago's not only thoroughly enjoyable but in fact joyous, at least to my mind (other critics accorded it those dreaded "mixed reviews"), is that its creator allows us to momentarily imagine an eternal version of the only paradise worth having, life itself. For a stretch of just under two hundred pages we are permitted to doff the unbearable weightiness of being that is contained in the perpetual reminder of mortality. All the while, of course, we continue to know what's in store for us, though as Saramago said in a late interview, "The worst that death has is that you were here, and now you're not."

5

Finally, there's Philip Roth. Or perhaps I should say, best of all, there's Philip Roth. Of all the writers of the decade whose late works invite consideration, no account of a writer's development is more remarkable than that of Roth. For many readers, fellow writers, and critics (including myself), Roth, who marked his 75th year in 2008, is regarded as the pre-eminent living novelist in the United States.

Born in 1933, Roth was recognized as early as his first books, *Goodbye, Columbus* (1959) and *Letting Go* (1962), as a leading literary figure of his generation, as well as the heir to the Jewish-American novelists of the preceding period, Bellow, Bernard Malamud, and Henry Roth.

With his scandalous bestseller *Portnoy's Complaint* (1969), which appeared in the midst of the so-called sexual revolution, and ever since, through a dozen subsequent volumes that brought him into mid-life, Roth has been something of a controversial figure, often described as a disloyal troublemaker within his own ethnic community. It was that infra-Jewish discomfiture that partially inspired Roth to pen *The Ghost Writer* (1979), the first of what would turn out to be a nine-volume cycle of novels featuring a sort of literary alter ego, Nathan Zuckerman.

In that brief novel, set in the mid-1950s, a retrospectively seen account written some two decades after the events it depicts, the young Zuckerman, who has published only his first troublemaking-among-his-Jewish-kin stories, visits the New England rural retreat of his literary hero, E.I. Lonoff, a short-story author of exquisite restraint, thought to be partly modeled on Malamud. The aesthetic argument of the book in fact turns on Lonoff's controlled passion and isolated operating mode, turning a sentence over again and again, versus Zuckerman's raging exuberance.

By the way, the question of the relationship or identity between Zuckerman and Roth, or even between "Philip Roth" and Roth (the former turns up as a narrator in several of Roth's books), or even of that between the fictional Lonoff and his real-life sources, is, as the critic Clive James notes, "a Mobius striptease" issue that has no resolution, and really doesn't need one.

The living muse of *The Ghost Writer*, a young woman graduate student of Lonoff's, is named Amy Bellette. In the uproarious course of this one-night sleepover at the backwoods home of Lonoff and his wife of some 30 years, young Zuckerman witnesses the breakup of Lonoff's marriage in favour of life with his mistress. In addition, the exuberant Zuckerman conjures up an erotic fantasy of his own about Amy Bellette in which the 20-something European immigrant is somehow transformed into the Holocaust martyr Anne Frank (who has survived, and resurfaced, incognito, in literary America). What better solution to Zuckerman's problem with the Jews than to out-do his compatriots with a marriage to the ultimate orthodox Jewish heroine of the age? The whole tale, by now characteristic of Roth, the author of *Portnoy*, is blasphemous, disruptive, obscene, and hilarious.

In subsequent Zuckerman novels, *Zuckerman Unbound* (1981), *The Anatomy Lesson* (1983), and *The Prague Orgy* (1985), Zuckerman is the successful, indeed notorious, author of *Carnovsky*, a *Portnoy*-like sex-and-Jewish-troublemaking novel that he has to live down while figuring out how to write on. All of the tangles, rages, and rants, and the Mobius strip twists between biography and imagination are there with mischief aforethought.

Then, just as many writers of his era were tailing off, something remarkable happened in the work of Roth, then approaching 60. While the work of others was diminishing in intensity and perhaps relevance, Roth experienced an extraordinary late flowering. It wasn't a break, or comeback, or return after long silence, since Roth was a steady producer who could be counted on for a book every couple of years.

I think I first noticed it when Roth published *Patrimony: A True Story* (1991), a memoir and meditation about the recent death of his 85-year-old father. It read as unembellished reportage, written with classic restraint and great beauty, about the death of an ordinary, aged, former insurance salesman. It was, as Edward Said says about other mature works, a "miraculous transfiguration of common reality."

If *Patrimony* was Roth's soberest work, the subsequent *Operation Shylock* (1993) was his most riotous. The protagonist is a troubled "Philip Roth" who goes to Israel to cover the trial of an alleged Nazi concentration camp guard but is shadowed by an imposter "Philip Roth" who can reproduce the real Roth's every mannerism. This rococo satire on Israel and Palestine not only plays on Roth's own shifting identity but also drags in the Israeli novelist Aharon Appelfeld for a cameo role as well as a Palestinian figure who bears a disconcerting resemblance to Edward Said. Its scope is near-epic, the competing rage of all its characters as unstoppable as the political conflict that motivates it. It's without question the great American novel about the seemingly perpetual and savage Israeli-Palestinian war.

As well, in the decade of the 1990s, Roth produced three more full-scale novels, *Sabbath's Theatre* (1995) and the first two volumes of a loose Zuckerman-narrated trilogy, *American Pastoral* (1997) and *I Married a Communist* (1998). The trilogy's concluding piece-de-resistance was *The Human Stain* (2000), a brilliant investigation of racial identity, old age, late desire, and American national and academic politics during the Bill Clinton era (discussed here in chapter 2).

The *Human Stain* was merely Roth's opening salvo in the first decade of the new century, a decade in which Roth's astonishing rate of productivity continued apace. The prolificness is notable, but other writers have been prolific, especially Roth's contemporary John Updike who, until his death, almost obsessively published a volume or more per year. What's remarkable about Roth is the variety, quality, and pertinence of each new book

The indelible *Human Stain* was followed by *The Dying Animal* (2001), the first of several meditations about death; then another "Roth" novel, *The Plot Against America* (2004); followed by *Everyman* (2006) and *Exit Ghost* (2007). Roth continued with *Indignation* (2008), *The Humbling* (2009), and *Nemesis* (2010).

Exit Ghost takes its title from a terse stage direction in *Hamlet*. Roth declares that old age isn't a battle, it's a massacre, and in this likely final Zuckerman novel, he's not the least bit squeamish about providing the details. The 71-year-old Zuckerman, having been holed up for the past decade in nearly total seclusion in his Berkshire Hills retreat, doggedly writing away and doing little else, suddenly comes to New York in autumn 2004 for medical treatment to repair some of the damage, particularly incontinence, caused by a prostatectomy operation several years before. A young clinician is offering a technique that supposedly reduces the leakage, and which will hopefully do away with Zuckerman's mortification at having to trundle around in adult diapers. It's not only Zuckerman's leaky, impotent spigot at issue, there's also the leakage of his mind: forgotten names, faces, telephone numbers, even pages from Zuckerman's own hand.

The plot is about the return of *The Ghost Writer*, a half-century later, and Zuckerman's "rash moments" in attempting to revivify his life. Amy Bellette turns up, the former muse a now 75-year-old woman with a partially shaved head and a disfiguring scar across her skull from a recent brain cancer operation. Lonoff, now literally a ghost, is there, too, on the urine-reeking stairs of a Lower East Side walk-up.

When Zuckerman rashly decides to answer an ad to exchange residences for a year (a New York apartment in return for his rural hermitage), he meets a young couple, both aspiring writers, Billy Davidoff and Jamie Logan, and through them the noxious Richard Kliman, a would-be biographer of the forgotten Lonoff, who intends to reveal the ghost writer's darkest sexual secrets, apparently an adolescent incestuous affair with his older stepsister. (Here, Roth is merging Lonoff-Malamud with Henry Roth, whose belated last novels suggested such an affair.)

Of course, once Zuckerman sets eyes on the langourous but troubled Jamie, the insane infatuation is inevitable and produces not only futile/fertile desire but a "He and She" playlet, penned by Zuckerman, that imagines even further twists and near-erotic turns. Against all this is the loosely sketched-in background of 2004 America in which people are ceaselessly jabbering into their cell phones, and the hopes of young liberals like Billy and Jamie are crushed by the re-election of George W. Bush. There are resemblances to Bellow's *Ravelstein*, though no one would ever accuse Roth of being laid-back, and in the afflictions of desire, there are parallels to Coetzee's *Diary of a Bad Year*.

Perhaps *Exit Ghost* is a novel more for devotees of the Zuckerman series than for a general readership, but, even at worst, it almost works. It sets out Lonoff's spare credo: "The end is so immense, it is its own poetry. It requires little rhetoric. Just state it plainly." To which it counterposes the rage of the toothless old lion and the handsome virile bull, Zuckerman and Kliman screaming at each other in the middle of New York's Central Park over the fate of Lonoff's ghost. Zuckerman's Rip van Winkle–like return to New York and the quick-sketch of the depths of the Bush era and a vacuous, trivial culture, the embattled ruminations on biography and identity, the massacre of old age, the absence of "serenity and reconciliation" (in Said's sense), all that seems pretty much right.

It makes sense that late works address the frailties of the flesh and mind, cast a cold eye on the passing caravan, play endgames with ever fewer pieces on the board. "Late style"? Well, it can be both timely and untimely. Milosz's grave serenity and Saramago's critical playfulness are as possible, as plausible as Coetzee's and Roth's raging against the dying of the light. Yeats was right that "No single story would they find / Of an unbroken happy mind, / A finish worthy of the start. Young men know nothing of this sort, / Observant old men know it well." We've been graced, this past decade, with "observant old men." And, as Yeats also asked, in the title of that poem, "Why Should Not Old Men Be Mad?"

12

Other Voices, Other Realms

I

Azar Nafisi, *Reading Lolita in Tehran: A Memoir in Books* (2003)

The university where I've taught for many years is located in a Vancouver suburb that also happens to be home, by virtue of historical accident, to a community of several thousand former Iranians. They've arrived on Canada's west coast in successive waves reflective of the cataclysms of Iranian politics in the last half-century. Since quite a few of them have been students of mine, I've fortuitously learned more about Iranian history, politics, theocracy, and Persian cooking than I otherwise would have in the ordinary course of things.

Some of my students, and/or their families, fled Iran during the reign of the Shah, others in the wake of Ayatollah Khomeini and the Islamic Revolution of 1979, still others came following various failed attempts to "reform" the regime during the last decade, and some arrived as recently as mid-2009 after the current Iranian president, Mahmoud Ahmadinejad, was fraudulently re-elected and hundreds of thousands of protestors who filled the streets of Tehran were violently suppressed by the Islamic Republic's security forces, both official and para-military. There are now communities and enclaves of former Iranians similar to the one in North Vancouver scattered around the world.

The members of those communities, like Azar Nafisi, the author of *Reading Lolita in Tehran*, are people who no longer look through living room windows "framing my beloved Elburz Mountains" at the edge of the Iranian capital, but instead find themselves "in another room, in another country," disturbed by the whirling dervishes of memory.

Nafisi's book, one of the notable ones of the 21st century's first decade, is a memoir of the author's life in Iran from the late 1970s, the moment of the Islamic revolution, to the late 1990s, when she emigrated to the United States, but, as *New York Times* reviewer Michiko Kakutani notes, "it is also many other things." Nafisi, a professor of literature and the daughter of a prominent Iranian family (her father was once mayor of Tehran, her mother was one of the first women members of parliament), returned to Iran in 1979 after an education in Europe and the U.S. Among the "many other things" Nafisi's book is, says Kakutani, "it is a visceral and often harrowing portrait of the Islamic revolution in that country and its fallout on the day-to-day lives" of Nafisi and her students. As another reviewer, *The Guardian's* Paul Allen, explains, "After teaching literature at three universities in Tehran (and being expelled or resigning in despair from each), Nafisi picked seven of her best students and invited them to come to her home every week to discuss books." *Reading Lolita in Tehran* tells the story of that remarkable group of readers.

As Kakutani says, Nafisi's book is also "a thoughtful account of the novels they studied together" – works by F. Scott Fitzgerald, Jane Austen, Henry James, and *Lolita* novelist Vladimir Nabokov, as well as the classic stories of Scheherazade in *A Thousand and One Nights* – "and the unexpected parallels they drew between those books and their own experiences as women living under the unforgiving rule of the mullahs. And it is, finally, an eloquent brief on the transformative powers of fiction." Or, as Paul Allen puts it, Nafisi "and her students, all women, began to think of these classes as an escape from the reality of Iran's totalitarian theocracy; but the picture her book paints is of an escape to a true republic where they are able to discover another reality." Nafisi sometimes refers to that place as the Republic of Imagination (Michiko Kakutani, "Book Study as Insubordination Under the Mullahs," *New York Times*, April 15, 2003; Paul Allen, "Through the Veil," *The Guardian*, Sept. 13, 2003).

Early on in her "memoir in books," Nafisi declares, "What we search for in fiction is not so much reality but the epiphany of truth." But what do you do if the reality in which you live is so distorted that the only epiphany it offers is the reality to be found in semi-clandestine fiction? That's why, although it is of *Lolita* (and other books) that Nafisi wants to write, "there is no way I can write about that novel without also writing about Tehran." What follows, then, "is the story of *Lolita* in Tehran, how *Lolita* gave a different colour to Tehran and how Tehran helped redefine Nabokov's novel."

The "different colour" that literature gives to Nafisi's Tehran is paralleled by a literal contrast between the black-and-white colours of veiled, "black-scarved, timid faces in the city" that sprawls below the mountains, and the students who arrived at Nafisi's home each Thursday for nearly two years, as they "shed their mandatory veils and robes and burst into colour." Writing her memoir from the U.S., where she now teaches at Johns Hopkins University, the exiled Nafisi has two photographs of her students and herself in front of her, taken days before her departure from Iran in 1997. In the first there's a gathering of women who are, "according to the law of the land, dressed in black robes and head scarves, covered except for the oval of their faces and their hands." In the second picture, the same women, in the same poses, "have taken off their coverings. Splashes of colour separate one from the next. Each has become distinct through the colour and style of her clothes, the colour and length of her hair; not even the two who are still wearing their head scarves look the same."

Vladimir Nabokov's *Lolita* (1955), the story of the "poet/criminal," as Nafisi calls its oddly named protagonist, Humbert Humbert, and his obsession with a 12-year-old all-American nymphet has always been a difficult book to read, and not just in Tehran. Nafisi reads Nabokov's notoriously disturbing novel as the "confiscation" of one individual's life by another, and it is not hard to see how a reading group in Tehran might interpret Humbert's seizure of Lolita's life as a metaphor for the way women are being treated in the radical Islamic state.

Nafisi emphasizes that "*we* were *not* Lolita, the Ayatollah was *not* Humbert and this republic was *not* what Humbert called his princedom by the sea." Although *Lolita* was not a critique of the Islamic Republic, nonetheless it was a work of art that "went against the grain of all totalitarian perspectives."

"When I think of Lolita," Nafisi says, the recurrent image that comes to mind is of a "half-alive butterfly pinned to the wall."

Although there is not a simple parallel between the lives of Nafisi and her students and Humbert's "creation" of Lolita, his erasure of her real past, and the "perverse intimacy" that links jailor and victim, nonetheless, as she observes, "At some point, the truth of Iran's past became as immaterial to those who appropriated it as the truth of Lolita's is to Humbert."

Part of the unsettling power of Nabokov's *Lolita* lies in the ambiguity and multiplicity of its meanings. Nafisi discusses a range of interpretations, from Humbert's own crazed attempt to exonerate himself by painting Lolita as a knowing "little monster," to those of other readers who have seen Nabokov's book as everything from a brutal satire on the mores of suburban American life to a parable that explores the unidentifiable border between true love and obsession. Still others, Nafisi notes, condemn *Lolita* "because they feel Nabokov turned the rape of a 12-year-old into an aesthetic experience." Nabokov died in 1977, but the question of *Lolita* preoccupied him to the end of his life, as is clear from the fragments of his final unfinished novel, the story of a novelist who publishes a best-selling novel about an illicit affair with an underage girl and is pondering the "real-life" model for his "fictional" creation. The notes were only published decades later, in 2009, as *The Original of Laura* (See John Lanchester, "Flashes of Flora," *The New York Review of Books*, Dec. 17, 2009, and Martin Amis, "The Problem with Nabokov," *The Guardian*, Nov. 14, 2009).

Nafisi's framework of readings and group of readers is permeated by the totalitarian context in which the whole of the story is embedded. It is a scene, Nafisi says, where "the streets have been turned into a war zone, where young women who disobey the rules are hurled into patrol cars, taken to jail, flogged, fined, forced to wash the toilets and humiliated" in a hundred other ways. "Almost every day my students would recount such stories," Nafisi writes, including some of her own stories about not wearing the veil, or wearing it improperly, or being castigated for studying allegedly decadent Western texts, as well as refusing to take up a hard-line ideological stance. "We laughed over them, and later felt angry and sad, although we repeated them endlessly at parties and over cups of coffee, in bread-lines, in taxis. It was as if the sheer act of recounting these stories gave us some control over them."

But the reappropriation of a measure of intellectual freedom through storytelling is clearly limited for those who "had become the figment of someone else's dreams. A stern ayatollah, a self-proclaimed philosopher-king, had come to rule our land. He had come in the name of a past, a past that, he claimed, had been stolen from him," and "he now wanted to re-create us in the image of that illusory past." Nafisi describes in convincing detail the "tragedy and absurdity of the cruelty to which we were subjected," and the circumstances of a culture "that denied any merit to literary works" except as ideology, a country "where all gestures, even the most private, were interpreted in political terms," and where "the colours of my head scarf or my father's tie were symbols of Western decadence and imperialist tendendies." It's hardly necessary to add, though one of Nafisi's students does, that the criminal acts of Humbert Humbert are perfectly legal within the provisions of Islamic marriage law in Iran.

A few reviewers criticized Nafisi for "fictionalizing" her students, for referring to one of her confidantes throughout the book only as "my magician," and even for the mixture of personal memoir combined with literary criticism. But the students, whose own developing life-stories are poignantly crucial to the reality of the book, have been disguised for their own protection. As for the unidentified mentor that Nafisi calls "the magician" (a reference to another Nabokov story), his genie-like existence is no more surreal than the actual existence, also noted by Nafisi, of a blind cleric who was the official Iranian censor of television and movies for many years. The hybrid combination of autobiography and literary commentary seems to me expressive of the book's Shaherazade-like charm, and its creative reshaping of Persian literary tradition. In the end, against the niggling complaints, I prefer Nafisi's defiance against radical Islam's suppression of women and her stirring tale of inspired teaching and the encounter with great writing.

The quickest sketch of Nafisi as a teacher is provided by Jacki Lyden, a writer and reporter for National Public Radio in the U.S. "When I first saw Azar Nafisi teach," Lyden recalls, "she was standing in a university classroom in Tehran, holding a bunch of fake red poppies in one hand and a bouquet of daffodils in the other, and asking, what is kitsch." In *Reading Lolita*, says Lyden, Nafisi "mesmerizingly reveals the shimmering worlds she created in those classrooms, inside a revolution that was an apogee of kitsch and cruelty."

Finally, beyond the stories of coming home to the Islamic revolution, surviving the eight-year-long Iran-Iraq War, and ultimately departing for "another room, another country," Nafisi wonders "if you can imagine us." Can we imagine this extraordinary gathering, of what might be described, in a cliché of the era, as "the mother" of all book clubs?

"We are sitting around the iron-and-glass table on a cloudy November day, the yellow and red leaves reflected in the dining room mirror are drenched in a haze," Nafisi recalls. "I and perhaps two others have copies of *Lolita* on our laps. The rest have a heavy Xerox. There is no easy access to these books – you cannot buy them in the bookstores anymore. First the censors banned most of them, then the government stopped them from being sold: most of the foreign-language bookstores were closed ... We photocopied all 300 pages for those without copies. In an hour when we take a break, we will have tea or coffee with pastry. I don't remember whose turn it is for pastry. We take turns; every week one of us provides the pastry." And every week all of them engage in the act of quiet heroism that serious reading can be in a world that denies its worth.

2

The heading that I'm using here, "Other Voices, Other Realms," as some readers will recognize, echoes the title of Truman Capote's first book, *Other Voices, Other Rooms* (1948), in which heretofore unheard voices resounded, but it also points to a contemporary and equally notable debut, Pakistani-American writer Daniyal Mueenuddin's *In Other Rooms, Other Wonders* (2009). In a brief survey of interesting books from places around the world that appeared in the first decade of the present century, Azar Nafisi's *Reading Lolita in Tehran* provides one of the convenient bookends; the other will be Sharhiar Mandanipour's *Censoring an Iranian Love Story* (2009).

It is not immediately clear how to categorize these books from Africa, Asia, and the Middle East, or if we need to do so. They are, of course, "international" literature but, then, so are the works of Orhan Pamuk, Amos Oz, and Javier Cercas. For that matter, so are the books of Philip Roth and other writers "closer to home," depending on where home happens to be. In that sense, "international" is simply a relative term, an "elsewhere" from the perspective of where one is. In some instances, but not all, these books are translated from another language into English, but that isn't their distinguishing feature, since many of them are written in English, and some of those that aren't originally in English are written by authors now living in English-speaking countries. The implication of a notion of other voices, other rooms, and other countries is that we're hearing voices in literature that we haven't heard before, from rooms and realms that are elsewhere. But for the authors themselves, their voices aren't "other," and the other rooms in other countries in which they find themselves, willingly or not, are merely places distant from where they started out.

My point is that the increasing presence of books from all over the world at the beginning of the 21st century is an indicator that there is no longer an "elsewhere," except relatively speaking. Once we might have thought of these works as "exotic," but the notion of the exotic diminishes in a de-centred global society and becomes little more than an anachronistic colonialism of the imagination. Indeed, perhaps the only exotic reality now is "virtual reality," not the different customs, languages, and landscapes of places other than our own. Although the stories such books tell may be news to us, even "news from the front," we now recognize that the "front," the place of crucial encounters, is increasingly everywhere. What were once thought of as "other voices" are now more appropriately recognized as simply the author's own voice. In a sense, all voices are now "our voices," but I don't mean "our" to suggest a reductive homogenizing or to erase the distinctive differences that distinguish our voices. Here are just a few of them.

Chimamanda Ngozi Adichie, *Half of a Yellow Sun* (2006)

There was once an African country called Biafra in what is now eastern Nigeria. It existed precariously from 1967-1970. It doesn't exist anymore. And few people now remember that breakaway state whose flag bore the emblem of half of a yellow sun and whose inhabitants were mostly members of the Igbo ethnic group. The bloody civil war that resulted in the demise of Biafra, one of the worst conflicts in modern African history, caused the deaths of hundreds of thousands of people, by bombs, gunfire, starvation, and disease.

Chimamanda Ngozi Adichie's *Half of a Yellow Sun* tells the epic story of the secession and destruction of Biafra. It is intimately presented through the experiences of its three principal characters: Ugwu is a teenage, village-raised youth who becomes a houseboy in the home of a politically radical mathematics lecturer at the nearby University of Nsukka. Ugwu's middle-class "Master," as he styles himself, is the impetuous Odenigbo; and finally, there's Odenigbo's woman-friend, Olanna, British-educated and the daughter of a *nouveau riche* business family in Nigeria's capital, Lagos. The cast of main players is rounded out by Olanna's twin sister, Kainene, and her English boyfriend Richard, a would-be historian, as well as an assortment of academics, villagers, and servants. The time-line takes us from the promise of the early 1960s, through the growing political alienation of the Biafran secessionists, and into the bloody civil conflict at the end of the decade.

The novel is technically conventional in a realist mode, but it tells us something about a tragic patch of history we probably didn't know much about, and its characters, I noticed, remained memorable long after I'd finished reading Adichie's book. Maya Jaggi called it "a landmark novel, whose clear, undemonstrative prose can so precisely delineate nuance." She also praised the "rare emotional truth" in its sexual scenes, including "Ugwu's adolescent forays and the mature couples' passions"; it's an emotional truth that extends to the horrors of rape in a war-battered land where one sees, as Adichie writes, "vaguely familiar clothes on headless bodies," or the odd skin tone of corpses – "a flat sallow grey, like a poorly wiped blackboard" (Maya Jaggi, "The Master and His Houseboy," *The Guardian*, August 19, 2006).

"It's easy to forget what a big deal" Adichie is, notes one newspaper profile of the author (William Skidelsky, "The interview: Chimamanda Ngozi Adichie, *The Observer*, April 5, 2009). One thing that might be easily forgotten is that her "hugely accomplished and harrowing drama" is literally a historical novel, in that its events all occurred before the birth of the then 29-year-old Adichie. The skills displayed in her well-received first novel, *Purple Hibiscus* (2003), the coming-of-age story of a Nigerian girl, were confirmed by the reception of the book that made Adichie a literary sensation in Britain. *Half of a Yellow Sun* won the 2007 Orange Prize, the prestigious award for women writers, and the book sold close to the three-quarters of a million copies in Britain alone. In addition to enthusiastic reviews, it received the imprimatur of Nigeria's most famous writer, Chinua Achebe, author of *Things Fall Apart* (1958), who said, "We do not usually associate wisdom with beginners, but here is a new writer endowed with the gift of ancient storytellers ... She is fearless, or she would not have taken on the intimidating horror of Nigeria's civil war. Adichie came almost fully made."

Adichie, the daughter of Nigerian academics, went to school in the United States, completing a graduate degree at Yale, while working on a third book, a volume of stories, *The Thing Around Your Neck* (2009). One of the stories, "Jumping Monkey Hill," is about an African writer's workshop held in South Africa, presided over by an unpleasant Englishman who tells the students what kinds of fiction they should be writing. "For me, the story is about the larger question of who determines what an African story is," says Adichie, which is precisely one of the sub-themes of her Biafran novel. "I remember feeling helpless. You're sitting there thinking, this is the result of two hundred years of history: we can sit here and be told what our story is."

As I was reading Adichie's work in mid-2009, her effort to define "what an African story is" was made all the more poignant by events in Nigeria itself. Some four decades after the brutal events in Biafra she brings to life in her prose, the day's news began with an account of a deadly clash between Nigerian government forces and religious fundamentalists. The location of the incident was far north of the now vanished Biafra, religious extremism had displaced ethnic and tribal politics as the issue of the day, but the troubled character of the Nigerian regime had not markedly improved, and the need for African storytellers remained urgent.

Khaled Hosseini, *The Kite Runner* (2003)

Afghan-American writer Khaled Hosseini's multi-million copy bestseller, *The Kite Runner*, as well as the successful film version of it made in 2007, is probably more of a cultural phenomenon than strictly a matter of literary merit. Still, thousands of readers found it to be a gripping page-turner, and it certainly deserves mention as a notable instance of literary news from "home and abroad," concepts that, as I've said, seem to be converging.

The melodramatic first novel by a then 38-year-old Afghan-born physician now living in California "tells a story of fierce cruelty and fierce yet redeeming love," wrote one of the many enthusiastic reviewers who, along with extensive word-of-mouth praise, helped propel the book to unexpected best-seller status in the U.S. (Edward Hower, "*The Kite Runner*: A Servant's Son," *The New York Times*, August 3, 2003). The story of two boys, Amir and Hassan, begins in Kabul, Afghanistan, in the late 1970s, during the last days of the country's shaky monarchy, before the society was brutally transfigured by, successively, civil war, invasion by the Soviet Union, and the mid-1990s triumph of the Islamic fundamentalist movement known as the Taliban.

Hosseini presents a sort of traditional "boy's own" tale of passionate adolescent friendship and betrayal, set against the background of competitive kite flying in Kabul that provides the book's title image, as well as a metaphor for freedom lost. The story reflects the class and ethnic tensions of Afghanistan, with Amir, the son of a wealthy Pashtun businessman, representing the ruling elite, while his devoted companion and servant, Hassan, is a member of a minority tribe, the Hazara, fated for poverty and subservience.

The intricate plot twists, complete with sociopathic villain, can be left to interested readers. But between the acts of moral and physical violence that launch the story and a dramatic denouement of moral redemption in contemporary Afghanistan, Hosseini tells an intriguing tale of Afghan refugees in America. Indeed, the best writing in the book is "a lively and well-observed section about Afghan expatriates setting up flea markets in Fremont, California," as one reviewer notes (Meghan O'Rourke, "*The Kite Runner*: Do I Really Have to Read It?", *Slate*, July 25, 2005).

The question that intrigues critic O'Rourke is, "Why have Americans, who traditionally avoid foreign literature like the plague, made *The Kite Runner* into a cultural touchstone?" She eventually finds a clue to the puzzle in a sentence spoken to Amir, many years after his forced emigration, by one of his childhood mentors: "There is a way to be good again." It serves as a mantra-like promise of moral renewal, and, in "the appealingly familiar story at the heart of the novel," a "struggle of personal recovery and unconditional love, couched in redemptive language," there is something "immediately legible to Americans."

While the "vocabulary of psychotherapeutic spiritual recovery" likely explains the book's popular success, critics like O'Rourke credit Hosseini with "wisely steer[ing] clear of merely exoticizing Afghanistan as a monolithically foreign place." While O'Rourke retains her doubts about the book's literary and other merits, she concedes that "one shouldn't underrate the complexity of the task facing Hosseini, who understandably wanted to make the human predicament at the core of his novel seem universal, not remote. There's something to be said for *The Kite Runner's* strategy."

That was my sense when I taught the book one semester. While the more sophisticated students, in terms of writing, were disdainful of the pot boiler elements of Hosseini's book, other students were enthralled by the melodrama and no doubt learned something about a contemporary political crisis to which they otherwise might not have paid attention. Whether Hosseini succeeds in achieving all his humanist political aims, either here or in his follow-up novel, *A Thousand Splendid Suns* (2007), his writing provides an intimate glimpse of a society with which a good part of the world was militarily and politically embroiled through the whole of the first decade of the present century.

Hisham Matar, *In the Country of Men* (2006)

If Khaled Hosseini's *Kite Runner* offers a populist redemptive narrative, Hisham Matar's Booker Prize–nominated first novel, *In the Country of Men*, while bearing some similarities to Hosseini's bestseller, presents a starker view of politics and love under conditions of totalitarianism. Matar's poignant novel is set in Tripoli, Libya, in 1979, and is written (like Hosseini's book) by an exiled author in his mid-30s.

One obvious feature that distinguishes the two books is political history itself. Unlike the fluid, volatile politics of Afghanistan, the North African country of Libya was ruled, then as now, by Colonel Muammar al-Qaddafi, who came to power in a 1969 military coup. By the end of the first decade of the present century, Qaddafi had marked four decades as the absolutist, and sometimes absurdist, "Guide" of one the longest-running regimes in the Arab world. It's not only a lengthy dictatorship that has engaged in both extensive internal violence and international terrorism, but it's one that explains itself by means of a bizarre brew of revolutionary socialist rhetoric, pan-Arabist nationalism, and the Guide's own idiosyncrasies, which range from goofy to deadly. Even at the time of the events depicted by Matar, Libya was already one of the stranger modern human hells. It had a zero tolerance policy for dissidents, many of whom it executed in gruesome, televised rituals.

Nine-year-old Suleiman, whose adult self is the narrator of *In the Country of Men*, is the son of a Libyan dissident, Faraj. His father's public life as a well-to-do entrepreneur provides cover for his frequent absences, which are written off as business trips. But one day, in Tripoli's Martyr's Square, when Suleiman spots his father (who is supposed to be away on business), the boy gets his first glimpse of the mysteries of political and domestic life that will shape his youth.

In an astute and admiring review of *In the Country of Men*, Indian writer Pankaj Mishra notes that Matar includes a description of the statue of the Roman emperor Septimius Severus that stands in Tripoli's main square. The North African–born emperor's arm points toward the sea, as though "urging Libya to look toward Rome" and the promise of Europe. When Suleiman eventually visits Lepcis Magna, the Roman seaside colony in Libya where Septimius was born, the boy finds that "absence was everywhere," a phrase that registers the distance between the ancient world and the debased present-day dictatorship. In the antique city's ruins, Suleiman is accompanied by Ustath Rashid, the father of the boy's best friend and next-door neighbour, Kareem. Rashid, one of the political liberals stealthily opposing Qaddafi's regime, recites an old Arab poem: "Why this nothingness where once was a city? / Who will answer? Only the wind." It doesn't give away any secrets to say that naive dissidents like Rashid and Suleiman's father will face variously grim fates (Pankaj Mishra, "Muslims in the Dark," *The New York Review of Books*, April 12, 2007).

The menace of Libyan politics and its effects on private life that Matar so effectively conveys no doubt reflect his own childhood. Born in New York in 1970 to a diplomatic family working in the Libyan delegation to the United Nations, Matar grew up in an upper-class Tripoli suburb, but when his father fell out with the regime, the family sought refuge in Egypt. Although Matar himself settled in England as a teenager, and lives there today, his father, who remained in Cairo, was "disappeared" in 1990, presumably by agents of Qaddafi, and has not been seen since, although rumours of his imprisonment have sporadically surfaced.

"For all the grim news it brings us from a murky region," Mishra observes, Matar's novel is neither "overtly political [n]or polemical." As in *The Kite Runner*, much of the story is devoted to boyhood friendship and betrayal, and the usual run of childhood activities, from soccer in the streets and swimming at the nearby beach to climbing the mulberry tree in the backyard of Suleiman's friend, Kareem. All of it is shadowed by the unexplained absences of Suleiman's father and the mysterious "illness" of his mother, which the reader quickly recognizes to be alcoholism, caused by the bottled substance in paper bags that Mama illicitly purchases from the local baker. "At the heart of the novel," Mishra says, "is Suleiman's great love for his mother, who, in a country dominated by men, faces both domestic and political oppression."

Unlike Khaled Hosseini's best-seller, while Matar offers painful, poignant love, there is little redemption possible here and "even fewer comforts," as Mishra says. What practically all the reviewers of Matar's novel noticed, however, is the quality of the prose. "Whatever his subject, Matar writes beautifully," says *Guardian* critic and novelist Kamila Shamsie. "In describing the world of seas and mulberries, he is a sensualist; when writing of executions and arrests he is a nuanced observer with a gift for conveying both absurdity and raw emotion." She cites Matar's sentence about a man trying to resist being taken to the gallows, which reminds Suleiman of "the way a shy woman would resist her friends' invitation to dance, pulling her shoulders up to her ears and waving her index finger nervously in front of her mouth" (Kamila Shamsie, "Where the mulberries grow," *The Guardian*, July 29, 2006).

Lorraine Adams's review of Matar warns readers not to confuse melodramatic populism with the sublimity of art. "The wonderfully original is anathema to most marketing campaigns, so don't let anyone tell you, as publicists in Britain did ... when *In the Country of Men* first appeared, that this is a Libyan *Kite Runner*," Adams says. Matar's "exceptional first novel ... yields something rare in contemporary fiction: a sophisticated storybook inhabited by archetypes, told with a 9-year-old's logic, written with the emphatic and memorable lyricism of verse ... free of both cliché and padding" (Lorraine Adams, "The Dissident's Son," *The New York Times*, March 4, 2007).

Pankaj Mishra makes the most interesting of comparative suggestions. In praising Matar's "clean supple prose, which vividly evokes
days of idleness, long warm afternoons, the sensations of extreme
heat, and the coolness of shuttered interiors," Mishra says, "Matar
resembles the lyrical Camus of *The First Man*." After invoking Albert
Camus, Matar's fellow North African–born writer, Mishra adds
that, given the "darkening ambiguities" of North Africa and its relation to the West, Matar's first novel makes "Septimius Severus's antique exhortation to learn from Europe look touchingly innocent."

Ma Jian, *Beijing Coma* (translated by Flora Drew, 2008)

One of the most ambitious books of the decade under review comes
from China. Ma Jian's *Beijing Coma* is an epic-sized novel that tells
the story of what happened in Tiananmen Square in 1989, where
the Chinese revolution not only ate its children but subsequently attempted to wipe out the memories of the citizens of the world's largest republic.

The London-based Ma Jian, a writer in his mid-50s, recreates the
day-by-day developments of the largest, most sustained political
demonstration against the Chinese Communist government in its
history. The events, now two-decades old, involved a huge number
of mostly young people and began with a burgeoning camp-like occupation of Beijing's main square in spring 1989 that gathered
around a polystyrene replica of the Statue of Liberty. The extended
protest was forcibly ended only in early June when the Chinese army
crushed the demonstrators with tanks and guns, and killed a still
unknown number of protesters. In a 2009 essay commemorating the
twentieth anniversary of the events in Tiananmen Square, Ma says
the massacre "killed thousands of unarmed citizens, and altered the
lives of millions," but the events seem "to be locked in the twentieth
century, forgotten or ignored … The amnesia to which China has
succumbed is not the result of natural memory-loss but of state-
enforced erasure. China's Communist regime tolerates no mention
of the massacre." (Ma Jian, "The great Tiananmen taboo," *The
Guardian*, June 2, 2009).

Ma, already in disfavour with the regime as a result of his earlier
book of stories, *Stick Out Your Tongue*, left China in 1987, "shortly
before my books were banned there," but he's returned regularly

ever since, and in 1989, "I was on Tiananmen Square with the students, living in their makeshift tents and joining their jubilant singing of the 'Internationale'... They were pressing for dialogue with their Communist leaders, and ultimately for freedom and democracy." Indeed, at one point during the giant sit-in, the Communist Party's general secretary, Zhao Ziyang, visited the students and for a moment it seemed possible that the ending might have been different from what it turned out to be.

By happenstance, a few days before the violent denouement, Ma's brother had an accident in their hometown of Qingdao and fell into a coma. "I immediately left Beijing to look after him, so I didn't witness the massacre of 4 June," Ma says, then adds, "Perhaps if I had, I would never have been able to write about it."

His brother's coma provides the "guiding metaphor" of *Beijing Coma*, as *Guardian* reviewer James Lasdun calls it. The book's protagonist and narrator, Dai Wai, a former biology student, is shot in the head during the military crackdown, falls into a coma, and for the following decade exists in a comatose state, lying in his mother's spare apartment. The title conceit, as Lasdun notes, refers to "the systematic erasure of the event from public consciousness as the hardliners in the government consolidated their victory ... Mention of the troops' massacre of unarmed civilians remains forbidden, as does all reporting that differs in any way from the official version. Many young people in China know nothing about the events at all, and with their new prosperity, perhaps few care."

As Lasdun sums it up, "A comatose mind within a terrifyingly vigorous body is the analogy for post-Tiananmen China that emerges from Ma Jian's book. In the classic tradition of satire, it opposes this image by turning it on its head." In the novel, Dai Wai's "body is comatose, but his mind is coruscatingly alert" (James Lasdun, "Children of the revolution," *The Guardian*, May 3, 2008). Another reviewer notes that Ma, in creating a protagonist who is conscious but immobile, takes James Joyce's famous dictum literally: "History is a nightmare from which I am trying to awake" (Jess Row, "Circling the Square," *The New York Times*, July 13, 2008).

Ma's account of China's political and social history over the past quarter-century is often stomach-churningly brutal. The phrase about a revolution that ate its children is unfortunately not just metaphorical, as Ma recounts instances of grotesque indignities inflicted on the protagonist's paralyzed body, as well as gruesome stories about forced organ donation and even cannibalism. Nor is Ma sentimental about his student heroes. "Alongside their heroism," notes Lasdun, "runs the whole gamut of human flaws." The student leaders are frequently portrayed as "full of posturing and petty squabbling ... Different factions make power grabs even as the tanks roll in." Nor is the novel itself entirely satisfactory. Even otherwise sympathetic critics recognized that several longish scenes of political debate featuring hard to distinguish personalities "may stretch some readers' patience," but as Lasdun ultimately argues, the flaws are outweighed by a "vivid, pungent, often blackly funny book [that] is a mighty gesture of remembrance against the encroaching forces of silence."

Notwithstanding what I said earlier about global familiarity gradually eroding a notion of the exotic, China may be the partial exception to the rule. While everyday life in China's cities, including its pace, production, and consumption of commodities, resembles that of other advanced industrial societies, the degree of authoritarian political secrecy and the state's control of virtual reality (such that a Chinese citizen is unable to "google" an independent account of the events of Tiananmen Square) lend China a chilling sort of political exoticism. What James Lasdun refers to as "silence" was briefly broken in 2009 by the publication of an unusual volume of memoirs that deserves at least brief mention here.

Although the Communist Party's Zhao Ziyang made a sympathetic visit to the demonstrating students in Tiananmen Square, he represented a minority view within the party leadership. Despite his prominence and seniority, he was thrown out of office in 1989 and kept under house arrest for almost sixteen years until his death in 2005, at age 85. *Prisoner of the State: The Secret Journal of Zhao Ziyang* (2009) is the secretly recorded reflections of the former Chinese official and is considered to be an authentic document by most China specialists. (See Jonathan Mirsky, "China's Dictators at Work: The Secret Story," *The New York Review of Books*, July 2, 2009.) In addition to lifting a corner of the curtain by which the Chinese leadership is insulated from scrutiny, the political conclusion of the elderly life-long communist, though couched in characteristically cautious language, proclaims, "In fact, it is the Western parliamentary democratic system that has demonstrated the most vitality. This system is currently the best one available."

By the time of his death, Zhao was pretty much a forgotten figure, as were the events Ma Jian depicts in *Beijing Coma*. Nonetheless, in December 2008, a document called "Charter 08," signed by several thousand Chinese dissidents, called for democratic freedom of assembly and a multi-party political system. Although the prospects for the enactment of the charter's hopes were minimal in the first decade of the century, there exist at least some home-grown "other" voices who seek to break China's "exotic" political silence.

Daniyal Mueenuddin, *In Other Rooms, Other Wonders* (2009)

The "link" in Pakistani-American Daniyal Mueenuddin's debut book of "linked stories," *In Other Rooms, Other Wonders*, is the formidable figure of K.K. Harouni. The retired high-ranking Pakistani civil servant (with a mansion in Lahore) and feudal owner of extensive agricultural estates in the Punjab district of the country periodically inhabits the elegant pages of these "other rooms." He is glimpsed in passing as a favour-dispensing patron, or seen in cameo praising the lightness of a kitchen girl's *chapattis*, sometimes observed in three-quarter length portrait, and even felt posthumously. His life and passing affect the destinies of servants, managers, colleagues, and various children and heirs.

He first appears in the book's opening story, "Nawabdin Electrician," the tale of the man who maintains the electric motors of the wells that dot Harouni's fields of sugarcane, cotton, mango orchards, clover, and wheat.

> K.K. Harouni rarely went to his farms, but lived mostly in Lahore. Whenever the old man visited, Nawab would place himself night and day at the door leading from the servants' sitting area into the walled grove of banyan trees where the old farmhouse stood. Grizzled, his peculiar aviator glasses bent and smudged, Nawab tended the household machinery, the air conditioners, water heaters, refrigerators, and water pumps, like an engineer tending the boilers on a foundering steamer in an Atlantic gale. By his superhuman efforts he almost managed to maintain K.K. Harouni in the same mechanical cocoon, cooled and bathed and lighted and fed, that the landowner enjoyed in Lahore ... Finally, one evening at teatime, gauging the psychological

moment, Nawab asked if he might say a word. The landowner, who was cheerfully filing his nails in front of a crackling rose-wood fire, told him to go ahead.

Nawab delivers a flowery speech of lament about approaching old age and diminished capacity. "The old man, well accustomed to these sorts of speeches, though usually not this florid, filed away at his nails and waited for the breeze to stop. 'What's the matter, Nawabdin?'"

"Matter, sir?" Nawab disenguously asks. "O what could be the matter in your service." The matter, it turns out, is that Nawab wants a motorcycle as a replacement for his ancient bicycle, a proper motorcycle that will allow Nawab not only to get around the vast holdings of K.K. Harouni, but as well to arrive at his wife's bedside in a nearby village each evening. Equally important, possession of the motorcycle will enhance the electrician's status among his peers. In due course, Nawab receives his motorcycle, not because Harouni cares "one way or the other, except that it touched on his comfort – a matter of great interest to him." In any event, the crops had been good that year and Harouni "felt expansive." In the neo-feudal world, all that is dispensed depends merely on the whims, moods, or passing desires of the prince, or his modern successor, K.K. Harouni.

The motorcycle, with Nawab aboard, as we can easily anticipate, will lead to further adventures, landscapes, fateful encounters, and fatality itself. In the above passage and dozens of others, Mueenuddin demonstrates an utterly sure touch, and "touch" is perhaps the key to short-story writing. Mueenuddin succinctly conveys the nuances of the Pakistani social class spectrum and confronts its brutality (especially in the lives of impoverished women) with a restrained prose that is all the more effective for concentrating on the particulars rather than giving way to mere rhetoric. In that, he's reminiscent of V.S. Naipaul, when the Nobel Prize-winner was at the height of his powers.

In Mueenuddin's stories we learn not only of a crafty electrician's slightly shady freelance fiscal affairs (but then, everyone, of financial necessity, is doing deals on the side) or the blunt sexual facts of life in the "upstairs, downstairs" arrangements of the class structure, we also learn about the little things, like the source of the rosewood in the "crackling rosewood fire" in front of which Harouni is filing his nails. Nawab, aboard his new motorcycle, flies down the "long straight road ... through the heart of the K.K. Harouni lands."

> The road ran on the bed of an old highway built when these lands lay within a princely state. Some hundred and fifty years ago one of the princes had ridden this way, going to a wedding or funeral in this remote district, felt hot, and ordered that rosewood be planted to shade the passersby. He forgot that he had given the order, and in a few dozen years he in turn was forgotten, but these trees still stood, enormous now, some of them dead and looming without bark, white and leafless.

Mueenuddin's stories are often about power – the casual orders of princes and landowners, or the sexual subservience of the powerless – but they also give us a sense of feudalism's timeless time – those rosewood-lined roads whose dead tree branches crackle in Harouni's fireplace.

Mueenuddin's sketches of "other rooms" deservedly found their way to various literary prize and book of the year lists (the stories were nominated for both the National Book Award and the Pulitzer Prize), and critics enthusiastic as myself offered a wide range of flattering comparisons. While I see a certain kinship with the prose of Naaipaul, others linked Mueenuddin to writers as diverse as R.K. Narayan, Turgenev, Chekhov, Isaac Bashevis Singer, and the previous "other voices" writer, Truman Capote, as well as to such contemporaries as Jhumpa Lahiri and Alice Munro.

If Mueenuddin's "other wonders" elicited unconstrained praise (William Dalrymple writing in the *Financial Times* called it "the best fiction ever written in English about Pakistan"), the author is himself a rather wondrous character. The son of an Oxford-educated Pakistani civil servant and landowner and an American journalist mother, Mueenuddin, in his mid-40s (born in 1963), has spent roughly equal parts of his life in both countries. As a child he grew up in Lahore and on the family farms, went to boarding school and college in America, until he was urged to return to Pakistan by his elderly father (a man not unlike the fictional K.K. Harouni) to tend the family property. For the next seven years, he managed a farm in the southern Punjab, along the way learning the gritty details of the agricultural business and life in the harsh villages of the countryside and occasionally doing some writing on the side. Mueenuddin decided to return to the U.S., attended Yale law school, and became a New York lawyer for a while. Then one day he resigned, left his 42nd floor office in Manhattan, went back to his Punjab farm, and began writing stories.

That Mueenuddin's book of linked stories is as good as any volume of short stories published in the first decade of the century is, of course, the true wonder of this particular tale.

3

Shahriar Mandanipour, *Censoring an Iranian Love Story* (translated by Sara Khalili, 2009)

I read Shahriar Mandanipour's novel *Censoring an Iranian Love Story* in mid-2009, during Iran's distorted presidential election and its brutal aftermath, one eye on literature and the other on television as the country's military violently suppressed hundreds of thousands of demonstrators protesting the dubious vote count that resulted in the re-election of president Mahmoud Ahmadinejad. The experience was very much like that reported by critic Michiko Kakutani in her review of Mandanipour's book (Michiko Kakutani, "Where Romance Requires Courage," *The New York Times*, June 30, 2009).

While reading it, Kakutani recalled seeing on television that month the repeated video clip of the killing of an Iranian protestor, Neda Agha-Soltan, a young woman cut down by a bullet during the post-election demonstrations. "In what now reads like an eerie echo" of that incident, Kakutani says, Mandanipour "foresees the possible death of his heroine in the streets of Tehran," a chilling instance of art anticipating life (and death). As Mandanipour puts it at the outset of his novel, "The girl does not know that in precisely seven minutes and seven seconds, at the height of the clash between the students, the police, and the members of the Party of God, in the chaos of attacks and escapes, she will be knocked with great force, she will fall back, her head will hit against a cement edge, and her sad Oriental eyes will forever close." Or, since this is a thoroughly postmodern confection, perhaps not.

Mandanipour is a prominent Iranian novelist and short-story writer who was prohibited from publishing his fiction in his native country for most of the decade of the 1990s, critic James Wood informs us in an extended essay (James Wood, "Love, Iranian Style," *The New Yorker*, June 29, 2009). He went to the United States in 2006 for a fellowship at Brown University and stayed, going on to become a visiting scholar at Harvard. "This novel, his first major work to be translated into English, was written in Farsi but cannot be read in Iran," Wood says, and then adds, "His book is thus acutely displaced: it had to have been written with an audience outside of Iran in mind, but in a language that his audience would mostly not understand; it depends on translation for its being, yet its being is thoroughly Iranian, lovingly and allusively so, dense with local reference. And it takes as its subject exactly these paradoxes, for it is explicitly about what can and cannot be written in contemporary Iranian fiction." That, no doubt, explains a good deal of the book's convoluted moves, but they're also the result of Mandanipour's literary sophistication.

His multi-layered text, as Kakutani describes it, "is, at once, a novel about two young Iranians trying to conduct a covert romance in Tehran; a postmodern account of the efforts of their creator, or his fictional alter ego, to grapple with the harsh censorship rules of his homeland; and an Escher-like meditation on the interplay of life and art, reality and fiction."

The would-be lovers are named Sara and Dara, and they're a cross between Jack and Jill figures in a children's nursery rhyme and the protagonists of ancient Persian love epics. They spend a good portion of their virginal courtship dodging the eyes of parents, nosy neighbours, and the morality police, and contriving to meet in museums, movie theatres, and even hospital emergency rooms. The digressive Mandanipour, who frequently breaks into his narrative, throws in an aside about how he once wrote a story in which he led an amorous couple to a cemetery in order to provide a meeting place. Dara leaves Sara hidden messages in library books, placing purple dots under certain letters in certain words, which she must then decode.

Mandanipour depicts the extremes of censorship in both Iranian literature and life through elaborate typographical devices. The adventures of Dara and Sara are presented in boldface type, but whenever the story becomes unacceptably political or erotic, offending sentences and phrases are crossed out, struck through with a horizontal line, so that, as Wood notes, "the reader can examine what might constitute a literary offense in Iran. The text is veiled, but the author lifts the veil for his non-Iranian audience." Wood cites a typical passage that begins, "Sara is studying Iranian literature at Tehran University." But the following sentence, "However, in compliance with an unwritten law, teaching contemporary Iranian literature is forbidden in Iranian schools and universities," is crossed out. The owner of a store where Sara goes to buy sunglasses sighs, "What a shame for those beautiful eyes and that tantalizing face to be hidden behind those glasses." The phrase "and that tantalizing face" is struck through.

The mutilated bold-face text of Mandanipour's faltering attempts to write an Iranian love story is accompanied by another text printed in normal roman type. "Since the official love story can barely get off the ground," Wood says, "Mandanipour supplies the unofficial version, in an essayistic running commentary that often displaces the official tale for pages on end." There we learn about the revolution of 1979, the history of censorship in Iran, and the risky obstacle course facing any courtship. In the unofficial text, with its metafictional echoes of Milan Kundera and Salman Rushdie, the censor is conceived of not merely as one who prohibits but as a kind of co-author of the book. He makes frequent appearances, under the alias of Porfiry Petrovich (a character in Dostoyevsky's *Crime and Punishment*). He squabbles with Mandanipour, crosses out sentences, chats with other characters, and even has desires of his own. "One of the great successes of this book," says Wood, "is how thoroughly it persuades the reader that a novel about censorship could not help also being a novel about fiction making."

But if this is a novel whose first hundred pages are "exciting," and whose writing is "exuberant, bonhomous, clever" (Wood), it eventually becomes a bit too much. Not only is the authorial commentary quickly of greater interest than the official love story, given that the lovers are simply present to show that it's impossible to write an Iranian love story, but the surreal, postmodern, magical elements increasingly "feel distinctly strained" (Kakutani). If Mandanipour's novel about writing and love falling apart has shortcomings, it nonetheless is more interesting as an attempt at what to do with writing in such circumstances than a host of other more conventional tales dealing with similar materials. In the end, critic Kakutani credits

Mandanipour with conjuring up "a clever Rubik's cube of a story, while at the same time giving readers a haunting portrait of life in the Islamic Republic of Iran: arduous, demoralizing and constricted even before the brutalities of the current crackdown." The crackdown has only become worse in the time since the publication of Mandanipour's book. I think it's a book that might be both recognizable and revealing to not only my Iranian students in a Vancouver university classroom but to a far broader readership.

In considering these other voices, places, regimes, I should underscore again that my reflections are a minuscule sampling of what became available in the first decade of the new century. There are dozens of other books, both fiction and non-fiction, that would reward comparable attention. Such works range from British-born Jhumpa Lahiri's Pulizter Prize-winning stories, *Interpreter of Maladies* (1999), and subsequent volumes; and include Suketu Mehta's portrait of Bombay, *Maximum City* (2005); Kiran Desai's *The Inheritance of Loss* (2006), winner of both the Booker and National Book Critics Circle awards; Mohsin Hamid's Booker-nominated *The Reluctant Fundamentalist* (2007), an elegant monologue about the anxieties of the 9/11 era; and Aravind Adiga's *The White Tiger* (2008), a novel of news from India which also won the Booker Prize, among other honours.

Among the threads and themes that bring many of these books together is that they invariably present political and class structures that contrast sharply to the relatively placid politics of countries like Canada or, in Europe, Germany, and France. For those whose "grand tour was only through the gently borderless continent of Google," we may find ourselves looking almost enviously, as James Wood says, "at those who have the misfortune to live in countries where literature is taken seriously enough to be censored, and writers venerated with imprisonment." In more bucolic politics, as a result of cultural and commercial indifference rather than repression, it is literature itself that seems an endangered and exotic species.

13

Haunted by a Spectre:
Krugman, Klein, Stiglitz

I

Paul Krugman, *The Return of Depression Economics and the Crisis of 2008* (2009)

The one literary prediction that could be safely made at the beginning of 2009 was that we would all be reading a lot more books about what was formerly known as The Economy, and was currently variously called The Crisis, The Collapse, Things Are Going to Get Worse Before They Get Better, The Brink of Great Depression II, and "A Spectre Is Haunting …" The spectre is haunting not just Europe, as the famous opening line of Marx's and Engels' *Communist Manifesto* of 1848 had it, but the entire globe, though it's not the "spectre of Communism" that's doing the haunting, as the mid-19th century revolutionaries claimed. What to call the spectre is merely a minor terminological aspect of the substantive investigation of political economy that was the subject of many of the books marking the conclusion of the first decade of the 21st century.

Personally, the book I was looking forward to was the tell-all tale about the aptly named Bernie Madoff, the New York financial wizard who made off with $50 billion in investors' money in the biggest Ponzi scheme in history and was eventually sentenced to several lifetimes in jail. More important, one wanted to know the inside story of that night in September 2008 when then President George W. Bush, the enemy of big government and lifelong proponent of unregulated cowboy capitalism, was told by Treasury Secretary Hank Paulson and Federal Reserve chair Ben Bernanke that the U.S. would have to, more or less, bail out the entire finance and banking sector, or else ... or else the American economy would collapse. Various first drafts of history were soon underway.

While awaiting these nasty-pieces-of-work-in-progress, we already had available a range of tempting titles that includes Canadian journalist Naomi Klein's *The Shock Doctrine* (2007), trade union economist Jim Stanford's useful primer *Economics for Everyone: A Short Guide to the Economics of Capitalism* (2008), and the British-born conservative Harvard historian Niall Ferguson's latest TV-series-text *The Ascent of Money: A Financial History of the World* (2008). For those still catching up with the last century, there was Robert Skidelsky's suddenly relevant-again massive biography *John Maynard Keynes (1883-1946): Economist, Philosopher, Statesman* (2003).

My own favourite Virgil-like guide to our present economic Hell is Paul Krugman, winner of the 2008 Nobel Prize for Economics. He's also a Princeton professor, a *New York Times* columnist, and a self-declared Keynesian economist, author of *The Conscience of a Liberal* (2007). It was Krugman who asked in one of his columns ("The Madoff Economy," *New York Times*, Dec. 19, 2008), "How different, really, is Mr. Madoff's tale from the story of the investment industry as a whole?" But before contemplating the possibility that much of capitalism is itself a Ponzi swindle writ large, we need a little background.

That's provided by Krugman in his slim and cautionary book *The Return of Depression Economics*. Actually, as Krugman explains in his introductory chapter, *Depression Economics* is a recycled version of his not-much-noticed 1999 text about the bursting of the Asian monetary bubble and other warning signs ignored, hence the add-on subtitle *... and the Crisis of 2008*, for the new edition. It's a literary example of "doing more with less," a conception that millions of unemployed and foreclosed people already had adopted by the time Krugman's book appeared.

As recently as the beginning of the 21st century, as Krugman reminds us, it was believed that "nothing like the Great Depression can ever happen again." The monumental slump of the 1930s was now seen by economists and other policy makers as a "gratuitous, unnecessary tragedy." If only the U.S. president of the day, Herbert Hoover, "hadn't tried to balance the budget in the face of an enormous economic slump"; if only "officials had rushed cash to threatened banks and thus calmed the bank panic"; if only ... But in today's enlightened era, claimed many prominent economists, we know better. Or do we?

Krugman sets up his account of the present crisis by reviewing various economic disasters and near-disasters of the past two decades in Mexico, Japan, Thailand, and other points east and south, as well as doing the forensics on recent American economic "bubbles" that eventually burst. He also explains some of the machinations of the stock market and other frightening institutions. Occasionally my eyes glazed over as Krugman explained how fortunes were made by turning Thai bahts and Mexican pesos into other currencies, but for the most part the analysis is pretty accessible, thanks to his commitment to ensuring that "there are no equations, no inscrutable diagrams, and (I hope) no impenetrable jargon" in his little treatise.

In due course, Krugman gets to the irrational housing bubble that initiated the present crisis. "Americans have long been in the habit of buying houses with borrowed money," Krugman notes, then adds, "but it's hard to see why anyone should have believed, circa 2003, that the basic principles of such borrowing had been repealed. From long experience we knew that home buyers shouldn't take on mortgages whose payments they couldn't afford, and they should put enough money down so that they can sustain a moderate drop in home prices and still have positive equity."

Instead, "what actually happened was a complete abandonment of traditional principles." A small part of the blame can be pinned on "the irrational exuberance of individual families who saw house prices rising ever higher and decided that they should jump into the market, and not worry about how to make payments."

But the real culprits, says Krugman, were the lenders. "Buyers were given loans requiring little or no down payment, and with monthly bills that were well beyond their ability to afford – or, at least would be unaffordable once the initial low, teaser rate reset. Much though not all of this dubious lending went under the headng of 'subprime,' but the phenomenon was much broader than that," and the total amount of the loans was in the hundreds of billions.

Why did the lenders relax the traditional standards, and why were they allowed to do so? Well, first, they too bought into the psychological bubble of believing in ever-rising house prices. They didn't have to worry about whether the borrowers could make their monthly payments. If the new homeowners couldn't, they could either get more cash by taking out a home equity loan or else sell the house, at a higher price, and pay off their mortage.

But far more important – and here's where it gets interesting – the lenders didn't worry about the loans "because they didn't hold on to them. Instead, they sold them to investors, who didn't understand what they were buying." The process is known as "securitization" of home mortgages – "assembling large pools of mortgages, then selling investors shares in the payments received from borrowers." Previous "securitization" had been limited to "prime" mortgages, that is, loans to borrowers who could make a substantial down payment and had enough income to meet the mortgage payments. Defaults were rare.

As the bubble inflated, everyone reached for a piece of pie-in-the-sky. Construction boomed, materials for construction were in demand, low unemployment and money in hand fuelled consumer purchases on big ticket items such as SUVs and newly invented electronic gadgets (all aided and abetted by the availability of further borrowing via credit cards), and you could even call in for pizza. All boats were lifted in the rising tide of prosperity, including all those borrowed boats. Eventually, when the people who made the loans they couldn't afford stopped paying, the foreclosures on houses began, housing prices plummeted, construction and consumption stopped, the boats, whether bought or borrowed, ran aground, and the bubble had burst. It was only when the plug was pulled that we learned that these weren't real boats, but only children's toys in a bathtub. The boats may not have been real, but people's lives going down the fiscal drain surely were.

According to Krugman, the "financial innovation" that made this enormous conjuring trick possible was something called "collateralized debt obligation" (CDOs). The CDOs created "senior" shares that were supposedly secure and junior shares that were more speculative. The CDOs were touted as a very safe investment because "even if some mortgages defaulted, how likely was it that enough would default to pose problems for the cash flow to these senior shares?" The answer: "Quite likely, it turned out." But because of the hype, the supposed watchdog or rating agencies were willing to classify senior CDO shares as AAA, "even if the underlying mortgages were highly dubious." Of course, "as long as housing prices kept rising, everything looked fine and the Ponzi scheme kept rolling." Since the CDOs were rated safe, that "opened up large-scale funding of subprime lending" to such institutional investors as pension funds that "were quite willing to buy AAA-rated assets that yielded significantly higher returns" than ordinary bonds and other super-safe properties. But once the bubble burst, we got *this*, the present monstrous mess.

In order to make the scheme work, there had to be institutions to bundle together and peddle the ultimately worthless mortgages. At this point Krugman introduces us to the crucial concept of the "shadow banking system." Krugman asks, "But wasn't the age of banking crises supposed to have ended seventy years ago? Aren't banks regulated, insured, guaranteed up the wazoo? Yes and no. Yes for traditional banks; no for a large part of the modern, de facto banking system."

In his thumbnail history of banking, Krugman notes that something eerily similar to what went on in the first decade of the 21st century happened a hundred years earlier in the Panic of 1907. "The crisis originated in institutions … known as 'trusts,' bank-like institutions" originally intended to manage inheritance and estates for the wealthy. "Because they were supposed to engage only in low-risk activities trusts were less regulated and had lower reserve requirements and lower cash reserves than national banks." As the economy boomed in the first decade of the last century, "trusts began speculating in real estate and the stock market areas from which national banks were prohibited." As long as the bubble inflated, "trusts were able to pay their depositors higher returns." When the bubble burst, it took all the republic's bankers to restore a semblance of fiscal order. Even though the actual panic lasted only a week, "it and the stock market collapse decimated the economy. A four-year recession ensued, with production falling 11 per cent" and unemployment almost tripling.

Krugman then describes the far larger crisis of 2008, one that has a global rather a merely national reach, and along the way he discusses the various arcane instruments and institutions of investment from the "auction-rate security system" to "hedge funds" and all the rest of the shadowy shadow-banking system that ultimately caved in, beginning with the 2008 bankruptcy of Lehman Brothers. Krugman notes that the unsustainable risk of such institutions wasn't really a result of deregulation but rather of the shadow system, which, although almost as large as conventional banking, was never regulated in the first place, even though the top five investment banks had balance sheets totalling $4 trillion. The catastrophe is a result of what Krugman calls "malign neglect." Nonetheless, what permitted much of the malign neglect was an ideology of unregulated market capitalism and almost theological opposition to government.

My recurrent emotion while reading Krugman's account (and I've only reprised a small portion of the complexities) was one of shock. Again and again, I found myself gasping with astonishment, "They let them do *that*?!" Much of the operation of the financial system looks like little more than a besotted weekend of casino gambling. Though I can hardly claim to be utterly naïve about the workings of capitalism, Krugman's brief book repeatedly brings home how little most people (including me) really know about what's going on. I guess that as long as our credit cards still work with a simple swipe through a machine perhaps we don't want to know. But at this point, continued ignorance is not an option.

Krugman wraps up with the usual "What is to be done?" question. His solution, which is pretty close to that of the ideas of President Barack Obama's economics team, is straightforward and not especially radical. "What the world needs right now is a rescue operation. The global credit system is in a state of paralysis and a global slump is building momentum," Krugman declares. Reform "is essential, but it can wait a little while." Right now, policy-makers around the world "need to do two things: get credit flowing again and prop up spending."

Krugman guesses that "recapitalization" of the economy will come close to requiring "a full temporary nationalization of a significant part of the financial system." Other leading economics experts also openly discussed the same thing (see "Nationalizing the Bank Problem," *New York Times*, Jan. 22, 2009). Apart from loony-tune right-wing Republicans and neo-conservative think tanks, there was a near-consensus that temporary nationalization was not unthinkable. Since the spectre haunting global capitalism isn't a radical reorganization of economic life, Krugman underscores that he isn't advocating the long-term seizure of the economy's commanding heights, as the Marxists used to say, and insists that "finance should be reprivatized as soon as it's safe to do so, just as Sweden put banking back in the private sector after its big bailout in the early 1990s." He adds, however, "Nothing could be worse than failing to do what's necessary out of fear that acting to save the financial system is somehow 'socialist.'" Some of us might be tempted to further add, "So what's wrong with a little socialism?", but we can leave that debate for another occasion.

Even if the credit markets can be brought back to life, what to do about the gathering global depression? "The answer, almost surely," says Krugman, "is good old Keynesian fiscal stimulus." That is, the next plan "should focus on sustaining and expanding government spending – sustaining it by providing aid to state and local governments, expanding it with spending on roads, bridges, and other forms of infrastructure." That's pretty much what the newly elected Barack Obama proposed at the beginning of his term in 2009, with an $800 billion stimulus package, including such other forms of "infrastructure" as education and green technology. In his subsequent columns, Krugman agreed with the direction of Obama's plan, but demurred on the sums involved. He thought they were far too small and feared that an insufficient stimulus would only lead to greater problems.

Krugman says, more than once, "We're not in a depression now, and despite everything, I don't think we're heading into one," then parenthetically adds, "although I'm not as sure of that as I'd like to be." If depression itself has not returned, depression economics – meaning, "the kinds of problems that characterized much of the world economy in the 1930s" – is back with a vengeance. Krugman's useful discussion is hardly deathless prose, nor is it meant to be. It's more on the order of "dispatches from the front," a front that's not located in some distant land but is as close as your local haunting spectre. While the ongoing immediate crisis inspired a cascade of explanatory books, there were other important investigations of political economy that marked the decade.

2. NAOMI KLEIN'S EXCELLENT ADVENTURES

Naomi Klein, *The Shock Doctrine: The Rise of Disaster Capitalism* (2007); *No Logo: Taking Aim at the Brand Bullies* (1999/2000; 2010)

If you're a teacher, what your students are wearing tells you something about what's going on in the culture. In the 1980s and 90s, I noticed that walking into a classroom was like hitting a stretch of highway crowded with advertising billboards. The students were wearing T-shirts, sweatshirts, and other paraphernalia that brazenly bore the names of the corporations that manufactured them. Unlike earlier displays of brand logos, such as the discreet crocodile insignia of a Lacoste shirt or the little horseman and mallet that decorated Ralph Lauren's Polo shirts, which were meant to subtly but publicly indicate the wearer's good taste and purchasing power, the new T-shirts were emblazoned with giant corporate names and company colours – Calvin Klein, Tommy Hilfiger, The Gap, and others – that tended to cover most of the surface of the garment being worn.

Puzzled as to why the students wanted to turn themselves into walking advertisements, I'd occasionally ask them what it all meant. Often as not, they would deny it meant anything and blandly declare, "It's just a fashion thing." Yes, I'd mildly persist, but how and why does a "fashion thing" *become* a fashion thing? And does the "thing" mean anything? Mainly, what I wondered was, how did the corporations get the consumers to not only advertise the corporation, but to pay for the privilege of doing so? The students were pretty resistant to my pointy-headed attempts at sociological analysis and my "lessons from everyday life" tended to fall flat.

Lots of subsequent "fashion statements" have come and gone since the era of big logos. In the first decade of the 21st century, I've noticed that students and other "dedicated followers of fashion" (to recall a phrase from an old pop song by The Kinks), tend to express their fashion sense less by haberdashery and bodily decorations (tattoos and other skin piercings) and more by technological accoutrements, such as iPods, cell phones, and all sorts of mobile computer gadgets. It's fairly *de rigueur* these days to be armed to the teeth with technology designed to facilitate multi-tasking, although spoilsport teachers often ask the students to turn off all electronic devices while the classroom is in session on the grounds that education is engaged in concentrating on the subject at hand or what might be called "mono-tasking."

All of these passing observations (by myself and others) remained idle speculation until the beginning of the new millennium when a then 29-year-old Canadian journalist, Naomi Klein, in a brilliant stroke of "pattern recognition," published No Logo: Taking Aim at the Brand Bullies (1999/2000; 2010). It quickly became an international, multi-lingual, million-copy bestseller, and it told readers a lot about the corporations that plastered their brands on the backs and fronts of their consumers, focusing as much on production and ideology as on the more familiar discussion of consumption. In the introduction to the 2010 tenth anniversary edition of *No Logo* – and it should be noted that a tenth anniversary edition of any work of non-fiction is a pretty rare publishing event these days – Klein points out that from the beginning of her writing career, she's always been interested in the relationship between power and business, or what was once called "political economy." (Small disclosure here: although I don't know Klein, we were both members of the editorial collective of Toronto's *This Magazine* at the end of the 1980s; she was the publication's precocious managing editor; I was its Vancouver-based West Coast correspondent.)

Among the first articles Klein published as a journalist "were [those] about the limited job options available to me and my peers – the rise of short-term contracts and McJobs, as well as the ubiquitous use of sweatshop labour to produce the branded gear sold to us." What's more, Klein also picked up on "how an increasingly voracious marketing culture was encroaching on previously protected non-corporate spaces – schools, museums, parks – while ideas that my friends and I had considered radical were absorbed almost instantly into the latest marketing campaigns for Nike, Benetton and Apple."

The notion about Klein's ability to connect-the-dots hidden in otherwise disparate phenomena is borrowed from the title of *Pattern Recognition* (2003), a novel by Vancouver writer William Gibson, who's best known for his "cyberpunk" speculative fiction. Klein mentions Gibson's book in her retrospective reflections on the genesis of *No Logo* and the kind of aha!-experience to which it refers. It's something like the sociological acuity found in Douglas Coupland's *Generation X* (1991) and other of his novels, but Klein's recognitions tend to be more pointedly political. As she recalls, "I decided to write *No Logo* when I realized these seemingly disparate trends were connected by a single idea – that corporations should produce brands, not products." Says Klein:

> This was the era when corporate epiphanies were striking CEOs like lightning bolts from the heavens: Nike isn't running a shoe company, it is about the idea of transcendence through sports,

Starbucks isn't a coffee shop chain, it's about the idea of community. Down on earth these epiphanies meant that many companies that had manufactured their products in their own factories, and had maintained large, stable workforces, embraced the now ubiquitous Nike model: close your factories, produce your products through an intricate web of contractors and subcontractors and pour your resources into the design and marketing required to project your big ideas … Some called these restructured companies "hollow corporations" because their goal seemed to be to transcend the corporeal world of things so they could be an utterly unencumbered brand.

In her 2010 *No Logo* essay, Klein explains that the move from the sociology of marketing to her later works doesn't represent a break in her thinking. "For me," she says, "the appeal of X-raying brands such as Nike or Starbucks was that pretty soon you were talking about everything except marketing – from how products are made in the deregulated global supply chain to industrial agriculture and commodity prices. Next thing you knew you were also talking about the nexus of politics and money that locked in these wild-west rules through free-trade deals and at the World Trade Organization (WTO), and made following them the precondition of receiving much-needed loans from the International Monetary Fund (IMF). In short, you were talking about how the world works."

The enormous success of *No Logo* was rooted not only in Klein's astute recognition of social patterns and their causes. It was also the result of intrepid on-the-scene reporting. "She ventures into sweatshops in the Philippines, attends classes for anticorporate crusaders and goes 'culture jamming' with groups who deface billboards in the middle of the night," as one enthusiastic reviewer described Klein's global beat (James Ledbetter, "Brand Names," *The New York Times*, April 23, 2000). The reviewer also noted that "the book's conclusions are largely grim. Klein links the development of multinational branding to the growth of international sweatshops, corporate censorship and the disappearance of the steady job," but added, "She is careful not to equate her criticisms with a false nostalgia for an ad-free past; instead, Klein takes the fairly unassailable position that our lives ought to have at least some 'unbranded space'." Although the classrooms where I was teaching were no longer among those unbranded spaces, Klein's book helped make sense of how they got to be crammed with displays of brand loyalties.

Klein notes that by the time *No Logo* came out (a first Canadian edition appeared at the very end of 1999, other editions shortly afterwards, in 2000), a popular political movement had emerged and "was already at the gates of the powerful institutions that were spreading corporatism around the world. Tens and then hundreds of thousands of demonstrators were making their case outside trade summits and G8 meetings from Seattle to New Delhi." Klein was soon amid the demonstrators and occasionally spotlighted as a spokesperson for what was called the "anti-globalisation movement." Klein regards the term as a misnomer. The spectrum of the movement, she says, ranged from anti-corporatism at the reformist end to anti-capitalism at the radical end. It was, far from being "anti-global," insistently internationalist. Klein's point is that "globalisation" was a bland euphemism for a "ruthless strain" of corporate capitalism.

For the next few years Klein joined protesters before the "gates of the powerful" and huddled in the conference rooms of various "counter-summits" as an advocacy journalist and political participant. The reportage appeared as *Fences and Windows: Dispatches from the Front Lines of the Globalisation Debate* (2002). As a collection of columns and talks, while it drew far less attention than *No Logo*, it helped develop the images and metaphors of Klein's thinking. She noticed that, despite the promise that post-Communist global economic integration would mean barriers coming down, the opposite appeared to be happening.

What's more, the fences and gates were increasingly literal. There are now, says Klein, "armies of locked-out people, whose services are no longer needed, whose lifestyles are written off as 'backward,' whose basic needs go unmet. These fences of social exclusion can discard an entire industry, and they can also write off an entire country" or even a continent. As for the protesters at global summits, they too find themselves behind actual fences, and "heavy-handed security measures ... become metaphors for an economic model that exiles billions to poverty and exclusion."

There were also less frequent glimpses through "windows," occasions where Klein experienced the feeling that "some sort of political portal was opening up – a gateway, a window, 'a crack in history'" (the phrase is that of the Mexican revolutionary, Subcomandante

Marcos), but most of all, a perspective where "the prospect of a radical change in political course does not seem like an odd and anachronistic idea but the most logical thought in the world." If you're of the party that wants to change the world, hope is probably an occupational hazard, as well as a necessity.

Naomi Klein begins her alternate history of the unregulated global free market, *The Shock Doctrine: The Rise of Disaster Capitalism* (2007), on the ground, interviewing survivors at a Red Cross shelter in Baton Rouge, Louisiana, shortly after the 2005 Hurricane Katrina that devastated the city of New Orleans. Although the efforts of President George Bush's federal emergency teams fell woefully short of the intended rescue of citizens and reconstruction of their habitations, one of the most curious things to emerge from the catastrophe, Klein reports, was educational reform.

The idea came from Nobel Prize winning economist Milton Friedman. The then 93-year-old doyen of free market economists (he died a year later, in 2006), author of *Freedom and Capitalism* (1962) and many other books, penned an op-ed piece in *The Wall Street Journal* (Dec. 5, 2005) lamenting the destruction of New Orleans' schools but also seeing the ruins as "an opportunity to radically reform the educational system."

Friedman's radical idea, Klein explains, "was that instead of spending a portion of the billions of dollars in reconstruction money on rebuilding and improving New Orleans' existing public school system, the government should provide families with vouchers, which they could spend at private institutions, many run at a profit, that would be subsidized by the state." The notion of "charter" or voucher-funded schools was an old hobbyhorse of Friedman's, who regarded the entire concept of a state-run school system as smacking of socialism. The odd idea of implementing this "radical reform" in the midst of a disaster is what Naomi Klein's book is about.

The idea was seized upon by right-wing think tanks, supported by the Bush administration, and "in sharp contrast to the glacial pace with which the levees were repaired and the electricity grid was brought back online, the auctioning off of New Orleans' school system took place with military speed and precision." Within 18 months of the hurricane, with most of the city's poor population still "in exile," as Klein says, the 123 school board–run public schools had been reduced to 4; the half-dozen existing pre-storm charter schools had burgeoned to over 30. The teachers' union's contract had been revoked and the union's 4,700 members had all been fired. Naturally, since a lot of what Klein has to say in this 600-page book is going to hinge on such facts, it's useful to note that her claims and interpretations are consistently documented, although her interpretations no doubt are subject to debate.

Neither the discussion of the New Orleans catastrophe nor the appearance of economist Friedman are tangential to Klein's concerns. Noting that the *New York Times* was soon calling New Orleans "the nation's preeminent laboratory for the widespread use of charter schools," Klein defines "these orchestrated raids on the public sphere in the wake of catastrophic events, combined with the treatment of disasters as exciting market opportunities" as the eponymous "disaster capitalism" whose history she is tracking.

Nor is Friedman just a passer-by. For more than three decades, Klein notes, Friedman and his many followers had been perfecting this disaster strategy, "waiting for a major crisis, then selling off pieces of the state to private players." She cites his *Freedom and Capitalism* as articulating "capitalism's core nostrum, what I have come to understand as the shock doctrine." There, Friedman wrote that "only a crisis – actual or perceived – produces real changes. When that crisis occurs, the actions that are taken depend on the ideas that are lying around. That, I believe, is our basic function: to develop alternatives to existing policies, to keep them alive and available until the politically impossible becomes politically inevitable."

Friedman became, unarguably, the most influential post–World War II economist in the world, displacing John Maynard Keynes, who had provided the outlines of the "welfare state" in response to the Great Depression of the 1930s. However, it wasn't until the ascension, in the 1970s and 80s, of Margaret Thatcher and Ronald Reagan to the offices of British prime minister and U.S. president, respectively, that Freidman's theories became official, mainstream, economic policy, emphasising reduction of the size of government, cuts in public spending, and the privatization of as many of the previous functions of the public sector as possible.

Friedman's ideas, however, had received their try-out a decade earlier in Latin America, and from his academic base at the University of Chicago, he and like-minded colleagues had produced a generation of so-called "Chicago Boys," economists who soon populated influential governmental posts throughout the region. Klein isn't making the claim, as she is sometimes accused of doing by critics, that Friedman was personally engaged in or even supportive of every instance of economic shock therapy. For instance, his commitment to more or less unfettered free markets would mean that he disapproved of various moves by the International Money Fund and other institutions as government interference, even when the IMF policies followed his prescriptions and were administered by economists trained at Chicago. Rather, Klein's point is that Friedman was the inspiration for a variety of free market "disaster" initiatives, irrespective of whether the governments taking them were nominally democratic or authoritarian. What's more, Friedman was often on hand to provide advice on just such occasions.

The first instance of the exploitation of a large scale shock or crisis occurred in the mid-1970s, when Friedman acted as an adviser to the Chilean dictator General Augusto Pinochet, who, in a violent coup, covertly supported by the United States, had overthrown the democratically elected socialist government of President Salvador Allende. Klein describes Friedman's proposals for tax cuts, free trade, privatized services, cuts to social spending, and deregulation (even Chilean public schools were replaced with voucher-funded private institutions) as "the most extreme capitalist makeover ever attempted anywhere." Since so many of Pinochet's economists had studied under Friedman at the University of Chicago, the transformation, which Friedman dubbed "shock treatment," was known as a "Chicago School" revolution.

The economic shock treatment in Chile was accompanied by more literal versions "performed in the regime's many torture cells." If "disaster capitalism" is the primary pattern Klein detects in her book, the use of torture and execution is a secondary, frequently interwoven, pattern that she identifies in a plethora of historical instances. "Many in Latin America," Klein declares, "saw a direct connection between the economic shocks that impoverished millions and the epidemic of torture that punished hundreds of thousands of people who believed in a different kind of society." Again and again, throughout Latin America in the 1970s, Klein documents authoritarian, violent takeovers of government, quickly followed by the shock of extreme capitalism implemented by policy makers trained by Friedman's Chicago School.

Klein, who began writing her book while the U.S. was in the midst of its self-proclaimed "Shock and Awe" attack on Iraq and the subsequent free market "reconstruction" of the country, gives herself a broader investigatory mandate than the gruesome events of Latin America. In New Orleans, Iraq, Sri Lanka in the wake of the 2004 tsunami, Poland and Russia in the post-Berlin Wall period, East Asia during its fiscal crisis of the late 1990s, and even in China and post-apartheid South Africa, she traces similar shocks and reconstructions. The circumstances of disaster she examines are various and "economics was by no means the sole motivator," she admits, nor were the traumatic episodes always overtly violent, "but in each case a major collective shock was exploited to prepare the ground for economic shock therapy." In almost all the cases she explores, there is little evidence that the free market policies improved the lives of the inhabitants affected by them.

Klein's book, finally, is conceived as "a challenge to the central and most cherished claim in the official story – that the triumph of deregulated capitalism has been born of freedom, that unfettered free markets go hand in hand with democracy itself." In making that challenge, she also offers some sensible cautions: "I am not arguing that all forms of market systems are inherently violent. It is eminently possible to have a market-based economy ... [that] coexists with free public health care, with public schools, with a large segment of the economy – like a national oil company – held in state hands." It's equally possible, she adds, to require decent wages, workers' rights, and redistribution of wealth. "Markets need not be fundamentalist." But in instance after instance, she demonstrates that the imposition of radical free market policies seldom occurs in conditions of enhanced democracy; indeed such policies, whether implemented by authoritarian regimes or the dictates of the International Monetary Fund, tend to be accompanied by a brutal curtailment of freedom.

What follows Klein's initial overview is an ambitious account that need not be reprised in detail here (but needs to be read in all its devilish detail), a panoramic story that ranges from military coups in Brazil and Chile in the 1960s and 70s to the terrorism, wars, tsunamis, and hurricanes of the last decade. Whether or not one entirely agrees with the delineation of the macro-economic "patterns" that Klein claims to recognize, her book offers a bold thesis, substantial research as well as first-hand reporting, and popular readability, all at the right political moment in the decade. For her generation, Klein conveys something of the urgency and astuteness that a previous era of radical readers had found in the work of Noam Chomsky.

The reception of *The Shock Doctrine* is also noteworthy. Klein had again written a best-seller, one that was widely reviewed, promptly translated into multiple languages, and named to numerous book-of-the-year lists. Succeeding editions carried an impressive roster of endorsements from economists, historians, and political journalists, as well as writers and other cultural figures. Novelist Arundhati Roy hailed the book as "nothing less than the secret history of what we call the 'free market'"; William Kowinski saw it as a possible revelation of "the master narrative of our time"; John Berger praised Klein as "an accusing angel."

Even discounting for the hyperbole, thoughtful analysts reckoned that Klein had recognized something important. The British social critic John Gray saw Klein's critique of neo-liberalism as both timely and devastating. "Many of the ideas of the far left," he writes, "have found new homes on the right." Once upon a time, it was the communist revolutionary Lenin who believed that conditions of catastrophic upheaval were crucial to social transformation; today, "the devastation of entire societies has been a key part of the neo-liberal cult of the free market," says Gray.

Throughout the world, Gray argues, "policies of wholesale privatisation and structural adjustment have led to declining economic activity and social dislocation on a massive scale. Anyone who has watched a country lurch from one crisis to another as the bureaucrats of the IMF impose cut after cut in pursuit of the holy grail of stabilisation will recognize the process Naomi Klein describes in her latest and most important book to date." *The Shock Doctrine*, he says, is one of those "very few books that really help us understand the present." Disaster capitalism, Gray foresees, writing exactly one year before the collapse of Lehman Brothers and the beginning of a global Great Recession, "is now creating disasters larger than it can handle" (John Gray, "The End of the World as We Know It," *The Guardian*, Sept. 15, 2007).

Joseph Stiglitz, a former World Bank and Bill Clinton administration economist, also thought "Klein's ambitious look at the economic history of the last 50 years and the rise of free-market fundamentalism around the world" a significant accomplishment. "Klein provides a rich description of the political machinations required to force un-savory economic policies on resisting countries, and of the human toll," Stiglitz writes, adding, "she paints a disturbing portrait of hu-bris, not only on the part of Milton Friedman but also of those who adopted his doctrines, sometimes to pursue more corporatist object-ives. It is striking to be reminded how many of the people involved in the Iraq War were involved earlier in other shameful episodes in United States foreign policy history. She draws a clear line from the torture in Latin America in the 1970s to that at Abu Ghraib and Guantanamo Bay," the two most notorious allegedly anti-terrorist prisons of the last decade.

As for the economics of the book, Stiglitz admits that "Klein is not an academic and cannot be judged as one. There are many places in her book where she oversimplifies. But Friedman and the other shock therapists were also guilty of oversimplification, basing their belief in the perfection of market economies on models that assumed perfect information, perfect competition, perfect risk markets. Indeed, the case against these policies is even stronger than the one Klein makes." Some of that case is made in Stiglitz's own subsequent book, *Freefall: America, Free Markets, and the Sinking of the World Economy* (2010).

Stiglitz recognizes that Klein isn't a professional economist but a journalist, and what he likes about her work is that "she travels the world to find out firsthand what really happened on the ground dur-ing the privatization of Iraq, the aftermath of the Asian tsunami, the continuing Polish transition to capitalism and the years after the African National Congress took power in South Africa, when it failed to pursue redistributionist policies." Stiglitz anticipates that Klein will be viewed by opponents as a mere conspiracy theorist. He points out that it's "not the conspiracies that wreck the world but the series of wrong turns, failed policies, and little and big unfair-nesses that add up." Not conspiracies, but a mind-set: "Market fun-damentalists never really appreciated the institutions required to make an economy function well, let alone the broader social fabric that civilizations require to prosper and flourish." (Joseph Stiglitz, "Bleakonomics," *The New York Times*, Sept. 30, 2007.)

Klein's book also had no shortage of detractors, even among left-liberals who otherwise provided much of the chorus of praise.

Perhaps the most dismissive of the criticisms was a lengthy essay in the *New Republic* (Jonathan Chait, "Dead Left," July 30, 2008), but Klein was also shrugged off by Doug Henwood in his newsletter *Left Business Observer* ("Awe, Shocks," March 2008), and frequently seen as a dupe of conspiracy theories (Tom Redburn, "It's All a Grand Capitalist Conspiracy," *The New York Times*, Sept. 29, 2007).

The most substantial of the critiques, Jonathan Chait's, is also notable for a tone that mixes ill-disguised resentment (and perhaps some envy) at Klein's prominence as a social critic, with a dismissal of her intellectual capability that tends to equate her with the nitwit teenagers who featured in the 1989 movie comedy *Bill and Ted's Excellent Adventure*. In that justly forgotten nerdish epic, the boys make use of a fortuitously available time machine in a desperate bid to pass their history exam. "It seems like a very long time – though in truth only a few years have passed – since the most sinister force on the planet that the left could imagine was Nike," is Chait's heavy-handed sardonic opener.

There's a thumbnail sketch of Klein's progress from "red diaper baby" (she comes from a leftist family and is married to Avi Lewis, a younger member of a prominent Canadian social democratic lineage) to spokesperson for the "defining causes" of the era (she writes for the *Guardian*, the *Nation,* and other lefty publications), and "darling of the left." (For interested readers, the most extensive profile of Klein in the mainstream media is Larissa MacFarquhar, "Outside Agitator," *The New Yorker*, Dec. 8, 2008.) But under it all, Chait's point appears to be that Klein is a simply a "classic Marxist-materialist" analyst with a bit of derivative Frankfurt School cultural critique tossed in. It's not clear whether Chait's claim that she "managed to make old notions feel new" is an observation or a complaint, and it's never said what exactly is wrong with Klein's rediscovery of the evils of capitalism.

Other critics, such as Tom Redburn, charge Klein with seeing "everything" as an opportunity "for a particularly ruthless form of capitalism to succeed where it otherwise would never take hold." He admits that "there's a measure of truth about the dark side of globalization in all this, but that's a lot to lay on poor Milton [Friedman]." Doug Henwood of *Left Business Observer* thinks that there's little new or "secret" in Klein and that it's simplistic to put such varied instances into a single theory. Henwood is a bit more-leftist-than-thou, chiding Klein for not including more pre-1970 history (particularly the Vietnam War) and for being nostalgic "for the Keynesian welfare state model," implying that more than Scandinavian-style social democracy is going to be required to solve the deeper crisis.

It may be that Klein's "pattern recognition" of "disaster capitalism" is over-extended. I share some of the reservations of Klein's critics and, as we've all learned in recent years, the situation is always more complicated than it appears. Still, I'm disposed to give her the benefit of the doubt in most instances, and I'm not much interested in whether her manner or fame are irritating to some. If anything, the years of the global capitalist crisis since *The Shock Doctrine* was published tend to bear out Klein's and others' arguments about unregulated free-market capitalism. The accuracy of Klein's "pattern recognition" is important, but it's outweighed, in my view, by the overall substance of her narrative.

For myself, Klein's work in the last decade inspires reflection about history and memory. As one of the readers of *The Shock Doctrine* who has lived through all of the historical events adumbrated in its pages, I'm surprised by both how much I've forgotten and how much I never understood. Much of Klein's writing works as an *aide-memoire* to our own era. Whether or not Klein has absolutely correctly recognized the patterns of the past half century, her tour of benighted and brutalized places on the globe is a historical reminder of the horrors of our time. It's as if all lands, including the "homeland," are now among the "dark places of the earth" that Joseph Conrad first traced in *Heart of Darkness* more than a century ago.

In terms of writing in the last decade, the most prominent literary figures among Naomi Klein's Canadian compatriots are undoubtedly Margaret Atwood, Alice Munro, and Michael Ondaatje. But I think a case can be made that Klein is not only one of her country's best-selling authors of the last ten years but also its most relevant writer.

3. WHAT DO YOU GET?

Barbara Ehrenreich, *Nickel and Dimed: On (Not) Getting By in America* (2001)

Sometime around the turn of the century, from the 20th to the 21st, the veteran journalist Barbara Ehrenreich was taken to lunch at an "understated" but expensive French restaurant by Lewis Lapham, the editor of *Harper's*, to discuss possible articles Ehrenreich might write for his magazine. The conversation drifted to one of the familiar themes that Ehrenreich frequently wrote about – poverty.

As Ehrenreich subsequently recounted the table talk at the French eatery, they wondered, "How does anyone live on the wages available to the unskilled?" Given that the Clinton administration had recently passed stringent new welfare restriction laws, they asked, "How were the roughly four million women about to be booted into the labor market by welfare reform going to make it on $6 or $7 an hour?" At which point, Ehrenreich "said something that I have since had many opportunities to regret." She said, "Someone ought to do the old-fashioned kind of journalism – you know, go out there and try it for themselves." Ehrenreich, then in her mid-50s, "meant someone much younger than myself, some hungry neophyte journalist with time on her hands. But Lapham got this crazy-looking half smile on his face and ended life as I knew it, for long stretches at least, with the single word '*You*'."

The outcome of that conversation is one of the most poignant, well-written, and important books of the decade, Barbara Ehrenreich's *Nickel and Dimed: On (Not) Getting By in America* (2001). I think it's fair to say that no discussion of either the economic crises of the last decade, or of writing that probed the resultant disruptions in the lives of millions of people, would be adequate without recognition of the work of Ehrenreich.

The radical, muckraking, intrepid reporter who, since the 1960s, has been publishing two, three, and more books a decade about everyday life in America, is something of a role model to younger understudies, like Naomi Klein. Ehrenreich's early scientific publications (she received a Ph.D. in cellular biology from Rockefeller University in 1968) were quickly succeeded by political, economic, and feminist writings, beginning with *Long March, Short Spring: The Student Uprising at Home and Abroad* (1969), written with her first husband John Ehrenreich, and continuing right up to *Bright-Sided: How the Relentless Promotion of Positive Thinking Has Undermined America* (2009), an acerbic debunking of the sentimentalities of the U.S. "happiness" industry.

The project Ehrenreich conceived for *Nickel and Dimed* was simply to do the kind of ordinary work that millions of people do every day, and then to write it up. The "rules" she invented for herself included finding jobs that didn't rely on her skills or education; taking "the highest-paying job that was offered to me and do[ing] my best to hold it: no Marxist rants or sneaking off to read novels in the ladies' room"; and living in the cheapest accommodations she could find, commensurate with "an acceptable level of safety and privacy, though my standards in this regard were hazy and, as it turned out, prone to deterioration over time." The last is a polite way of saying that she occasionally ended up in flea-bitten firetraps through no choice of her own. Ehrenreich pretty much stuck to her self-imposed rules, but points out that "this is not a story of some death-defying 'undercover' adventure. Almost anyone could do what I did – look for jobs, work those jobs, try to make ends meet. In fact, millions of Americans do it every day, and with a lot less fanfare and dithering."

At the time Ehrenreich began, it was estimated that it took, "on average nationwide, an hourly wage of $8.89 to afford a one-bedroom apartment," and yet, about 30 per cent of the American workforce at the time was earning only $8 an hour or less. How did they do it? What were their lives like? Ehrenreich begins her low-wage life in Key West, Florida, the town closest to where she lives, as a waitress in a "family restaurant" attached to a chain discount hotel. It's "a dismal looking spot looking out on a parking garage, which is featuring 'Polish sausage and BBQ sauce' on this 95-degree day," and it pays $2.43 an hour plus tips. In Portland, Maine, Ehrenreich becomes part of a female housecleaning crew, and in Minneapolis, Minnesota, she lands a sales job at Wal-Mart (a job that doesn't involve sales so much as picking up and refolding clothes in the wake of disorderly shoppers). There are a few other paying gigs along the way, and at the end an evaluation of the obvious: "You don't need a degree in economics to see that wages are too low and rents too high."

What makes *Nickel and Dimed* so compelling is that Ehrenreich renders visible a very large chunk of working class reality that readers outside of that reality seldom see or think about. It is a portrait of injustice, of course. At the same time, it is a beautifully written book, part of whose literary quality is that its congenial prose is almost invisible. It is both tempered and brought into high relief by the precision of Ehrenreich's eye, which includes the details of the believable lives of her harried co-workers, all the relevant facts and figures down to the penny (in situations where pennies count), and a sense of humour that even includes those occasional hallucinogenic moments at the Wal-Mart's women's wear department where she briefly achieves "a magical flow state in which the clothes start putting *themselves* away." But those fleeting instants are about as much magical realism as Enrenreich permits herself; for the rest, it's a daily grind of bone-tiring, ill-paid work. As the mid-20th century coal-miners' song, "Sixteen Tons" has it,

> You load sixteen tons, what do you get?
> Another day older and deeper in debt.
> Saint Peter, don't you call me, 'cause I can't go;
> I owe my soul to the company store.

Wal-Mart is the company store of our times. "If it's hard to think 'out of the box,' it may be almost impossible to think out of the Big Box," Ehrenreich says in explaining why and how people put up with living lives in which they're barely able to get along. "Wal-Mart, when you're in it, is total – a closed system, a world unto itself," she discovers, and recounts an eerie but ordinary incident in which,

> watching TV in the break room one afternoon [she] sees ... *a commercial for Wal-Mart.* When a Wal-Mart shows up within a television within a Wal-Mart, you have to question the existence of an outer world. Sure, you can drive for five minutes and get somewhere else – to Kmart, that is, or Home Depot, or Target, or Burger King, or Wendy's, or KFC. Wherever you look, there is no alternative to the megascale corporate order ... Even the woods and meadows have been stripped of disorderly life forms and forced into a uniform made of concrete. What you see – highways, parking lots, stores – is all there is, or all that's left to us here in the reign of globalized, totalized, paved-over, corporatized everything.

Maybe this is the "Marxist rant" Ehrenreich promised to refrain from while on the job. If so, it's justified at the conclusion of a book about the lives of the "working poor," a way of life that was marginal even before the capitalist meltdown at the end of the decade.

4. THAT SINKING FEELING

Joseph Stiglitz, *Freefall: America, Free Markets, and the Sinking of the World Economy* (2010)

One of the many disquieting things about the Great Recession that began in 2008 is how much the theory and practice of "business as usual" survived intact, not only in the world of business but in politics and the public forum as well. "One might have thought," says Joseph Stiglitz, near the beginning of *Freefall*, "that with the crisis of 2008, the debate over market fundamentalism – the notion that unfettered markets by themselves can ensure economic prosperity and growth – would be over. One might have thought that no one ever again – or at least until memories of this crisis have receded into the distant past – would argue that markets are self-correcting and that we can rely on the self-interested behaviour of market participants to ensure that everything works well." Instead, on Wall Street and in the American Congress, as well as in other global centres of power and finance, we heard once again the theology of the marketplace and its corollary damnation of government intrusion.

Joseph Stiglitz is the 2001 winner of the Nobel Prize in economics, former chief economist of the World Bank, an advisor to the Clinton administration, a Columbia University professor, and one of the thinkers who predicted and warned against the impending recession well in advance of its advent. In *Freefall*, he attempts to explain some of what went wrong. His book is both an interim report on the causes of the crisis and a running assessment of the remedial measures taken by the Obama administration in its first year in office. Stiglitz's book joins a growing (and perhaps groaning) shelf of works that try to explain the extraordinary economic events of the first decade of the new century, events that proved contagious in a "globalized" world where, as we're frequently reminded, national economies are interconnected.

The profusion of books inspired by the economic crisis that deserve at least mention here present both detailed narrative accounts of the capitalist meltdown, such as William Cohan's *House of Cards: How Wall Street Gamblers Broke Capitalism* (2009), *New York Times* financial reporter Andrew Ross Sorkin's thriller-paced *Too Big To Fail* (2009), and Michael Lewis's *The Big Short: Inside the*

Doomsday Machine (2010), as well as more analytical forays. The fiscal investigations and autopsies range from those that probe historical precedents, such as Liaquat Ahamed's *Lords of Finance: The Bankers Who Broke the World* (2009), a re-telling of the run-up to the 1930s Great Depression, to works attempting a broader overview of the present. Among the more readable volumes about the market are English novelist John Lanchester's populist *Whoops!: Why Everyone Owes Everyone and No One Can Pay* (2010; the American edition is titled, *I.O.U.*), Paul Krugman's writings (cited above), Jeff Madrick's *The Case for Big Government* (2009), Nouriel Roubini and Stephen Mihm's *Crisis Economics: A Crash Course in the Future of Finance* (2010), and Stiglitz's own *Freefall*. I'm focusing on the latter as something of a stand-in for an impressive array of analyses that necessarily cover similar and overlapping ground.

Stiglitz's book "is about a battle of ideas, about the ideas that led to the failed policies that precipitated the crisis and about the lessons that we take away from it." It's a critique of shattered illusions and, in terms of what might be learned, an argument for what can be called "social democratic" economics and politics. "Economics need a balance between the role of markets and the role of government – with important contributions by nonmarket and nongovernmental institutions. In the last twenty-five years, America lost that balance, and it pushed its unbalanced perspective on countries around the world," says Stiglitz.

In looking at "the making of a crisis," Stiglitz warns against "too facile explanations" that begin and end "with the excessive greed of the bankers." Yes, the bankers were greedy, but in part that's because they had "incentives and opportunities" to be greedy. Stiglitz emphasizes the interconnectedness of the elements that produced the crisis: a phantasmal housing bubble generated by worthless "sub-prime" mortgages; the bundling or "securitization" of those mortgages through instruments of fiscal "innovation" invented by very clever operators; the sale of those packages by both mainstream and "shadow bank" sectors to large investors, including mutual funds, pensions, and other banks around the world; the absence of regulation of both institutions and innovations, or the collusion of regulators who gave their imprimatur to Ponzi-scheme-like speculation; and the inevitable, even predictable, bust that followed the artificial boom.

It was mortgage securitization, the bundling and sale of "toxic" mortgages, "that proved lethal," says Stiglitz, who likens the whole process to the attempts of medieval alchemists to turn base metals into gold. Here, "modern alchemy entailed the transformation of risky sub-prime mortgages into AAA-rated products safe enough to be held by pension funds. And the ratings agencies blessed what the banks had done. Finally, the banks got directly involved in gambling – including not just acting as middlemen for the risky assets that they were creating, but actually holding the assets." When the day of reckoning came, it was not just investor institutions and individuals who were stuck with worthless assets; it turned out that the banks, both mainstream and shadow, had also been caught off guard.

Summing it up, Stiglitz charges that "America's financial markets had failed to perform their essential societal functions of managing risk, allocating capital, and mobilizing savings, while keeping transaction costs low. Instead, they had created risk, misallocated capital, and encouraged excessive indebtedness while imposing high transaction costs." The high transaction costs made for ballooning profits and instant multi-million dollar bonus compensation for the money managers. "At their peak in 2007," notes Stiglitz, "the bloated financial markets absorbed 41 per cent of profits in the corporate sector." That's a number worth thinking about. It's a reminder that in the midst of all the razzmatazz, the economic system wasn't making money from making things, but making profit by moving money around (often, imaginary money).

While the details of the story are fascinating, the fiscal innovations downright exotic, and Stiglitz's telling of the tale engrossing, there's something more going on here, and the shrewder observers, like Stiglitz, Krugman, and Roubini are quick to see it. "The current crisis," says Stiglitz, "has uncovered fundamental flaws in the capitalist system, or at least the peculiar version of capitalism that emerged in the latter part of the twentieth century in the United States. It is not just a matter of flawed individuals or specific mistakes, nor is it a matter of fixing a few minor problems or tweaking a few policies." Rather, there's something wrong with capitalism. However, none of the major analysts at hand is proposing anything more than a social democratic reform of capitalism. This is not Karl Marx and *The Communist Manifesto* of 1848.

In arguing that the "problems are more deep-seated," Stiglitz notes that even in the last quarter-century, "this supposedly self-regulating apparatus, our financial system" has repeatedly required government rescue from crisis. As for the world outside the U.S., Stiglitz, who once worked for the World Bank and is something of a "crisis veteran," reports that "crises in developing countries have occurred with an alarming regularity – by one count, 124 between 1970 and 2007." Stiglitz also has the virtue of not treating the numbers as abstractions; repeatedly, he points to the toll caused by these crises on actual human beings.

Nouriel Roubini, an economics professor at New York University, where his gloomy but prescient predictions of the collapse earned him the sobriquet of "Dr. Doom," goes further in underscoring the point that crisis is inherent in capitalism. He describes the idea that markets are stable, solid, dependable, self-regulating entities as a "simple, quaint belief." His book, *Crisis Economics*, as he and his co-author Stephen Mihm explain, "returns crises to the front and center of economic inquiry ... It shows that far from being the exception, crises are the norm, not only in emerging but in advanced industrial economies. Crises – unsustainable booms followed by calamitous busts – have always been with us ... Though they arguably predate the rise of capitalism, they have a particular relationship to it. Indeed, in many important ways, crises are hardwired into the capitalist genome."

In his focus on the nature of "crisis economics," Roubini indirectly echoes some of the ideas in Naomi Klein's *The Shock Doctrine*. Roubini says that, beyond the exploitation of crises by a particular school of capitalists, economic instability is part of what capitalism is all about. The amelioration of capitalist crises, insofar as it is available, is state regulation of capitalism to prevent "bubbles" and the use of government as an instrument of economic stimulus in hard times. Stiglitz, Krugman, and Roubini represent themselves as proponents of capitalist markets but insist on the reform of such markets in the name of democracy, justice, and a morality that is seldom heard about outside of certain church pews and select university classrooms.

Stiglitz's *Freefall* provides an on-going evaluation of the Obama administration's measures in response to the present recession as well as to the systemic flaws of capitalism. His account is hardly reassuring. Stiglitz says that his experience as an analyst of Obama's policies has been "painful." The "spirit of hope" that marked the arrival of a new, more liberal president has substantially diminished. Neither Stiglitz, Krugman, or Roubini, three of the most prestigious economists working in the U.S., is satisfied that the American or global response to the crisis amounts to more than half-measures and muddling through. Although they call for policies that are much stronger than the programs and rules established to date, there's a political problem.

It is not clear that the Obama administration, even if wanted to implement stronger measures, has the political clout to do so. What is most evident about American politics in the first years of the new century is how deeply divided the world's most powerful empire is, riven by seemingly unreconcilable economic, cultural, and political values. No doubt, it's too much to demand that economists like Stiglitz and his intellectual peers offer not only economic remedies but political formulas that will permit their implementation. Roubini cites a line from John Maynard Keynes, one of the mentors of the age. Keynes criticised economists who, "in tempestuous seasons ... can only tell us that when the storm is long past, the ocean is flat again." So far, the ocean is not yet flat again, and even the best economists, to echo the sub-title of Stiglitz's book, tend to leave us with a familiar sinking feeling.

5. P.S.

When economist Jeff Madrick's *The Case for Big Government* was published at the beginning of 2009, in the midst of the largest global capitalist crash since the 1930s, and just as U.S. President Barack Obama was being inaugurated, I thought that events had pretty much surpassed the pitch made in the book's title. As one reviewer wryly noted, Madrick's defence of the importance of government arrived at a moment "when one might imagine that Wall Street has made the case quite persuasively on its own."

Even if Madrick's title was half-ironic, playing on the frequent conservative denunciation of "big government," the capitalist meltdown signalled by the bankruptcy of Lehman Brothers' bank in September 2008 showed that the market was neither beneficent, self-correcting, or rational, as its proponents had long trumpeted, and that the rescue of Wall Street as well as cleaning up the broader mess could only be done by an institution devoted to the public good rather than private profit, namely, the state.

In short, it seemed fairly obvious that government was back. And not a moment too soon, considering the greed-fuelled, reckless, crisis. But that's not what happened in the first two years of the Obama administration. Wall Street and the other global centres of finance didn't appreciably change their way of doing business, and in the U.S., the financial sector, while happy to accept taxpayer bailouts, stubbornly resisted even minimal forms of government regulation, investing substantial sums of money in lobbying efforts to prevent constraints on its methods of transacting business.

Not until mid-2010 was a moderate fiscal regulation law levered into place. Earlier, Obama and the Democratic Party representatives in the American Congress passed modest but significant health care reform legislation as well as a stimulus package in an effort to refurbish infrastructure, maintain public services, especially schools, and ultimately reduce a nearly ten per cent official unemployment rate (the "real" numbers, it's claimed, may be half again as high). Every initiative of the new president was almost unanimously opposed by the Republican Party opposition. Moreover, conservative political forces in the U.S. moved further to the populist right under the banner of a "Tea Party" movement, accompanied by a ratcheting up of the decibel level in the public forum, thanks to a rabid right-wing media.

If the recession and near collapse of the economy might have been expected to instil a new respect for the role of government in public affairs, given that government action is what averted catastrophe, there has been little evidence of it. Nor has there been much of a swing away from the libertarian ideas and rhetoric that have had free play ever since the era of President Ronald Reagan in the 1980s. Even though the effects of the recession are visible everywhere, the debate in the U.S., Europe, and elsewhere, some two years after the "freefall" of the economy, focused not on further measures to alleviate joblessness, home foreclosure, and diminishing public services but instead concentrated on fears about government deficits. The resulting proposals to "tame" those deficits would further reduce services, government revenues, and consumption exactly at the moment when, according to many economic thinkers, further stimulus is precisely what is called for.

By the end of 2010, mid-term elections in the U.S. had resulted in a significant political shift in favour of right-wing representatives in the government. Anti-government rhetoric, often promoted by recently elected government officeholders themselves, was as loud as ever. While the "recession" was statistically and officially over, it remained a stubborn reality for millions of under- and unemployed citizens. Large numbers of people continued to experience the economic crisis on a daily basis but, paradoxically, the lessons that the financial cataclysm offered about the necessary role of government were either denied or, worse, forgotten. The economic near-collapse left in its wake, along with large-scale joblessness and empty, foreclosed homes, a volatile mixture of amnesia and ignorance.

Code Red

For most of the first decade of the 21st century, the U.S. government deployed a colour-coded terrorism threat scale known as the Homeland Security Advisory System. The colour red was used to denote the highest degree of anticipated danger, and the scale then shaded toward cooler hues, green and blue, to indicate reduced levels of threat – although the less threatening colours were never, as far as I know, used. During much of the decade, the threat level remained high, oscillating between orange and yellow.

Many saw the scale as merely a rhetorical device and, like the somewhat similar attempt to popularise the ungainly acronym "GWOT" (for "Global War on Terror"), the colour-coded threat scheme came in for considerable derision. As a character in Tom Rachman's novel *The Imperfectionists* (2010) says about GWOT, "[S]ince conflict against an abstraction is, to be polite, tough to execute, the term should be understood as marketing gibberish." Critics of the colour-code scale took a similar line, dubious that a warning system originally designed to signal the level of danger of a forest fire occurring could be usefully applied to the complexities of politics. Ultimately, the colour code was seen more as a propaganda device to ratchet up popular anxiety than as a source of useful information and it was quietly phased out of use by the Obama administration in early 2011.

I suspect that a "code red" system to depict threats to the condition of our culture would be similarly ineffective. Still, the thought of issuing "red alerts" or raising rippling coloured flags has some appeal. There were certainly alert-worthy political conflicts, metaphysical disputes, economic crises, natural catastrophes and cultural productions during the decade 2000-2009, some of which are the subject of my book. But it is the deteriorating state of the "cultural context," primarily in North America, that particularly caught my attention as I considered the books of the decade.

The state of our overall cultural context is obscured for many by the present technological revolution in digital information and entertainment devices, which is itself part of the cultural context. Yet, there's trouble in our virtual paradise. I've argued in this book, both overtly and as a sub-textual theme, that we find ourselves in a paradoxical dilemma in which writing flourishes, which is just cause for celebration, but book reading is in decline, especially among younger people. That situation ought to set off alarms, even if not yet of the code red variety.

These discouraging words about reading will seldom be heard in the glittering emporia where the latest infotainment devices are on sale but they are easily located in contemporary writing. For example, in Gary Shteyngart's satiric *Super Sad True Love Story* (2010), a doleful romance is embedded in a dystopian "very near future (oh, let's say next Tuesday) ... [in a] functionally illiterate America" which is just about to collapse. Due to a temporary power outage, the "elderly" protagonist Lenny (he's 39) resorts to the antiquated practice of reading aloud to his younger girlfriend, Eunice, from an old "printed, bound media artifact" titled *The Unbearable Lightness of Being* by the long-forgotten author Milan Kundera. Sensing that Eunice has drifted off, Lenny asks, "Are you following all this? Maybe we should stop." "I'm listening," she murmurs. "But are you *understanding*?" he wants to know. "I've never really learned how to read texts," she admits. "Just to scan them for info."

For those of us who haven't drifted off, the poignancy of that scene is not in the intellectually desolate imagined future but in its chilling proximity to present reality. By "cultural context," I mean something more than the reading of serious books, even bitterly brilliant novels like Shteyngart's all-too-plausible speculative fiction. Rather, "cultural context" refers to an entire ensemble of activities and artifacts that occupies significant portions of our lives. It includes book reading but it also takes in playing video games, chatting on cellphones (or "texting" and "sexting"), Internet surfing, watching YouTube, or "friending" people on Facebook and other social network sites. It includes much of the political apparatus, the entire education system, television, films, advertising, pornography, and the vast, lucrative realm of sports spectatorship – much of it accompanied by the ubiquitous iPod soundtrack that provides the pulse of many people's lives. Examination of our cultural context inevitably involves judgments about the quality of the materials with which we're engaged (even if those judgments are no more than libertarian pronouncements that deny that there are judgments to be made). Finally, as I've suggested by discussing a broad range of books about current events, evaluation of our cultural condition is inseparable from politics, economics, moral progress (or the lack thereof), and our understanding of our own historical situation.

It's likely that this crucial evaluation will be one of the themes of the writing of the second decade of the 21st century. Already, books that I've discussed here, such as Bauerlein's *The Dumbest Generation*, Jacoby's *The Age of American Unreason*, and Judt's *Reappraisals*, as well as books that have appeared subsequently, including Nicholas Carr's *The Shallows: What the Internet Is Doing to Our Brains* (2010), Jaron Lanier's *You Are Not a Gadget* (2010), and Clay Shirky's *Cognitive Surplus: Creativity and Generosity in a Connected Age* (2010), have contributed to the debate. I should note that I'm certainly not claiming that this debate is unique to our era. Each generation in every culture faces its own intellectual challenges, but how we succeed or fail in addressing the particular issues of our time is what's at stake here.

Much of the discussion to date strikes me as too narrow to adequately assess what I'm calling the cultural context, and the responses to the debate often tend to be dismissive, ranging from outright denial that there's a problem to scoffing at what are seen as the perennial complaints of the elderly about the behaviour of the young. The weary murmurs of "it was ever thus" are offset by the clamour of competing sales pitches for new technological utopias.

Some of the discussion is also misguided. The question of whether we read our books in the form of a "printed codex" or on an e-reader can obscure the issue of whether we're reading at all and, if we are, whether what we're reading is any good. The effort to understand what the Internet and other devices are doing to our brains is interesting, but it shouldn't divert us from critically examining the contents of the information systems we're employing. Marshall McLuhan's celebrated claim that "the medium is the message" needs to be corrected to acknowledge that the message is *also* part of the message, irrespective of how it is transmitted by various media. We too often forget that it is the real world that constitutes the "world wide web" and that the designation www. on our computers points only to a virtual world.

Throughout this "reading" of the beginning of the 21st century, while I've emphasized that there's plenty to read (and that there will continue to be worthwhile books being written for the foreseeable future), I've taken the view that the general decline of book reading is a symptom of a larger cultural and political crisis. It has been denied that there is a decline in reading, but I've yet to see a persuasive refutation of the statistics I've cited from the various books I've discussed here or of the anecdotal evidence I've accumulated over a long teaching career, evidence that is consistently corroborated by colleagues.

Nor is the decline in book reading simply a matter of shifting tastes and the replacement of books by other forms of equally valuable materials. The data indicates that the decline in book reading is associated with other "knowledge deficits" (in history, science, politics, and culture) as well as with diminishing participation in the cultural and civic activities necessary to flourishing democracies. My experience with post-secondary students, who at least formally share a more intense intellectual engagement with the world than that experienced by two-thirds of their agemates, indicates that while they maintain a variety of individual identities, their sense of being citizens of a democracy, if it ever existed, has atrophied.

Further, we have considerable data about what young people are doing with their time: they are studying less than students two decades ago and their minds are occupied with undemanding entertainments. There's little point to arguing over, say, the virtues or deficiencies of video games without putting the usage of such games and their effects into the larger cultural context in order to see the quality of the minds being developed in contemporary society. It's not sufficient to inveigh against violent video games or debate the fine points of the hand-and-eye coordination skills that may be acquired through *World of Warcraft*. Specific concerns about one aspect or another of the culture must be considered in relation to the whole. Just as thinkers in the past have presented overviews of the cultural, political, and moral condition of their times, I expect that writers of the present decade will attempt to broadly analyze, evaluate, and even remedy the failings of the current conjuncture.

I'm neither persuaded by the denial of a cultural crisis, no matter how confidently articulated, nor consoled by the claim that the degree of ignorance is more or less a historical constant. However, I'm distrustful of people who know with certainty either the truth or the future, my inclination being less toward the declarative sentence and more toward the interrogative one. Rather than ranting about "the end of the world as we know it" (to cite both the title of an old R.E.M. song and the sub-title of Ken Auletta's business history, *Googled* (2009)), I'm drawn to examining and evaluating the available evidence, even if it leads to a Samuel Beckett-like gloom.

Occasionally, I'm surprised by how sanguine some people are who might be expected to know better. For example, the *New York Times* convened a symposium under the heading "Why Criticism Matters" (Dec. 31, 2010), in which a half-dozen well-known literary critics and writers were invited to evaluate the state of the critical craft. The cleverest of the essays was by Katie Roiphe, who began by affecting an air of mock alarm, asking, "Is it time to write about the Death of the Critic, the proliferation of the app, the rise of the screen ...?" (Katie Roiphe, "With Clarity and Beauty, the Weight of Authority," *New York Times*, Dec. 31, 2010.)

But "before the requiem begins," she cautions us to remember that critics "have always decried the decline of standards, the end of reading ... the virtually apocalyptic state of literature and culture. Yet somehow the bruised and embattled figures of both the writer and the critic have survived lo these many centuries." Roiphe goes on in this gently mocking vein at some length, recommending that we take "with a grain of salt our definite sense and encroaching fear that our audience of educated readers is shrinking." In short, no problem, or none that can't be solved by the critic writing "dramatically, vividly, beautifully." Roiphe sees the "seductions of Facebook" as simply healthy competition. "The answer to the angry Amazon reviewer who mangles sentences in an effort to berate or praise an author is the perfectly constructed old-fashioned essay," she advises. Thus will critical authority be preserved. "The secret function of the critic today," Roiphe concludes, "is to write beautifully, and in so doing protect beautiful writing." Even as someone whose childhood was happily poisoned by *Mad* magazine's emblematic character

Alfred E. Newman and his proclamation, "What, me worry?", I can only admire Roiphe's insouciance as the ranks of literary critics are being decimated.

Fortunately, Roiphe's is not the only note struck. The Indian writer and critic Pankaj Mishra reminds us that both Liu Xiaobo, the imprisoned 2010 Nobel Peace winner from China, who is a literary critic by trade, and Mario Vargas Llosa, the Peruvian winner of the 2010 Nobel Prize for Literature, "testify to the impossibility of considering aesthetic matters in isolation from social and political movements. They confirm that a writer's individual self-awareness is always historically determined, and that one cannot assess a writer's work without examining her particular quarrel with the world, the rage or discontent that took her to writing in the first place." (Pankaj Mishra, "The Intellectual at Play in the Wider World," *New York Times*, Dec. 31, 2010.) While Mishra doesn't speak directly to the fate of literary criticism, he recalls us to the critic's subject matter. Mishra, however, is the exception – most of the musing about the future of criticism sounds more like whistling past the graveyard.

The problem is that while we have some idea of what is to be done to produce desirable and diverse public mentalities, we have very little idea of *how* to do it. We see more clearly the power of political and economic resistance to such changes than the means to countermand or subvert those powers. Against the present prospect of ignorance and amnesia, I counterpose the books and ideas I've written about in *Reading the 21st Century*. The schematic version of what is a far more complex argument that can be essayed in a brief conclusion is that if a sufficient number of people read the "books of the decade," ignorance would be diminished, the threat of amnesia averted, and the possibility of sustaining a democratic society and significant intellectual life would be enhanced. (My use of "books" here serves as a metonym for the larger cultural context.)

If facing our situation inspires a form of Beckettian despair, those of us who are already readers (and participants in democratic societies) can take solace in the fact that there's plenty to read, now and in the immediate future. The readership for serious books may be shrinking and the "saving remnant" may be increasingly isolated or restricted to book clubs and literary fairs. However, the "end of reading" is not an imminent prospect. What's more, as those of us who work in education observe, there continues to be a proportion of the present generation who are readers and citizens. They may amount to only a future elite, but better a democratic elite than barbarism. The now-classic closing lines of Beckett's *The Unnamable* (1953), "You must go on, I can't go on, I'll go on," are suggestive not only of the gravity of our situation but also of determination, if not quite hope.

Some Prize Lists

Appended here are some lists of prize-winning authors and books that were honoured in the first decade of the 21st century. They will also serve as a reminder of the gaps and lacunae in my discussion of writing from 2000–2010, or, more positively, as a suggestion for further exploration.

NOBEL PRIZE IN LITERATURE

2000	Gao Xingjian
2001	V.S. Naipaul
2002	Imrc Kertesz
2003	J.M. Coetzee
2004	Elfriede Jelinek
2005	Harold Pinter
2006	Orhan Pamuk
2007	Doris Lessing
2008	J.M. Le Clezio
2009	Herta Muller

THE PULITZER PRIZE (U.S.)

Fiction

2000	Jhumpa Lahiri, *Interpreter of Maladies*
2001	Michael Chabon, *The Amazing Adventures of Kavalier & Clay*
2002	Richard Russo, *Empire Falls*

2003 Jeffrey Eugenides, *Middlesex*
2004 Edward P. Jones, *The Known World*
2005 Marilynne Robinson, *Gilead*
2006 Geraldine Brooks, *March*
2007 Cormac McCarthy, *The Road*
2008 Junot Diaz, *The Brief Wondrous Life of Oscar Wao*
2009 Elizabeth Strout, *Olive Kitteridge*

General Nonfiction

2000 John W. Dower, *Embracing Defeat: Japan in the Wake of World War II*
2001 Herbert P. Bix, *Hirohito and the Making of Modern Japan*
2002 Diane McWhorter, *Carry Me Home: Birmingham, Alabama: The Climactic Battle of the Civil Rights Revolution*
2003 Samantha Power, *A Problem from Hell: America and the Age of Genocide*
2004 Anne Applebaum, *Gulag: A History*
2005 Steve Coll, *Ghost Wars: The Secret History of the CIA, Afghanistan and Bin Laden*
2006 Caroline Elkins, *Imperial Reckoning: The Untold Story of Britain's Gulag in Kenya*
2007 Lawrence Wright, *The Looming Tower: Al-Qaeda and the Road to 9/11*
2008 Saul Friedlander, *The Years of Extermination: Nazi Germany and the Jews, 1939–1945*
2009 Douglas Blackmon, *Slavery by Another Name: The Re-Enslavement of Black Americans from the Civil War to World War II*

NATIONAL BOOK CRITICS CIRCLE AWARDS (U.S.)

Fiction

2000 Jim Crace, *Being Dead*
2001 W.G. Sebald, *Austerlitz*
2002 Ian McEwan, *Atonement*
2003 Edward P. Jones, *The Known World*

2004   Marilynne Robinson, *Gilead*
2005   E.L. Doctorow, *The March*
2006   Kiran Desai, *The Inheritance of Loss*
2007   Junot Diaz, *The Brief Wondrous Life of Oscar Wao*
2008   Roberto Bolaño, *2666*
2009   Hilary Mantel, *Wolf Hall*

General Nonfiction

2000   Ted Conover, *Newjack: Guarding Sing Sing*
2001   Nicholson Baker, *Double Fold: Libraries and the Assault on Paper*
2002   Samantha Power, *A Problem from Hell: America and the Age of Genocide*
2003   Paul Hendrickson, *Sons of Mississippi: A Story of Race and Its Legacy*
2004   Diarmaid MacCulloch, *The Reformation: A History*
2005   Svetiana Alexievich, *Voices from Chernobyl*
2006   Simon Schama, *Rough Crossings*
2007   Harriet Washington, *Medical Apartheid: The Dark History of Medical Experimentation on Black Americans from Colonial Times to the Present*
2008   Dexter Filkins, *The Forever War*
2009   Richard Holmes, *The Age of Wonders*

NATIONAL BOOK AWARD (U.S.)

Fiction

2000   Susan Sontag, *In America*
2001   Jonathan Franzen, *The Corrections*
2002   Julia Glass, *Three Junes*
2003   Shirley Hazzard, *The Great Fire*
2004   Lily Tuck, *The News from Paraguay*
2005   William Vollman, *Europe Central*
2006   Richard Powers, *The Echo Maker*
2007   Denis Johnson, *Tree of Smoke*
2008   Peter Matthiessen, *Shadow Country*
2009   Colum McCann, *Let the Great World Spin*

Nonfiction

2000 Nathaniel Philbrick, *In the Heart of the Sea: The Tragedy of the Whaleship Essex*

2001 Andrew Solomon, *The Noonday Demon: An Atlas of Depression*

2002 Robert A. Caro, *Master of the Senate: The Years of Lyndon Johnson*

2003 Carlos Eire, *Waiting for Snow in Havana: Confessions of a Cuban Boy*

2004 Kevin Boyle, *Arc of Justice: A Saga of Race, Civil Rights, and Murder in the Jazz Age*

2005 Joan Didion, *The Year of Magical Thinking*

2006 Timothy Egan, *The Worst Hard Time: The Untold Story of Those Who Survived the Great American Dust Bowl*

2007 Tim Weiner, *Legacy of Ashes: The History of the* CIA

2008 Annette Gordon-Reed, *The Hemingses of Monticello: An American Family*

2009 T.J. Stiles, *The First Tycoon: The Epic Life of Cornelius Vanderbilt*

IMPAC DUBLIN LITERARY AWARD (U.K.)

2000 Nicola Barker, *Wide Open*

2001 Alistair MacLeod, *No Great Mischief*

2002 Michel Houellebecq, *The Elementary Particles*

2003 Orhan Pamuk, *My Name Is Red*

2004 Tahar Ben Jelloun, *This Blinding Absence of Light*

2005 Edward P. Jones, *The Known World*

2006 Colm Toibin, *The Master*

2007 Per Petterson, *Out Stealing Horses*

2008 Rawi Hage, *De Niro's Game*

2009 Michael Thomas, *Man Gone Down*

THE MAN BOOKER PRIZE (U.K.)

2000 Margaret Atwood, *The Blind Assassin*

2001 Peter Carey, *True History of the Kelly Gang*

2002 Yann Martel, *Life of Pi*

2003   D.B.C. Pierre, *Vernon God Little*
2004   Alan Hollinghurst, *The Line of Beauty*
2005   John Banville, *The Sea*
2006   Kiran Desai, *The Inheritance of Loss*
2007   Anne Enright, *The Gathering*
2008   Aravind Adiga, *The White Tiger*
2009   Hilary Mantel, *Wolf Hall*

ORANGE PRIZE FOR FICTION (U.K.)

2000   Linda Grant, *When I Lived in Modern Times*
2001   Kate Grenville, *The Idea of Perfection*
2002   Ann Patchett, *Bel Canto*
2003   Valerie Martin, *Property*
2004   Andrea Levy, *Small Island*
2005   Lionel Shriver, *We Need to Talk About Kevin*
2006   Zadie Smith, *On Beauty*
2007   Chimamanda Ngozi Adichie, *Half of a Yellow Sun*
2008   Rose Tremain, *The Road Home*
2009   Marilynne Robinson, *Home*

GOVERNOR GENERAL'S LITERARY AWARDS (CANADA)

Fiction

2000   Michael Ondaatje, *Anil's Ghost*
2001   Richard B. Wright, *Clara Callan*
2002   Gloria Sawai, *A Song for Nettie Johnson*
2003   Douglas Glover, *Elle*
2004   Miriam Toews, *A Complicated Kindness*
2005   David Gilmour, *A Perfect Night to Go to China*
2006   Peter Behrens, *The Law of Dreams*
2007   Michael Ondaatje, *Divisadero*
2008   Nino Ricci, *The Origin of Species*
2009   Kate Pullinger, *The Mistress of Nothing*

Nonfiction

2000   Nega Mezlekia, *Notes from the Hyena's Belly*

2001   Thomas Homer-Dixon, *The Ingenuity Gap*
2002   Andrew Nikiforuk, *Saboteurs: Wiebe Ludwig's War Against Big Oil*
2003   Margaret MacMillan, *Paris 1919*
2004   Romeo Dallaire, *Shake Hands with the Devil*
2005   John Vaillant, *The Golden Spruce*
2006   Ross King, *The Judgment of Paris*
2007   Karolyn Smardz Frost, *I've Got a Home in Glory Land: A Lost Tale of the Underground Railroad*
2008   Christie Blatchford, *Fifteen Days: Stories... from Inside the New Canadian Army*
2009   M.G. Vassanji, *A Place Within: Rediscovering India*

Index

Note: The names of fictional characters are in quotation marks, followed by the title of the book in which they appear.

Achebe, Chinua, 209

Adams, Lorraine, 213

Adichie, Chimamanda Ngozi, xiii, 207

Adiga, Aravind, 223

Adorno, Theodor, 181; on Beethoven, 182

Adventures of Augie March, The (Bellow), 185

Afghanistan, 109; *Kite Runner, The*, 209–11; legality of invasion, 119; political developments, 114; women in, 131–2

After Lorca (Spicer), 77

Against All Enemies (Clarke), 106–12

Age of American Unreason, The (Jacoby), 40–5, 255

Age of Reason, The (Paine), 40

Agnon, S.Y., 93, 95

Aguirre, Miquel, 26–7

Ahamed, Liaquat, 247

Ahmadinejad, Mahmoud, 201, 220

Alfred Kazin (Cook), xvii

All Quiet on the Western Front (Remarque), 134

Allawi, Alli, 106, 134–5

Allen, Paul, 202

Allende, Salvador, 29, 34–5, 237

American Idol, 43, 47

American Pastoral (Roth), 198

Amis, Martin, 204

Amos Oz Reader, The (Oz), 100

Anatomy Lesson, The (Roth), 197

Anderson, Sherwood, 97

Anselm, 173

Anti-Intellectualism in American Life (Hofstadter), 40

Appelfeld, Aharon, 83, 197

Aquinas, Thomas, 174

Arendt, Hannah, 59, 63, 143

Armies of the Night (Mailer), 31

Aron, Raymond, 65

Ascent of Money, The (Ferguson), 225

Assassins' Gate, The (Packer), 106, 121–7

Ataturk, Mustafa Kemal, 72–3; reform program, 73

atheism, xv, 160–79
Atheism (Baggini), 160
Atta, Mohamed, 113
Atwood, Margaret, xiii, 150, 242; on *Snow*, 71, 80
Auletta, Ken, 257

Baggini, Julian, 160, 172; and evidence, 175–6
Banna, Hassan al-, 116
Barnes, Julian, 177
Battle for Spain, The (Beevor), 29
battle of Salamis, 29
Bauerlein, Mark, 45–51, 255; and National Endowment for the Arts, 47
Baum, L. Frank, 127
Beauvoir, Simone de, xiv
Beckett, Samuel, 153, 259
Beethoven, Ludwig van, 182
Beevor, Antony, 29
Begin, Menachem, 99
Beijing Coma (Ma), 214–16
Bellow, Saul, xi, 184–6
Benda, Julian, 50
Ben-Dov, Nitza, 100
Ben-Gurion, David, 99–100
Berger, John, 4, 147, 239
Berger, Sandy, 107
"Berlin Chronicle, A" (Benjamin), 8
Berman, Paul, 124
Bernanke, Ben, 224
Bernhard, Thomas, 189
Biafra, 207–9
Big Bang (Singh), 174
Big Short, The (Lewis), 246
Bill and Ted's Excellent Adventure, 241
Blair, Tony, 63–4
Blaser, Robin, 77, 193

Blind Watchmaker, The (Dawkins), 161
blindness, 152–6
Blindness (Saramago), 193
Bloom, Allen, 31, 185
Bloom, Harold, xii, 47, 194
Bolaño, Roberto, 34
Books in Canada, x, xvi
Borges, Jorge Luis, 153, 156
Boru, Brian, 146
Breaking the Spell (Dennett), 160
Bremer, Paul, 126–7
Bright-Sided (Ehrenreich), 57, 243
Brokaw, Tom, 50
Brokeback Mountain (McMurtry, Proulx), 7
Bush, George W., 60, 105, 224; and focus on terrorism, 108; obsession with Iraq, 110
Bush at War (Woodward), 108
Byrne, Rhona, 57

Cambodia (Fawcett), 148
Camus, Albert, 31, 59, 214; on Spanish Civil War, 29
Capilano University, x, 152
Capote, Truman, 31, 206
Carr, Nicholas, 255
Carter, Jimmy, 114
Caryl, Christian, 80–1
Case for Big Government, The (Madrick), 247, 250
Castle, The (Kafka), 68
Cavafy, C.P., 138, 181
Censoring an Iranian Love Story (Mandanipour), 206, 220–3
Cercas, Javier, xi, xv, 22–38, 77; as narrator, 22–3; *Soldiers of Salamis*, 22–38
Cervantes, Miguel de, 32

Chait, Jonathan, 241
Chandrasekaran, Rajiv, 106, 127–9
Chen, Joanna, 98
Cheney, Dick, 107, 111, 123
Chile, 29, 34; CIA in, 29
China, 214–17
Chomsky, Noam, 237
Clancy, Tom, 109
Clarke, Richard, 106–12
Clinton, Bill, 10
Closing of the American Mind,
    The (Bloom), 185
Cockeyed (Knighton), 152–6
Coetzee, J.M., xi, 79, 184, 189–93
Cognitive Surplus (Shirky), 255
Cohan, William, 246
Coll, Steve, 106, 112–15
Collins, Francis, 171
Communist Manifesto, The (Marx
    and Engels), 224, 248
Conrad, Joseph, 242
Conscience of a Liberal, The
    (Krugman), 225
Cook, Richard, xvii
Costa, Margaret Jull, 193
"Costello, Elizabeth" (Elizabeth
    Costello), xi
Coupland, Douglas, 232
Crisis Economics (Roubini and
    Mihm), 247–8
Cult of the Amateur (Keen), 54
cultural condition: of young people,
    47–8; paradox of, ix
cultural context, 253–5; capitalist,
    51
cultural crisis, ix, 39, 253–5;
    remedies for, 57
culture: celebrity, 54; of distraction,
    43; pop, 53; middlebrow, 42–3,
    167; and nature, 148

Culture and Imperialism (Said), 180
culture wars, 9, 13; in the 1960s,
    51; and sanctimony, 11

Dabney, Lewis, xvii
Dalrymple, William, 219
Danai, Alex, 140
Darwin, Charles, 161, 173
Dawkins, Richard, xv, 160–79;
    God Hypothesis, the, 164
Dead Reckoning (Glavin), 147
Death with Interruptions
    (Saramago), xi, 193–5
Deathfeast in Dimlahamid,
    A (Glavin), 147
Defoe, Daniel, 32, 190
DeLillo, Don, xiii
Dennett, Daniel, 160
Desai, Kirin, 223
Dewey, John, 73
Diary of a Bad Year (Coetzee), xi,
    189
Diderot, Denis, 32
Dillon, Sam, 44
Dispatches (Herr), 31, 134
Dixon, John, x
Dooneyscafe.com, x
Drabble, Margaret, 184
Drew, Flora, 214
Dumbest Generation, The
    (Bauerlein), 45–51, 255
Duras, Marguerite, xiv
Dying Animal, The (Roth), 198
Dylan, Bob, 51

Eagleton, Terry, xii, 160; criticism
    of Dawkins, 165–7
economic crisis, ix, 224–52
Economics for Everyone (Stanford),
    225

Edemariam, Aida, 102

Edmund Wilson (Dabney), xvii

Ehrenreich, Barbara, xiii, 57, 242–5

Ehrenreich, John, 243

Eichmann in Jerusalem (Arendt), 143

Elizabeth Costello (Coetzee), xi,
   189–91

Elon, Amos, 83–4

Elusive Embrace, The (Mendelsohn),
   138

Emperor, The (Kapuscinski), 187

Empire of Illusion (Hedges), 52–8

End of Faith, The (Harris), 160

End of Iraq, The (Galbraith), 127

Everyman (Roth), 198

evolution, 41–2, 161–2, 172

Exit Ghost (Roth), 198–9

experience, 7; decline of, 5

Fabric of the Cosmos, The (Greene),
   174

Facebook, 55

fascism, 14

Fawcett, Brian, 148

Feith, Douglas, 123

Fences and Windows (Klein), 234

Ferguson, Niall, 225

fiction: and censorship, 222; and
   facts, 37; self-reflexiveness in, 32

Filkins, Dexter, 106, 118, 132–4

First Man, The (Camus), 214

Flannery, Tim, xiii

Forever War, The (Filkins), 106;
   battle in Iraq, 132–4

Fragments (Wilkomirski), 32

Franco, Francisco, 24, 30

Franklin, Benjamin, 42

Freedom and Capitalism
   (Friedman), 235

Freefall (Stiglitz), 240, 246–9

Freeley, Maureen, 68

Freethinkers (Jacoby), 40

French, Patrick, 84

Frey, James, 32, 155

Friedman, Milton, 235–7

Galbraith, Peter, 127

Galileo, 161

Garcia Lorca, Federico, 28

Garcia Marquez, Gabriel, 84, 184

Generation X (Coupland), 232

Genet, Jean, 181

genre-bending, 31; and Cercas's
   "true tale," 36. *See also:* stories

Gil, Jaime, 26

Ghost in the Water, A (Glavin), 147

Ghost Wars (Coll), 106, 112–15

Ghost Writer, The (Roth), 12,
   196–7

Gibson, William, 232

Glavin, Terry, 145–52

Globe and Mail, The, x, xvi

Glowczewska, Klara, 187

God Delusion, The (Dawkins), xv,
   160–79

God Is Not Great (Hitchens), 160

Gomorrah (Saviano), xiii

Good Calories, Bad Calories
   (Taubes), xiii

Goodbye, Columbus (Roth), 196

Goodman, Paul, 40

Googled (Auletta), 257

Gorbachev, Mikhail, 115

Gordimer, Nadine, xiv, 184

Gore, Al, 107

Gould, Glenn, 181

Grammars of Creation (Steiner),
   137

Grand Theft Auto, 55
Grandmothers, The (Lessing), 184
Grant, Linda, 84
Gray, John, 239
Grass, Gunter, 184
Greatest Generation, The (Brokaw),
    50
Greene, Brian, 174
Grossman, David, 83
Grossman, Edith, 84
Grown Up Digital (Tapscott), 49

Half of a Yellow Sun (Adichie),
    207–9
Hamid, Mohsin, 223
Harris, Sam, 160
Havel, Vaclav, 179
Hawkins, Bobby Louise, 3
Hawthorne, Nathaniel, 11
Heart of Darkness, (Conrad),
    242
Hedges, Chris, 52–8
Hekmatyar, Gulbuddin, 113
Henwood, Doug, 241–2
hero, 35, 37
Herodotus, 29, 187–8
Herr, Michael, 31, 134
Herzog (Bellow), 185
historical memory, 29–30; and
    Herodotus, 187–8; and
    Reappraisals, 59–60. *See also:*
    memory
Histories, The (Herodotus), 29, 187–8
History of Reading, A (Manguel),
    158
*History of the Second Temple,
    The* (Klausner), 91
*History of the Siege of Lisbon,
    The* (Saramago), 193

Hitchens, Christopher, 81, 124, 160
Hobbes, Thomas, 184
Hobsbawm, Eric, 63
Hofstadter, Richard, 40
Holocaust, 137
Homage to Barcelona (Toibin), 30
Homage to Catalonia (Orwell), 23,
    29
Home Alone, 106
Homer, 9, 18, 153, 157
Horseman, Pass By (McMurtry), 7
Hosseini, Khaled, 209–11
House of Cards (Cohan), 246
housing bubble, 226–7
How Beautiful It Is ...
    (Mendelsohn), 138
Hower, Edward, 210
Hud (McMurtry), 7
Human Stain, The (Roth), xi, 9–21,
    198
Humbling, The (Roth), 198
Humboldt's Gift (Bellow), 185
Hussein, Saddam, 107, 111, 114

I Married a Communist (Roth),
    198
I.O.U. (Lanchester), 247
identity politics, 13–15
Ignatieff, Michael, 124
Iliad (Homer), 9–10, 157
Imperfectionists, The (Rachman),
    253
Imperial Life in the Emerald City
    (Chandrasekaran), 106, 127–9
In Cold Blood (Capote), 31
In Other Rooms, Other Wonders
    (Mueenuddin), xi, 206, 217–20
In the Country of Men (Matar),
    211–14

In the Land of Israel (Oz), 83
In the Realm of Hungry Ghosts (Mate), xiii
Indignation (Roth), 198
Inheritance of Loss, The (Desai), 223
Internet, 159
Interpreter of Maladies (Lahiri), 223
Iran, 201–6, 220–3
Iraq, 109; failure of occupation, 125–6, 128–9; legality of invasion, 121–2
Israel, Richard, 161
Israel: and Judt, 64–5; life in, 83–104; and Said, 65
Istanbul (Pamuk), 79

Jacoby, Susan, 40–5, 255
Jaeger, Abraham, 138
Jaeger, Shmiel, 138
Jaggi, Maya, 208
James, Clive, 196
Jefferson, Thomas, 42, 161
Jesus the Jew (Klausner), 91
Jones, Ann, 106, 130–2
Joyce, James, 215
Judt, Tony, 58–66, 255

"Ka" (*Snow*), 67–78
Kabul in Winter (Jones), 106, 130–2
Kafka, Franz, 68
Kakutani, Michiko, 44, 118, 202, 221, 223
Kant, Immanuel, 158
Kapuscinski, Ryszard, 184, 187–9
Kazin, Alfred, xvii
Keen, Andrew, 54

Keynes, John Maynard, 236, 250
Keynes, John Maynard (Skidelsky), 225
Khalili, Sara, 220
Khomeini, Ayatollah, 113, 201
Khoury, Elias, 103
Khoury, George, 103
Kiddie Porn, On (Persky and Dixon), x
Kite Runner, The (Hosseini), 209–11
Klausner, Arieh, 85–6, 89
Klausner, Joseph, 86, 91–3
Klein, Naomi, 225, 230–42, 249
Knighton, Ryan, 152–6
knowledge deficits, ix, 47, 54; Bauerlein assessment of, 49
Koestler, Arthur, 59, 63
Kolakowski, Leszek, 63
Kowinski, William, 239
Krugman, Paul, 224–30
Kundera, Milan, 254
Kurzweil, Ray, 178

Laden, Osama bin, 105, 108, 113, 117
Lahiri, Jhumpa, 223
Lampedusa, Tomasi di, 181
Lanchester, John, 204, 247
Lange, Nicholas de, 83
Language of God, The (Collins), 171
Lanier, Jaron, 255
Lapham, Lewis, 243
Lasdun, James, 215–16
Last Great Sea, The (Glavin), 147
Last Picture Show, The (McMurtry), 3
Lawless World (Sands), 121

Lea, Richard, 23
Leavis, F.R., xii
Ledbetter, James, 233
Leonard, John, 84, 89
Lessing, Doris, xiv, 79, 149, 184
Letter to a Christian Nation
    (Harris), 160
Letting Go (Roth), 196
Levi, Primo, 59, 63
Lewinsky, Monica, 11, 19
Lewis, Michael, 246
library, 45–7; aspects of, 158;
    unused, 46–7
Library at Night, The (Manguel)
    156–9
Libya, 211–14
literacy, 54
literary criticism, ix, xv-xvi; decline
    of, xvi; defense of, xvii; sympo-
    sium, 257
literary fiction: status, xi
Literary Review of Canada, xvi
Literary Theory (Eagleton), xii
Liu Xiaobo, 258
Living to Tell the Tale (Garcia
    Marquez), 84
Lolita (Nabokov), 202–4
Lonesome Dove (McMurtry), 7
Long March, Short Spring
    (Ehrenreich), 243
Longest War, The (Timerman), 139
"Lonoff, E.I." (*Ghost Writer, The*),
    11–12, 196
Looming Tower, The (Wright), 106,
    112, 115–19
Lords of Finance (Ahamed), 247
Lost, The (Mendelsohn), 84,
    137–43
Lyden, Jacki, 205

Ma Jian, 214–16
MacFarlane, Robert, 191
MacFarquhar, Larissa, 241
Machado, Antonio, 25
Madison, James, 42
Madoff, Bernie, 224
Madrick, Jeff, 247, 250
Mailer, Norman, 31, 184
Major, John, 64
Makiya, Kanan, 123–5
Malamud, Bernard, 196
Mandanipour, Sharhiar, 206, 220–3
Manguel, Alberto, 156–9
Mann, Thomas, 181
Marcuse, Herbert, 43
Martinez, Tomas Eloy, 32
Marx, Karl, 248
Massoud, Ahmed Shah, 113
Matar, Hisham, 211–14
Mate, Gabor, xiii
Maximum City (Mehta), xiii, 223
McCarthy, Cormac, xiii
McLean, Anne, 22, 28
McLuhan, Marshall, 255
McMurtry, Larry, xv, 3–8; as
    screenwriter, 7
Mehta, Suketu, xiii, 223
Melville, Herman, x
memory, 5, 6, 7, 91; as building
    in the ruins, 92; and Herodotus,
    187–8; obsolescence of, 4; of the
    Sixties, 42; of Spanish Civil War,
    30
Mendelsohn, Daniel, xv, 84,
    137–43
Mendelsohn, Matt, 141
Metamorphoses (Ovid), 153
Mihm, Stephen, 247–8
Million Little Pieces, A (Frey), 32

Milosz, Czeslaw, 184, 186–7

Milton, John, 153

Minima Moralia (Adorno), 183

"Miralles" (*Soldiers of Salamis*),
35–8

Mirsky, Jonathan, 216

Mishra, Pankaj, 212–14, 258

Moby Dick (Melville), x

Modern Warfare, 52

Morrison, Toni, xiii

"Moscow" (Benjamin), 8

Mozart, W.A., 181

Mueenuddin, Daniyal, xi, 206,
217–20

Munro, Alice, xiii, 242

Museum of Innocence, The
(Pamuk), 80

Mussman (Klausner), Fania, 85,
87–8; death, 89

Mussman, Sonia, 88

My Lives (White), 84

My Michael (Oz), 83

My Name Is Red (Pamuk), 79

Nabokov, Vladimir, 202–4

Nafisi, Azar, xiii, xv, 201–6

Nagel, Thomas, 160, 168, 170–1,
175

Naipaul, V.S., 79, 184, 218

Najibullah, 115

Nasser, Gamal Abdul, 116

National Endowment for the Arts, 47

Nemesis (Roth), 198

New Left, 15

New York Review of Books, xvi

New York Times Book Review, xvi

Nickel and Dimed (Ehrenreich),
242–5

Nineteen Eighty-Four (Orwell), 29

Nixon, Richard, 42

No Logo (Klein), 230–3

Notebook, The (Saramago), 193

Nothing To Be Frightened Of
(Barnes), 177

novels, xi; purpose of, xii

Oates, Joyce Carol, xiii

Obama, Barack, ix, 13, 57, 250;
and change, 66; withdrawal from
Iraq, 129

Occupation of Iraq, The (Allawi),
106, 134–5

Omar, Mullah, 115

On Late Style (Said), xii, 180–3

Ondaatje, Michael, 242

One Dimensional Man (Marcuse), 43

One Way Street (Benjamin), 8

O'Neill, John, 117–18

Operation Shylock (Roth), 31, 197

Oprah, 161

Orange Prize, xiv

Orientalism (Said), 180

Origin of Species, The (Darwin),
161, 173

O'Rourke, Meghan, 210–11

Orr, Allen, 160; criticism of
Dawkins, 167–8

Orwell, George, 22–3, 29

Oryx and Crake (Atwood), 150

Other Colors (Pamuk), 80

Other Voices, Other Rooms
(Capote), 206

Out of Place (Said), 180

Ovid, 153

Oz, Amos, 83–104; becoming a
writer, 96–8; on reading and
writing, 93–4

Oz, Fania, 100

Packer, George, 106, 121–7
Paine, Tom, 40
Pamuk, Orhan, xi, 67–82; and
   Dostoyevsky, 80–1; motives for
   writing, 81; Nobel Prize, 68,
   79–80
Patrimony (Roth), 197
Pattern in the Carpet, The
   (Drabble), 184
Pattern Recognition (Gibson), 232
Paulson, Hank, 224
Pelosi, Nancy, 47
Peres, Simon, 95
Perle, Richard, 123
Persig, Robert, 163
Pessoa, Fernando, 193–4
Philosophy and Social Hope
   (Rorty), 14
Philosophy as Cultural Politics
   (Rorty), xii
Pinochet, Augusto, 29, 34, 237
Pinter, Harold, 79
Plot Against America, The (Roth),
   198
poetry: serial, 77–8
political correctness, 15
pornography, 55–6
Portnoy's Complaint (Roth), 196
Postman, Neil, 40–1
postmodernists, 14
Postwar (Judt), 59
Powell, Colin, 128
Prague Orgy, The (Roth), 197
Prisoner of the State (Zhao), 216
Prose, Francine, 191
Proulx, E. Annie, 7
Purple Hibiscus (Adichie), 208
Putin, Vladimir, 48
Pynchon, Thomas, xiii

Qaddafi, Muammar al-, 211
Qutb, Sayyid, 115–17

Rachman, Tom, 253
Radical Enlightenment (Israel), 161
Ragged Place, This (Glavin), 147
railways: as public service, 64
Ravelstein (Bellow), xi, 31, 185–6
reading: and books, 90–1; decline
   of, ix, 39, 44, 47, 254; and
   e-readers, xvi, 256; and non-
   reading, 159; refutation of decline
   of, 49, 256; and writing, 44
Reading Diary, A (Manguel), 158
Reading Lolita in Tehran (Nafisi),
   201–6
Reading Pictures (Manguel), 158
Reading the 21st Century (Persky),
   xiv-xv
Reagan, Ronald 114, 236, 251
Reappraisals (Judt), 59–66, 255
Reason, Faith and Revolution
   (Eagleton), 167
Redburn, Tom, 241
Reluctant Fundamentalist, The
   (Hamid), 223
Remarque, Eric Maria, 134
Remnick, David, 86, 90, 100
Rest Is Noise, The (Ross), xiii
*Return of Depression Economics,
   The* (Krugman), 224–30
Rhyming Life and Death (Oz), 83,
   94
Rice, Condoleezza, 48, 107, 111
Road-side Dog (Milosz), 187
Robinson, Marilynne, xiii
Roiphe, Katie, 257–8
Romano, Carlin, 45
root causes debate, 119

Rorty, Richard, xii, 13; on culture wars, 14–15
Ross, Alex, xiii
Roth, Henry, 196
Roth, Philip, xi, xv, 9–21, 184, 195–9; as character, 32; *Exit Ghost*, 198–9; *Ghost Writer, The*, 12
Roubini, Nouriel, 247–8
Row, Jess, 215
Roy, Arundhati, 239
Rumsfeld, Donald, 107, 109, 111, 123, 128; envoy to Iraq, 114

Sabbath's Theatre (Roth), 198
Sadat, Anwar al-, 117
Sadr, Muqtada al-, 129
Said, Edward, xii, 59, 63, 180–3
Sanchez Ferlosio, Rafael, 23
Sanchez Mazas, Rafael, 22; life of, 33
sanctimony, 11
Sands, Philippe, 121
Santa Evita (Martinez), 32
Saramago, Jose, xi, 184, 193–5
Saturday Night, x, xvi
Saul, John Ralston, 63, 65
Savage Detectives, The (Bolaño), 34
Saviano, Roberto, xiii
Scarlet Letter, The (Hawthorne), 13, 16
Sebald, W.G., 141
Secret, The (Byrne), 57
Sedaris, David, 154
Selected Writings (Benjamin), 8
Selfish Gene, The (Dawkins), 161
Sense of Sight, The (Berger), 4
September 11, 2001, ix, 105; eye-witness account, 109

sexual harassment, 15–16
Shallows, The (Carr), 255
Shamsie, Camila, 213
Shirky, Clay, 255
Shock Doctrine, The (Klein), 225, 235–42, 249
Short Version, The (Persky), x
Shteyngart, Gary, 254
"Silk, Coleman" (*Human Stain, The*), 9–13, 19–21
Sinatra, Frank, 19
Singh, Simon, 174
Singularity Is Near, The (Kurzweil), 178
Six Impossible Things Before Breakfast (Wolpert), 160
"Sixteen Tons," 245
Sixties, the (1960s), 42, 50–1
Sixty Minutes, 110
Skidelsky, Robert, 225
Skidelsky, William, 208
Slow Man (Coetzee), 189, 191–2
Snow (Pamuk), xi, 67–78; doubles in, 70–1; and God, 74–5; and poetry, 74, 76–7; reviews of, 80–1
Soldiers of Salamis (Cercas), xi, 22–38
Sorkin, Andrew Ross, 246
Spanish Civil War, 22, 29; memories of, 30; and post-war transition, 30–1
Spanish Civil War, The (Thomas), 29
Sperber, Manes, 63
Spicer, Jack, 77–8
Spinoza, Baruch, 161
spooks, 12
Stahl, Lesley, 110

Stanford, Jim, 225
state, the, 61–2, 65; thinking about, 63
Steiner, George, 137
Sterne, Laurence, 32
Stick Out Your Tongue (Ma), 214
Stiglitz, Joseph, 239–40, 246
Stone Raft, The (Saramago), 193
stories, 5, 141–2, 149; arousing interest in, 23, 26; Holocaust, 139; landscape as, 146; of libraries, 156; and *Soldiers of Salamis*, 22; truth in, 31
"Storyteller, The" (Benjamin), 4
"Storyteller, The" (Berger), 4
Storyteller, The (Vargas Llosa), 4, 32–3
storytelling, xv, 4; in Iran, 204; and storytellers, 5; and tribal perspective, 33
studies: Geographic Literacy Survey, 49; National Assessment of Educational Progress history exam, 48; National Conference of State Legislatures citizenship study, 48; National Election study, 48; Pew Research report, 48
Super Sad True Love Story (Shteyngart), 254
Survivor, 43

Tale of Love and Darkness, A (Oz), 83–104
Taliban, 115
Tapscott, Don, 49
Task of the Critic, The (Eagleton), xii
Taubes, Gary, xiii

Tchernikowsky, Saul, 91
teaching, 28–9; and student fashion, 230–1; and video games, 52–3
Thatcher, Margaret, 63–4, 236
Thing Around Your Neck, The (Adichie), 209
Things Fall Apart (Achebe), 209
thinking politically, 62
Thomas, Hugh, 29
Thompson, J. Hunter, 31
Thousand Splendid Suns, A (Hosseini), 211
Tiananmen Square, 214
Timerman, Jacabo, 139
Times Literary Supplement, xvi
Toibin, Colm, 22; on Spanish transition, 30
Too Big To Fail (Sorkin), 246
Topic Sentence (Persky), x
Trapiello, Andres, 25
Travels with Herodotus (Kapuscinski), 187–9
Treason of the Intellectuals, The (Benda), 50
"Trotsky and the Wild Orchids" (Rorty), 14
Trueba, David, 28
Turkey: *Snow*, 67–82
Tyee, The, x

Ultimate Fighting Challenge, 55
Unbearable Lightness of Being, The (Kundera), 254
Uncle Joaquin, 27–8
Unconscious Civilization, The (Saul), 63
Under This Blazing Light (Oz), 87
universities, 56–7

Unnamable, The (Beckett), 259
"Unpacking My Library"
    (Benjamin), 8
Updike, John, 80, 184

"Valley of the Black Pig, The"
    (Yeats), 147
Vancouver Sun, x
Vargas Llosa, Mario, 4, 32–3, 258
Vidal, Gore, xii, 138, 184
View from Nowhere, The (Nagel),
    170
Vonnegut, Kurt, 184

Waiting for Godot (Beckett), 153,
    156
Waiting for the Macaws (Glavin),
    145–52
*Walter Benjamin at the Dairy
    Queen* (McMurtry), xv, 3–6
war: in 20th century, 60
*War Is a Force That Gives Us
    Meaning* (Hedges), 53
Washington Post, The, xvi
Weather Makers, The (Flannery),
    xiii
Weinberg, Steven, 160, 168–70,
    172
Weiseltier, Leon, 124
Western Canon, The (Bloom), xii
What Does It All Mean? (Nagel),
    170
*When a Nation Fights for its
    Freedom* (Klausner), 92
White, Edmund, 84
White Tiger, The (Adiga), 223
Whoops! (Lanchester), 247

Wilkomirski, Binjamin, 32
Wilson, Edmund, xvii, 45–6
Winesburg, Ohio (Anderson), 97
Wolf, Christa, xiv
Wolfe, Tom, 31
Wolfowitz, Paul, 123
Wolpert, Lewis (160)
women workers, 243–5
women writers, xiii-xivi
Wood, James, 192, 221–2
Wood, Michael, 180
Woodward, Bob, 108
Woolf, Virginia, xii
World Is What It Is, The (French),
    84
World of Warcraft, 256
World Wrestling Entertainment, 53
Wright, Lawrence, 106, 112,
    115–19
writing: as category, xi; motives for,
    81

*Year of the Death of Ricardo Reis,
    The* (Saramago), 193
Yeats, W.B., 82, 146–7, 200
Yehoshua, A.B., 83
You Are Not a Gadget (Lanier),
    255
YouTube, 55, 161

Zawahiri, Ayman al-, 113, 117
Zhao Ziyang, 215–17
Zionism, 100–1
"Zuckerman, Nathan" (*Human
    Stain, The; Exit Ghost*), 10,
    196–9
Zuckerman Unbound (Roth), 197